THE

JESUIT

AND THE

History, Languages, and Cultures of the
Spanish and Portuguese Worlds

This interdisciplinary series promotes scholarship
in studies on Iberian cultures and contacts from the premodern
and early modern periods.

SERIES EDITOR
Sabine MacCormack, Theodore M. Hesburgh Professor of Arts and Letters,
Departments of Classics and History, University of Notre Dame

SERIES BOARD
J. N. Hillgarth, emeritus, Pontifical Institute of Mediaeval Studies
Peggy K. Liss, Independent Scholar
David Nirenberg, Johns Hopkins University
Adeline Rucquoi, École des Hautes Études en Sciences Sociales

TITLES IN THE SERIES

The Mirror of Spain, 1500–1700: The Formation of a Myth
J. N. Hillgarth

Bishops, Councils, and Consensus in the Visigothic Kingdom, 589–633
Rachel L. Stocking

A Network of Converso Families in Early Modern Toledo: Assimilating a Minority
Linda Martz

Romans in a New World: Classical Models in Sixteenth-Century Spanish America
David A. Lupher

The Jesuit and the Incas: The Extraordinary Life of Padre Blas Valera, S.J.
Sabine Hyland

Upholding Justice: Society, State, and the Penal System of Quito (1650–1750)
Tamar Herzog

Conflict and Coexistence: Archbishop Rodrigo and the Muslims and Jews
of Medieval Spain
Lucy K. Pick

The Origins of Mexican Catholicism: Nahua Rituals and Christian Sacraments
in Sixteenth-Century Mexico
Osvaldo F. Pardo

Missionary Tropics: The Catholic Frontier in India (16th–17th Centuries)
Ines G. Županov

Jews, Christian Society, and Royal Power in Medieval Barcelona
Elka Klein

How the Incas Built Their Heartland: State Formation and the Innovation
of Imperial Strategies in the Sacred Valley, Peru
R. Alan Covey

THE

JESUIT

AND THE

INCAS

*The Extraordinay Life
of Padre Blas Valera, S.J.*

Sabine Hyland

THE UNIVERSITY OF MICHIGAN PRESS   ANN ARBOR

2011   2010   2009   2008   5   4   3   2

A CIP catalog record for this book is available from the British Library.

Library of Congress Cataloging-in-Publication Data

Hyland, Sabine, 1964–
    The Jesuit and the Incas : the extraordinary life of Padre Blas
Valera, S.J. / Sabine Hyland.
        p.   cm. — (History, languages, and cultures of the Spanish and
Portuguese worlds)
    Includes bibliographical references and index.
    ISBN 0-472-11353-4 (alk. paper)
    1. Valera, Blas, 1551–1597.   2. Incas—Missions.
3. Jesuits—Peru—History.   4. Jesuits—Spain—History.   I. Title.
II. Series.
BX4705.V2747 H95   2004
271'.5302—dc21   2003008359

    ISBN 978-0-472-11353-8 (alk. paper)
    ISBN 978-0-472-03041-5 (pbk. : alk. paper)
    ISBN 0-472-03041-8 (pbk. : alk. paper)

To my husband, William

We were like strangers in our own city, visitors who had lost their way. It was your books that, as it were, brought us back home, so that at last we could recognize who we were, and where we were. It was you who revealed to us the age of our country, and sequence of events, the laws of religious ceremonies and of the priesthoods, the traditional customs of private and public life, the position of geographical areas and of particular places, and the terminology of all matters, human and divine, with their various kinds, functions and causes.

—Cicero, writing about Marcus Terentius Varro,
quoted by St. Augustine in *The City of God*

Preface

This book grew out of my dissertation research on the debates over ordaining mestizos as Catholic priests in early colonial Peru. My dissertation, "Conversion, Custom, and 'Culture': Jesuit Racial Policies in Sixteenth-Century Peru" (Ph.D. dissertation, Yale University, 1994), focused specifically on the Jesuits' attitudes toward mestizos in the viceroyalty. When the first members of the Society of Jesus arrived in Lima in 1568, they intended to encourage mestizo vocations to the Society. It was believed that mestizos—the children of Spanish fathers and native mothers—would make ideal missionaries, combining a Christian heritage from their fathers with a knowledge of native culture and language from their mothers. Yet fourteen years after arriving in South America, the Jesuits in Peru voted unanimously against ever allowing any mestizo to join the Society; this legislation would remain in place until the Jesuits were forced out of South America in the 1770s.

As I explored the reasons for this change of policy, speculating on how the Jesuits' experience might shed light on the development of racial and cultural ideologies in Peru, I became intrigued with the story of one particular mestizo Jesuit—Blas Valera. Some Jesuits in Peru claimed that the reason for the ban on mestizos was Valera's misdeeds, which had proven mestizos to be unfit as priests. What were these heinous acts that Valera allegedly had committed? According to the Jesuits at the time, the Spanish Inquisition had convicted him of fornication and sentenced him to a long imprisonment. Yet, searching through Inquisition archives, I discovered that the Jesuits' story was false and that Valera had never even been brought before the Inquisition, let alone convicted by the Holy Office (see chap. 8 for the true story). Moreover, it became increasingly clear to me that Valera had been an ardent defender of the native peoples of Peru and had devoted his life to gathering the legends, histories, and myths of the native Andeans.

Therefore, I decided to write a biography of Valera, an entirely new book that would incorporate material from my dissertation. This biography was almost completed in 1996 when Laura Laurencich Minelli announced that a series of seventeenth-century documents had been discovered in Naples. These manuscripts make extraordinary claims about Blas Valera (see chaps. 9–10) that have inspired intense debates over the life of this mestizo priest. The passion behind these current controversies reveals how much the issues that dominated Valera's life—issues concerning native languages, cultures, and religion—are still vital today.

Many people have generously assisted me in writing this book. Richard Burger, as a dissertation director and colleague, has contributed his profound knowledge of Andean civilization and the Inca chroniclers; he is a model scholar and mentor, whose support and friendship over the years are deeply appreciated. This work has benefited also from numerous conversations with Mike Coe about Native American writing systems; his unwavering support during the writing of this book has meant a great deal to me. Noble David Cook trained me in Peruvian colonial history and paleography and helped to clarify my ideas about Blas Valera and mestizo ordination; his kindness is much appreciated.

This book owes a special debt of gratitude to Brian Bauer, who encouraged me to publish it and whose criticisms have improved the manuscript considerably. I am indebted also to Sabine MacCormack for her very careful and highly informed reading of the manuscript. Gary Urton's thoughtful comments have greatly improved the entire work, especially chapter 6—on language and writing. Frank

Salomon's suggestions for further clarifications have likewise benefited this work. Warren Church has provided insights into Chachapoya society, along with helpful comments on chapter 2.

I am very grateful to Laura Laurencich Minelli for her sincere friendship and support over the years of writing this book. Monica Barnes has contributed to this work in many ways, and her help is much appreciated. William Klimon provided invaluable bibliographic assistance. Many other friends and colleagues have provided assistance, criticism, and encouragement, including Harold Conklin, Davide Domenici, Maurizio Gnerre, Esther González, Teodoro Hampe Martínez, Bill Isbell, James John, Marti Lamar, Bruce Mannheim, René Millar Carvacho, Craig Morris, Jeremy Mumford, Joanne Pillsbury, Charles Reid, Elayne Zorn, and Tom Zuidema. My departmental colleagues, Cheryl Carpenter, Jim Benton, and Tom Faase, have patiently supported me through this endeavor.

Sabine MacCormack, Collin Ganio, and Chris Collins, of the University of Michigan Press, have been gracious and exemplary editors who have made this process as easy as possible. Erin Snoddy, Sarah Mann, and Jillian Downey have maintained their good humor while helping with the details of preparing the manuscript.

César Rodríguez, of Sterling Memorial Library at Yale University, has repeatedly given invaluable help with manuscripts at Yale. I would also like to thank the librarians and archivists at the Archivo Histórico Nacional in Madrid, the Biblioteca Nacional in Madrid, the Biblioteca de la Universidad de Sevilla, the Biblioteca de la Universidad de Salamanca, the Archivo General de Indias, the British Library, the Beinecke Rare Book and Manuscript Library, Manuscripts and Archives in Sterling Memorial Library, the Pius XII Microfilm Collection at St. Louis University, the Harkness Collection at the Library of Congress, the New York Public Library, the Lilly Library at Indiana University at Bloomington, and the Rare Books Collection at St. Benedict's Abbey, Kansas. My thanks also go to Lynn Orlowski, the head of interlibrary loan at St. Norbert College, and to Paul Spaeth, director of the library at St. Bonaventure University.

The book has benefited greatly from the prayers and friendship of the Benedictine monks of St. Benedict's Abbey, Kansas, especially Father Denis Meade, O.S.B.; Father Benedict Laroque, O.S.B.; and Brother John Peto, O.S.B. I am also deeply grateful to the monks of

PREFACE

Conception Abbey, Missouri, for their prayers and friendship, especially Father Patrick Caveglia, O.S.B., Abbot Gregory Polan, O.S.B., and Brother Thomas Sullivan, O.S.B.

Much of chapter 8 originally appeared as the article "The Imprisonment of Blas Valera: Heresy and Inca History in Colonial Peru" in *Colonial Latin American Historical Review* 7, no. 1 (1998): 43–58.

The research for this book was supported by grants from the National Science Foundation, the National Endowment for the Humanities, the Andrew W. Mellon Foundation, the Williams Fellowship (Yale University), the Yale University Dissertation Fellowship, and the St. Norbert College Faculty Development Fund.

Finally, my largest debt is to my family. My mother, Sigrid Campbell, read through the manuscript and provided very useful comments and encouragement. I would like to thank my lovely daughters, Margaret and Eleanor, for sharing their mom with Blas Valera. My husband, Bill, has been at my side throughout all phases of this work. He has critically read the manuscript many times, provided translations of Latin texts, and cheerfully endured countless conversations about Blas Valera and the Naples documents. To him I owe more than I can adequately express.

Note on Translations and Orthography

The English translations of selections from Garcilaso de la Vega's *Royal Commentaries of the Incas and General History of Peru* are from the translation by Harold V. Livermore (Garcilaso de la Vega 1987). Unless otherwise cited, all other translations from Spanish and Quechua are by the author. Translations from Latin are by William P. Hyland. To remain true to the spirit of the original sixteenth- and seventeenth-century documents, the spellings of Quechua words conform to the common usages of the colonial period.

Contents

Illustrations

EQUATOR

Quito

Puerto Viejo

▲ Chimborazo
Riobamba

Tumebamba

Tumbez

Rio Marañón

Chachapoyas

Cajamarca

Huamachuco

Trujillo

Huaylas

Rio Ucayali

Huánuco

Cajatambo

Chilón

Canta

Xuaxa

Lima

Huarochirí

Pachacamac

Huamanga

Rio Apurimac

Chincha

Andahuaylas

Cuzco

Urcos

Ica

Nazca

EL COLLAO

LAKE TITICACA

Chucuito

Copacabana

La Paz (Chuquiabo)

Arequipa

Sicasica

Cochabamba

PACIFIC OCEAN

La Plata
(Chuqisaca)

CHARCAS

Potosí

MAP
LOCATION

0   200 miles

0   200 km

Western South America

CHAPTER ONE

Introduction

On May 3, 1586, in a small underground prison cell beneath the Jesuit residence in Lima, Blas Valera penned an urgent letter to the general of the Society of Jesus, Claudio Aquaviva, asking for a release from his imprisonment and a transfer to Rome. Valera had already spent three years in jail, in a prison he shared with some of the unfortunate individuals being held by the Holy Office of the Inquisition in Lima. During the years of his incarceration, Valera was required to endure weekly floggings—"mortifications"—under the supervision of the Jesuit provincial, as well as weekly fasting. Not surprisingly, his health suffered under this harsh regime, and in his request to the general, he pleaded that his illness and poor health were principle reasons for his removal to Rome.

Yet it would be another year until Valera was released from the Jesuits' underground jail cells, and even then he would continue under house arrest for an additional six years. Forbidden to leave the Jesuit residence, to talk to outsiders, or to perform any of the sacraments of a priest, he presumably used these six years to write his monumental work, the *Historia Occidentalis* (History of the West), cited by the chroniclers Garcilaso de la Vega and Alonso de Sandoval but now lost. Only in 1593, at the urging of José de Acosta, did Aquaviva allow Valera to be transferred to Europe, albeit to Spain rather than to Rome. After an unintended delay in Quito of almost two years, Valera arrived in Cádiz in 1596, where he was permitted to resume teaching. He was not allowed to enjoy his newfound freedom for long, however; that same year, he was severely injured in the English pirate attack on Cádiz, and according to Jesuit sources, he died of his wounds on April 2, 1597.

What was Valera's crime, an infraction so heinous that he was forced to spend the latter fourteen years of his life in imprisonment and then exile? Humiliatingly for the priest and scholar, his Jesuit superiors claimed that he had been imprisoned by the Inquisition for the crime of fornication. But as newly discovered Inquisition documents reveal, the Jesuits themselves had imprisoned Valera—for the crime of heresy, not fornication. Through his teachings and writings, the Jesuit missionary staunchly defended the rights of the native peoples of Peru. His work lauded not only native Inca government, culture, and learning but Inca religion as well, suggesting that Andean Christianity should incorporate many aspects of the pre-Spanish native religiosity. His apologetics for the Inca faith, in fact, came dangerously close to heresy, a situation that the Jesuits, battling Inquisition efforts to destroy the Society in Spain, could not tolerate.

Born of a native woman and a Spanish father, Valera was able to use his fluency in his mother's language and culture to work with native peoples throughout Peru and eventually to lead "spiritual discussions" with Inca elites in Cuzco. Echoes of these discussions, which centered on the similarities between the Inca and Christian religions, can be found in the existing remnants of Valera's chronicles of the Andes. His work demonstrates that he dedicated most of his intellectual life to defending Inca civilization against defamation by Spanish authors: he condemned the Spanish conquest of the Incas as unjust; he praised Inca rule as legitimate and moral; he placed the Inca language, Quechua, on par with Latin for its civilizing influence; he claimed that Inca religion possessed an implicit knowledge of Christ; and he even portrayed the defeated Inca emperor, Atahuallpa, as a Christian saint in heaven.

By taking these stands in favor of the native peoples, Valera placed himself in the middle of one of the most controversial issues of his day in Peru. Spanish debates over the legitimacy of Iberian rule in the

Indies and the manner in which natives should be treated, begun in the 1520s with the influential teachings of Francisco de Vitoria (1483–1546) in the Universidad de Salamanca, continued unabated throughout Valera's lifetime. In Salamanca, Vitoria and his followers elaborated principles of "just-war theory," propounding fairly restrictive circumstances whereby a Christian ruler could justify the conquest of a pagan kingdom; the writings of the "Salamanca school" formed the basis of subsequent attempts to protect the Indians from Spanish abuse, most notably by Vitoria's fellow Dominican Bartolomé de las Casas. The debates that occurred in Peru during Valera's life over the character of Inca rule, Inca civilization, and Andean religion had extensive political and spiritual consequences. Such issues as the recognition and treatment of native nobility, the legitimacy of new conquests in the interior, the nature of native labor and tribute, the ordination of men of Indian descent as Catholic priests, the use of native rituals in Christian ceremonies, and the forgiveness of conquistadors' sins in the confessional hinged on the outcome of these controversies.[1]

Valera was one of the first chroniclers of the Incas to present a strongly pro-Indian position, one developed in conscious response to the negative depictions of the Inca state that were sponsored by the viceroy Francisco de Toledo. For the breadth and vigor of his writings, Valera merits comparison with the other great defender of the rights of the native Americans in the sixteenth century, Bartolomé de las Casas. Yet for his involvement in these controversies, Valera would suffer the imprisonment, slander to his reputation, exile, and obscurity of his latter years. In fact, when the Jesuits in Peru voted unanimously in 1582 to never again allow mestizos into the Society, some claimed that this policy was necessary because of the dangerous example provided by the mestizo Valera. Valera's story provides a remarkable example of courage in the defense of the native Peruvians and sheds valuable insights into the controversies over religion, language, and Inca culture among sixteenth-century missionaries and native elites.

Amazingly, over four centuries after his death, Valera's role in

---

1. Two recent, excellent treatments of Vitoria, Las Casas, and the Spanish struggle for justice are Tierney 1997 and Goti Ordeñana 1999.

controversy is far from over. When I began this study years ago, Valera was an overlooked chronicler of the Incas; his mysterious life was little known. Scholars knew none of the details of his imprisonment; his work with native confraternities; his theories of language, writing, and history; or his experimentation with quipus. No scholar had even attempted to prepare a comprehensive, comparative study of his writings. Then, in 1996, at the Fourth International Ethnohistory Conference in Lima, the Italian anthropologist Laura Laurencich Minelli announced that a seventeenth-century document about Valera had been discovered in a private collection in Naples. This new document, she claimed, made a host of extraordinary assertions, including that Valera's death in 1597 had been faked by the Jesuits; that after 1597, Valera returned secretly to Peru, where he authored the famous *Nueva corónica y buen gobierno* (New chronicle and good government), which has been attributed to the native writer Felipe Guaman Poma de Ayala; that Valera taught his followers that the Incas used a secret, phonetic quipu to record history; and that several of these special phonetic quipus had been sent to Garcilaso de la Vega, who, however, lied about them in his book *Comentarios reales de los Incas y historia general del Perú* (Royal commentaries of the Incas and general history of Peru).

Minelli's revelations about the "Naples documents," as they are called, created an international sensation and has led to bitter disputes among scholars over how these documents should be assessed. Numerous Andeanists have denounced the manuscripts as forgeries concocted by the owner, Clara Miccinelli, and her friend Carlo Animato, perhaps with the assistance of Minelli. Francesca Cantú, from the Universitá di Roma, and Maurizio Gnerre, from the Instituto Universitario Orientale, have both discovered additional documents in public archives in Italy that confirm aspects of the story found in the Naples materials; these established Italian scholars likewise have been accused of participating in an intentional fraud, by seeding the archives with fake texts.

Other Peruvianists have argued that the Naples documents, while authentic seventeenth-century manuscripts, were forged by Jesuit followers of Valera after the latter's death, possibly to express political theories censored by the Society. Those who belong to this school of opinion point out that while some of the assertions in the texts, such as the claim that Valera wrote the *Nueva corónica,* are clearly false, much of the manuscript fits into what is now known (but was still unpublished in 1996) about Valera and the Jesuits in Peru. Finally, there are those who maintain that the Naples documents are both authentic and true in their startling allegations about Valera's faked death and his subsequent activities in Spain and Peru.

With the discovery of the Naples documents, knowing the truth about Valera's life has taken on a heightened importance. Some of the claims in the Naples documents, if true, will have major repercussions for our understanding of Andean civilization. Did the Incas have a secret, phonetic writing system? Was the *Nueva corónica,* a major testament of indigenous resistance to Spanish hegemony and one of the most important written sources about Inca culture, actually written by a Jesuit in hiding? Establishing a firm understanding of Valera's life is necessary for evaluating the authenticity of these mysterious and troubling documents.

The purpose of this book is to present a discussion of both Valera's life and his writings about native Peruvian history, religion, and language. It represents the first full-length monograph devoted to studying the poorly understood history of this mestizo author and priest. First, his childhood amid the "cloud forests" of Chachapoyas, his formation as a Jesuit priest, and his missionary work throughout Peru are explored to assess the influences on his thought. Then, the content of his writings is examined to demonstrate the diverse ways in which he developed his apologetics for the Incas and the native peoples of Peru. Because the Naples documents are so controversial, chapters 1–8, describing Valera's life and work, are based entirely on material unrelated to the manuscripts from Naples. Chapters 9–10 focus on the Naples materials, explaining what the documents are and considering their authenticity and their implications for our knowledge of Valera and of the Incas. It is hoped that this approach will allow readers to judge the documents for themselves based on what is known about Valera from other independent sources. It will also allow the story of Valera to shine in its own right, without being marred by the recent controversy over the Naples documents. Valera was a Peruvian of great courage and importance in the struggle for native rights, and he deserves to be recognized for his achievements in this area.

Chapter 2, "In 'the land of strong men,'" describes Valera's early life in Chachapoyas as an illegitimate mestizo son of one of the most powerful Spanish *encomenderos* (beneficiary of a grant of native labor tribute) in the region. This chapter examines in detail the lives of his father, Luis Valera; his native mother, Francisca Pérez; and his younger brother, Jerónimo, who eventually became one of the leading Franciscan theologians in Lima. Valera's eventful career as a Jesuit missionary is discussed in chapter 3, ". . . to go without subterfuge or excuse . . ." Based on a variety of Jesuit and other sources, this chapter first explores Valera's formation in the Jesuit novitiate in Lima. His missionary endeavors brought him into contact with native communities throughout the Andes, including those of Huarochirí, Santiago del Cercado (outside of Lima), Cuzco, Juli, and Potosí. In this chapter, his experiences and contacts in these missions are analyzed in the context of changing Jesuit attitudes toward native Andean Christianity.

Chapter 4 provides an overview of Valera's writings. His four known texts—including his major work, the *Historia Occidentalis*—are described in this chapter. Particular attention is paid to the manner in which his lost works are cited by Garcilaso de la Vega, Alonso de Sandoval, and Giovanni Anello Oliva. This chapter also considers the diverse sources of Valera's work, from the writings of well-known chroniclers, such as Polo de Ondegardo; to lost manuscripts by Spanish, mestizo, and Indian authors, such as Francisco Falcón, Melchior Hernández, and Juan Huallpa Inca; to conversations with indigenous leaders, such as Don Sebastián de Quispe Ninavillca, a native *curaca* from Huarochirí.

Chapters 5–7 focus on Valera's ethnography of the Incas and of Andean life in his own time. Chapter 5, ". . . the age of our country and sequence of events . . . ," examines his complex view of native Peruvian history. This chapter begins by analyzing his highly unusual history of over ninety pre-Inca rulers, including the kings Capac Raymi Amauta, Capac Yupanqui Amauta, Capac Lluqui Yupanqui, and Cuis Manco. This list of pre-Inca kings was shared with the chronicler Fernando de Montesinos and appears to reflect the native traditions of the Quito region. Valera's writings about the Inca kings are studied next, along with the manner in which Valera used this history to defend the Incas against their Spanish critics. Chapter 6, ". . . the terminology of all matters, human and divine . . . ," treats Valera's theories about the Quechua language, his comparison of Quechua with other South American languages and with Latin and Hebrew, and his beliefs about Andean writing systems. Additionally, this chapter explores Valera's association with an invented, phonetic quipu writing system, the iconography of which expresses many of the chronicler's polemics about Andean religious belief.

The nature of Inca religion is the subject of chapter 7, ". . . the laws of religious ceremonies and of the priesthoods . . ." Valera based his apologetics for Inca religious beliefs and practices on the categories of natural theology propounded by the classical writer Marcus Terentius Varro; this chapter explains how Valera's vision of Andean faith is structured according to Varro's typology, elevating Inca religion to a level almost on par with Christianity. Valera's characterization of Andean religious practitioners—including Inca priests, hermits, and holy virgins *(aclla)*—is also considered. Finally, this chapter concludes with a comparison of Valera's writings on religion with those of José de Acosta, Valera's Jesuit superior.

Chapter 8, ". . . a danger to Peru . . . ," recounts the tragic events leading to Valera's imprisonment by the Jesuits for heresy, as well as their false claims that he was actually incarcerated by the Inquisition. The final years of the chronicler's life are described, along with his protestations of innocence and the ultimate decision by General Aquaviva that Valera never, under any circumstances, be allowed to teach grammar. Completing the chapter is an account of the 1596 sack of Cádiz by Robert Devereux, earl of Essex, and of Valera's subsequent death at the hands of the English pirates.

In the remaining two chapters, the controversy over the so-called Naples documents is explored. Chapter 9 provides a description of the manuscripts found in the private archives of Clara Miccinelli in Naples: the *Historia et Rudimenta Linguae Piruanorum* (History and rudiments of the Peruvian language); *Exsul Immeritus* (Undeserved exile), which includes an account—allegedly by Francisco de Chaves—of the Spanish conquest of Peru; and a woven portion of a "royal" quipu recounting the honorary poem in honor of "Sumac ñusta" (Beautiful princess). Juan Carlos Estenssoro's and Rolena Adorno's allegations of modern anachronisms in the texts are examined in chapter 10, followed by a discussion of the texts' instances of historical accuracy on matters otherwise unknown at the time of the *Historia et Rudimenta*'s first publication. A tentative solution to the mystery of these manuscripts is suggested, along with a reflection on how they may affect our perception of Blas Valera.

CHAPTER TWO

In "the land of strong men"

Chachapoyas—the South American Frontier

B las Valera, the native Peruvian historian, poet, and missionary, was brought into this world in the province of Chachapoyas in 1544 (Egaña 1954, 284). It is most likely that he was born in the town of Quitaya, owned by his father; this settlement has since been lost to the encroaching forest. Blas's father, Luis Valera, had been one of the original Spanish conquerors of Chachapoyas and was a prominent *encomendero* in the region. Little is known about Blas's native mother, Francisca Pérez. Various scholars have speculated that she was related to the emperor Atahuallpa (Santisteban Ochoa 1946; González de la Rosa 1907, 190). It is believed that she and Luis had at least one other illegitimate son together—Jerónimo, who became the leading Franciscan writer and theologian in Peru during the early seventeenth century (Jerónimo Valera 1610, prologue; Córdoba y Salinas 1651, 257–58).

The province of Chachapoyas, centered in the "cloud forest" east of Cajamarca, was a relatively remote region within the early Peruvian viceroyalty. Chachapoyas is a land of great natural beauty, with steep, craggy mountains, fast-moving rivers, and thick, tropical forests comprised of low trees, mosses, ferns, and wild orchids. Yet the same features that contribute to the region's charms also helped to isolate the area from the rest of Spanish Peru. The mountains, rivers, and dense vegetation hindered travel and trade between Chachapoyas and the major Spanish population centers in Peru's highlands and along its coast. The difficult climate—one of the rainiest on earth—also made Chachapoyas relatively less attractive to Spanish settlers. During the rainy season, from September to March, much of the region receives daily inundations of fog and rain; during the dry season, snowstorms, freezing rain, and hail can occur in the higher elevations.

According to Blas Valera, as he is cited by Garcilaso de la Vega in the *Comentarios reales* ([1609] 1987, 475), *chachapoyas* was a native, non-Inca term meaning "the land of strong men."[1] Garcilaso provides several other details about the Chachapoya people that presumably were taken from Valera's lost writings. For example, he tells us that the Chachas were a numerous and warlike people whose women were renowned for their beauty. The condor was their principle god, and they revered snakes as well. According to an unpublished missionary account from 1612 by Father Antonio Pardo (Pius XII Library 1612), the region contained numerous powerful shamans who were able to cure illness and divine the future through the use of hallucinogenic herbs. The power to be a shaman was hereditary, Pardo writes, and open to women as well as to men. Pardo adds that shamans were known to have engaged in magical warfare with each other and to have performed maleficent actions on others' behalf.

Valera, as cited by Garcilaso, also mentioned that the Chachas had built many strong fortresses along mountain passes throughout the region. In fact, archaeologists have discovered in Chachapoyas numerous fortified settlements having a distinctive stone architecture. Most Chachapoya settlements were built at thirty-five hundred meters, providing for both defense and access to pastures and farmlands (Church 1996, 129–94). It is believed that the Chachapoya people were not politically unified before their conquest by the Incas

---

1. More recently, scholars have speculated that the name *Chachapoyas* is derived from the Quechua words meaning "forest" *(sacha)* and "cloud" *(puya)* and was imposed on the natives of this area by the Inca (Muscutt 1998, 28). There is no evidence that Valera ever knew the Chachapoya languages.

(Espinosa Soriano 1967, 233–34; Schjellerup 1997; Church 1996). Rather, the Chachas lived in independent cities, led by a chief—known in the Chachapoyan tongue as the *protho* (Avalos y Figeroa 1602, colloquy 28, line 124b)—and a council of elders.

Chachapoya history from both before and after the conquest of Chachapoyas by the Spanish seems to have been plagued by war. According to local oral traditions, the Chachapoya peoples frequently warred among themselves (Church 1996, 129–94). The Chachapoya people had been conquered by the Inca emperor Topa Inca Yupanqui (Garcilaso de la Vega [1609] 1987, 475–77). During the reign of the next emperor, Huayna Capac, the Chachas unsuccessfully rebelled against their Inca overlords and were forced to sue for peace when confronted with invading Inca armies. In 1532, the armies of the Inca emperor Atahuallpa marched through the province, wreaking vengeance against the Chachas for having supported Atahuallpa's rival, Huascar, in a bloody civil war. However, Atahuallpa's retaliation was interrupted by his own imprisonment at the hands of the Spanish conquistador Francisco Pizarro. After Atahuallpa's execution by the Spanish, Guaman, a Chachapoya leader who acted as the Inca proxy ruler in Cochabamba, swore his loyalty to Pizarro, becoming one of the colonial government's most faithful collaborators (Espinosa Soriano 1967, 262–69).

In 1536, the marquis Francisco Pizarro granted to Captain Alonso de Alvarado the right to explore the land of Chachapoyas. Later that year, Alvarado and seven men set out for the province, where they were greeted by Guaman, who promised his fealty to the Spaniards (Alvarado [1550] 1965, 165; Espinosa Soriano 1967, 270). Alvarado then demanded treasures of gold and silver, which he received, and ordered a census of the province, before departing. The Spanish captain returned in 1537 and began dividing Chachapoyas into *repartimientos*—grants of Indian labor intended for the new Spanish overlords. However, at this juncture, war broke out between Pizarro and Diego de Almagro, and Alvarado hurried back to fight on the side of the marquis. Upon the defeat of Almagro's army in 1538, Pizarro granted to Alvarado the right to settle Chachapoyas, stating that Alvarado possessed "the requisite ability, diligence, fidelity, and discretion in such matters and thorough experience with the customs of the Indians for their conquest, through being a pioneer in these parts."[2] Alvarado immediately proceeded to Chachapoyas with a small army, which included Luis Valera as a captain of the crossbow-men. There, Alvarado founded the city of San Juan de la Frontera de Chachapoyas at the site of the native town of Levanto. He then marched against the numerous native groups in the province who refused to accept Spanish sovereignty. Eventually, the Spaniards were able to defeat their Chachapoya enemies in a series of battles in which Luis Valera gained distinction for his valor and fighting skill (Cieza de León [1553] 1986, 296–301, 314–17). The Spanish then began the task of forming their own culture on this frontier gained through blood-shed and battle. The nature of early colonial life on this frontier, it should be noted, has been little studied and merits greater investiga-tion. From existing records, we know that Luis Valera, Blas's father, was a leading figure in the creation of the colonial Spanish society of Chachapoyas, where Blas's earliest character would have formed.

Luis Valera

The picture of Luis Valera that emerges from the historical documents is one of a cultured, educated, ambitious, hospitable man. He wrote with an elegant hand, as the manuscript records from the town coun-cil *(cabildo)* of Chachapoyas reveal (fig. 1). We know that he encour-aged learning in his two sons. He paid for both boys to be schooled away from home, where the educational opportunities were still very limited. Blas was educated in Trujillo, in the college founded there by the marquis de Cañete in 1556,[3] and Jerónimo was educated by the Jesuits in Lima (Jerónimo Valera 1610, prologue). Luis also harbored an interest in Inca antiquities, which he was able to pass on to his son Blas. In his later writing, Blas noted that his father had received from his kinsman Francisco de Chaves a "copious" history of the Incas, which Luis eventually gave to his friend Diego de Olivares, who in turn passed it on to other friends in their circle (Blas Valera [1594] 1968, 155).

----

2. ". . . la avilidad diligençia, y fedelidad e buen rrecado que Conviene y toda ysperençia de las costumbres de las yndios para su conquista por ser antiguo en estas partes" (Harkness 1538–45, fol. 1a).

3. This information is taken from the Jesuit provincial catalog of 1569, published in Egaña 1958, 141.

Fig. 1. Luis Valera's signature, from the *Libro del cabildo . . . de Chachapoyas,* fol. 43b. (Courtesy of the Harkness Collection, Library of Congress.)

According to the catalog of passengers to the Indies, Luis Valera hailed from Aracena, a small town in the mountains of western Andalusia (Bermudez Plata 1940, 304). His parents were Bartolomé García Román and Catalina Hernández. The mountains of Aracena, with their cool forests and many fresh springs, form a pleasant, if impoverished, area. Aracena and its neighboring villages were known in the sixteenth century for their wines, honey, and ham, the latter considered the finest in all of Spain. The region's copper mines date to the time of the Phoenicians. Young Luis, who later would become an important rancher in Chachapoyas, would have had ample opportunity to observe the art of animal husbandry while growing up in this agricultural region.

On April 28, 1534, Luis and his friend Francisco Romano departed for the New World (Bermudez Plata 1940, 304).[4] Only nine men from

---

4. It has been asserted that Luis Valera was present at the capture of Atahuallpa in 1532 by Pizarro, but this clearly was not possible. Information on the other men from Aracena who went to the New World can be obtained from the catalog of passengers to the Indies (Bermudez Plata 1940, 1942, 1944).

Aracena had preceded the two friends to the Americas. Of these ear-lier travelers, Valera would maintain relations with at least one, Fran-cisco Hernández, who had gone to America in 1517 (Bermudez Plata 1940, 187). When Valera departed from his hometown, he left behind a wife, the noblewoman Catalina Rodríguez de Aldana, daughter of Rodrigo Alonso Gallego and Ana García. Catalina did not join her husband in Peru until 1559—twenty-five years after his departure (Bermudez Plata 1944, 324).[5]

Valera's activities in Peru between 1534 and 1538 are unclear. It is likely, however, that he was in contact with his relative and friend Francisco de Chaves, one of Francisco Pizarro's most trusted com-panions.[6] In 1537, Valera probably fought with Alvarado on the side of Pizarro against Almagro. By 1538, he had signed on as a captain under Alonso de Alvarado. As a captain of the crossbowmen, Valera was one of Alvarado's most valued subordinates, which suggests that the two men had shared some prior military involvement.

As a reward for his military service in the conquest of Chachapoyas, Valera was granted the *encomiendas* (grant of native labor tribute) of Chibalta and Tiapullu by Alvarado (Alvarado [1550] 1965, 159). The latter *encomienda* consisted of two native villages— San Andrés and Santo Tomás—in which some 770 Indians resided (Puente Brunke 1992, 479, 484).[7] Those who served the *encomienda* of Chibalta lived about twenty miles to the north of the city of Chachapoyas. The native peoples of the Chibalta *encomienda* were divided between two small villages, Quitaya and Chibalta (ibid.). Valera built his country estate in Quitaya, where it is likely that his son Blas was born. In 1591, the archbishop of Lima, St. Toribio de Mogrovejo, visited the *doctrina* (a type of missionary parish) of Chibalta, which would have included Valera's *encomienda*. Accord-ing to the archbishop, about fifteen hundred adult Indians lived in this *doctrina*, which was divided into seven villages. Four hundred and

---

5. As Noble David Cook and Alejandra Parma Cook have demonstrated (1991), it was far from uncommon for would-be conquistadors to leave behind wives in Spain.

6. Blas Valera ([1594] 1968, 155) tells us that Francisco de Chaves was the "amigo y deudo" of Don Luis Valera.

7. An estimate of the number of inhabitants was reached by multiplying the number of tributaries in 1575 (153) by a factor of five. During Valera's ownership of Tiapollo and Chibalta, the number of tributary natives declined markedly (Puente Brunke 1992, 479, 484).

twelve adult natives lived in Quitaya in 1591 (Mogrovejo [1593] 1921, 54). In Blas's day, the entire life of this small town and of the other towns in his father's *encomiendas* would have revolved around his father's manor house.

Like the other *encomenderos* of northern Chachapoyas and Moyobamba, Luis Valera would have raised livestock, including cattle and llamas (and possibly goats, horses, and mules). This livestock was transported overland, in seasonal drives, to the city of Santiago on the Marañón River. In Santiago, the Chachapoya *encomenderos* were able to purchase—for very inflated prices—Spanish goods brought to Santiago in canoes from the city of Jaén (Alvarado [1550] 1965, 149). Valera's estate also produced salt, one of the region's most lucrative industries. Gold, obtained through placer mining, was also an important product of this area, and it is likely that Luis made his native workers mine gold in the local streams and rivers.

In addition to the *encomienda* of Chibalta and Tiapullu, Luis Valera also owned property in Nieva, the small town where his son Jerónimo was born (Córdoba y Salinas 1651, 257). Nieva was located in the valleys of the Moyobamba region.[8] When St. Toribio visited Nieva in 1591, he described it as being in a region of "mountains with bad roads," where travel was very difficult (Mogrovejo [1593] 1921, 48). In 1538, an earlier explorer had described this region as "a country of dense forest, and many rivers, . . . and ravines full of great thickets and cane-brakes." That explorer noted, "There were a few habitations of natives throughout this region, but so poor that there was nothing in them but a stone on which to make bread, a pot for cooking, and a mat to sleep on" (Cieza de León [1553] 1923, 289). Living in the town of Nieva in 1591 were 220 natives, all apparently of the Ollero tribe (Mogrovejo [1593] 1921, 48–49). The *encomenderos* in the area of Moyobamba were primarily engaged in cattle ranching (ibid., 49–50), and it is probable that Valera's property here was related to that industry. He also might have been involved in trade between Chachapoyas and the lowlands east of Moyobamba.

Luis Valera spent only part of every year at his estate in Quitaya or his property in Nieva. At least half of the year was spent in his Inca

8. This pueblo should not be confused with the town of Santa Maria de Nieva, founded in 1564 along the Nieva River, some eighty kilometers southwest of Santiago.

house in the city of Chachapoyas, where he attended meetings of the city town council, or *cabildo*. Council meetings were most commonly held during the rainy season, between October and February, although the council would meet at other times of the year when necessary (Harkness 1538–45). The Chachapoya *encomenderos* apparently preferred to pass the season of drenching rains, hail, and snowstorms in the conviviality of town life, rather than in the relative isolation of their country estates.

The city of San Juan de la Frontera de Chachapoyas was founded on September 5, 1538, on the site called Xalca by the natives, whose chief was named Çuta. Ten days later, however, the city was moved to the native town of Levanto.[9] In Levanto, Alvarado and his men were greeted by the local Inca governor of Chachapoyas, Cayo Tupac Rimachi, a nephew of the deceased emperor Huayna Capac. Years later, in 1592, Luis Valera recounted the meeting in the following words.

> When I entered the province of Chachapoyas with Mariscal Don Alonso de Alvarado, we found the governor to be Cayo Tupac Rimachi, chosen by Huayna Capac, in the town of Levanto. The Incas whom we met told him [Alvarado] that he [Cayo Tupac Rimachi] was the nephew of Huayna Capac; [he was] courageous and a good leader and afterward was called by the name *Pedro Cayo Tupac Rimachi* (I see and know that this Don Pedro has two sons: Pasac Tupac Yupanqui and Tito Tupac Yupanqui, who was afterward called Juan). This governor was the one who gave the provinces to Alvarado and who afterward helped [Alvarado] to conquer the Luya Chillaos, the Chillaos, and the rest of the towns. They say that he gave the nation's obedience to Mariscal Alvarado and to His Majesty.[10]

---

9. On August 27, 1544, the city council petitioned for permission to move the city to a site that would offer greater protection from Indian attacks (Harkness 1538–45, fols. 1b–16a, 69a), but there is no further mention of this in the council minutes. Today, the town of Levanto lies about ten miles south of the modern city of Chachapoyas.

10. "Cuando entré con el mariscal Don Alonso de Alvarado a la provincia de Chachapoyas a la conquista de ella, encontramos de gobernador, puesto por Huayna Capac, a Cayo Tupac Rimachi en el pueblo de Levanto. Los yngas que encontraron le dijeron que era sobrino de Huayna Capac, que es valiente y buena autoridad, y que después le llamaron con el nombre de Pedro Cayo Tupac Rimachi (Que veo y conozco que este don Pedro tiene dos hijos: Pasac Tupac Yupanqui y Tito Tupac Yupanqui que le llamaron

Concerning the friendship between Alvarado and Cayo Tupac, Cristobal Maldepen, the leader *(curaca)* of the ethnic group the Chill-chos, reported, "on one occasion, Alvarado gave to Don Pedro Cayo Tupac Yupanqui a dog named Poma [and] also a pair of eyeglasses from Spain, from which I deduced that they had a great friendship."[11]

Although Cayo Tupac, the Inca governor in Levanto, had remained to befriend the Spaniards, many of the other Inca and native lords in Levanto had fled the city, leaving behind their abandoned homes. Luis Valera and the other important Spaniards with Alvarado took over the empty Inca residences for their own homes. Whenever Blas stayed at his father's house in Chachapoyas, therefore, he lived in a typical Inca domicile, made up of several single-storied stone build-ings grouped around a courtyard. One imagines that his native mother, Francisca, would have been quite at home here. A large, round, white stone building—typical of Chachapoya architecture—was converted by the Spaniards into the city's Catholic church. The first masses that young Blas attended would have been held in this cir-cular native building, into which a Christian altar and Christian images had been placed.

The seven or eight members of the city council, along with the *alcaldes* (judges), met regularly to set about the business of creating a Spanish city on the Amerindian frontier. Their first crisis came in June 1539, when the Chachapoya native elites prepared a major revolt against the Spaniards.[12] In November of the preceding year, Alonso de Alvarado had set out with 250 Spaniards to search for gold in the lands east of Moyobamba (Alvarado [1550] 1965, 167; Cieza de León [1553] 1923, 289–93). In June, while Captain Alvarado was still away, "the Indians who were subjects of the new city [i.e., Chachapoyas] had rebelled and thrown off the yoke of the Spaniards. . . . When the natives of Chachapoyas saw that the captain was absent, they would

---

después Juan). Que este gobernador fue quien le dio la provincia a Alvarado y que después le ayudó a conquistar Luya Chillaos, los Chillaos y demas pueblos, dicen que le dio obedi-encia del pueblo al mariscal Alvarado y a su magestad" (testimony of Luis Valera in favor of Don Juan Cayo Tupa Inga, Don Felipe Cayo Tupa Inga, and Doña Luisa Quisquima, November 1592, published in Lerche 1995, 111–12).

    11. ". . . en una oportunidad Alvarado le regalo a Don Pedro Cayo Tupac Yupanqui un perro llamado Poma también unos ojos de vidrio de España, deduciendo de esto que ten-ian mucha amistad" (ibid., 112).

    12. See Harkness 1538–45, fols. 9v–13r, for determining the date of the revolt.

not come to serve nor pay tribute, nor do anything for their masters" (Cieza de León [1553] 1923, 290). The council and the mayors tried to pacify the native leaders and meanwhile sent messengers to find Alvarado and inform him of the dangerous situation. Upon hearing of the uprising, Alvarado returned to Chachapoyas at once. The chronicler Cieza de León (ibid., 291) reports:

> he was received with great joy by the Spaniards, while many of the Indian leaders, fearing the consequences of their rising, came in peacefully, offering excuses although it was clear that they were neither just nor relevant. The captain told them that they should not rebel, but continue their friendship with the Spaniards, for they knew their great power, and that they could make war as well as maintain peace. They answered that they would never rebel again.

Despite the local leaders' assurances of peace, the dread of violence against the Spanish invaders was always a lurking fear in Chachapoyas. Minor rebellions, such as the 1576 revolt in Moyobamba during which a Mercedarian friar was murdered, occurred throughout the colonial era.[13] The records of the early Chachapoya council contain a 1544 letter addressed to the viceroy, in which Luis Valera and the other council members described the native people as "warlike and wild, as one can always see in the outlying districts of the city rebellious and insurgent native leaders."[14] Although Blas Valera had not yet been born by the time of the Chachapoya uprising of 1539, he would have experienced firsthand the climate of unease and violence that underlaid European rule on the Chachapoya frontier.

Most of the work of the city council was, of course, much more mundane than responding to native rebellions. Luis Valera and the other council members were more typically concerned with such matters as regulating the local markets, publishing mining ordinances, and maintaining the city roads (Harkness 1538–45, fols. 55a, 82b–83a, 59a). In 1543, the year before Blas was born, Valera was elected *alcalde* for the city, in addition to being named royal treasurer (ibid.,

---

13. The story of the murder of this friar can be found in Bartolomé de Santiago's 1577 account of his missionary journey through Chachapoyas, published in Egaña 1958, 232–39.

14. ". . . tan belicosa e yndomyta a ver siempre como los ay en los termynos desta cibdad al presente caçiques alçados e Rebelados" (Harkness 1538–45, fol. 76b).

fol. 51b). As an *alcalde*, Valera was a judge for minor crimes, as well as an advisor to the *lugarteniente*, Alonso de Alvarado.

For the next sixteen years, little is heard of Luis Valera, except for routine matters. In 1559, however, a major transformation occurred in the Valera household in Chachapoyas. In that year, Catalina Rodríguez de Aldana, Luis's wife, left Spain to join her husband in Peru (Bermudez Plata 1944, 324). She was accompanied by her two nieces, Isabel and Francisca de la Paz. We do not know why Catalina had spent twenty-five years apart from her husband or why she was finally going to join him now. A possible answer, however, is suggested by the party of people whom Luis sent to Spain to travel back with his wife. Included in this group was Luis's infant son Jerónimo, but not Jerónimo's mother, Francisca. Instead, the boy was cared for by two adult women—Catalina Ruiz, the daughter-in-law of Luis's original traveling companion Francisco Romano; and Isabel Bernal, the widowed daughter of Francisco Hernández, one of the first men from Aracena to venture to the New World. One wonders whether the mother of both Blas and Jerónimo had died or otherwise left Luis, causing their father to ask his wife to come and care for his sons and household.

The arrival of a stepmother must have marked a significant change for Blas, who was fifteen years old at the time; his father's legitimate wife was now in charge of the household. However, Blas would not remain in Chachapoyas for long after her arrival. Around this time, Blas was sent to school in Trujillo to study Latin and the liberal arts (Egaña 1958, 141). Jerónimo was raised in the household of his Spanish stepmother. Later, he was sent to the Jesuit College of San Martín in Lima to complete his education. Unlike Blas, Jerónimo never learned to speak Quechua; apparently, his mother was not there to teach it to him.

In 1577, Luis Valera appears again in Jesuit records. In the previous year, the Jesuit priest Miguel de Fuentes, accompanied by the mestizo lay brother Bartolomé de Santiago, went on a missionary journey to the Chachapoya region. Bartolomé de Santiago described his travels through the rugged Chachapoya mountains in a letter to the Jesuit provincial dated February 15, 1577.[15] Santiago wrote that,

---

15. See the account of this expedition published in Egaña 1958, 232–39.

while visiting the *doctrina* of Chibalta, Santiago wrote that he and Father Fuentes were very well received by Luis Valera, who invited them to stay in his home in Quitaya. Every day of the Jesuits' stay, the native lords of Valera's *encomienda* brought their children to the Jesuits for instruction in the faith. These were difficult times in the region, however, because of unrest among the native populations. In the city of Chachapoyas, Santiago wrote, the Christian teaching was opposed by a great many native "witches"—Indian priests and healers who actively discouraged native peoples from participating in Catholic rituals. Santiago also described a recent local uprising in which the natives of Moyobamba had murdered a friar. The Spanish wanted to take revenge for the killing on the local native population, Santiago continued, but the two Jesuits were able to bring at least a temporary peace to the situation (Egaña 1958, 232–39). Thirty-eight years after Alonso de Alvarado and his men founded the city of Chachapoyas, the region remained a challenging one in which to live and prosper.

Luis Valera had certainly come a long way from the mountains of western Andalusia. He had transformed himself into one of the most powerful men in Chachapoyas, an *encomendero* with sizable ranching and mining interests, as well as an *alcalde* and a royal treasurer. Yet he lived in a difficult frontier zone, where the culture, people, and material goods of home were scarce and were overshadowed by the Indian world on whose exploitation his wealth depended. He never left his newly found country of Peru, however—not even to bring home his Spanish wife. One wonders whether he ever missed his native soil in Aracena, or whether he was only too thankful to be gone from there forever.

Francisca Pérez

All that can be stated with absolute certainty about Blas Valera's mother is her Christian name—Francisca Pérez—and that she was an indigenous Peruvian; it is also most likely that she was of Inca ancestry.[16] As

---

16. Francisca's name and ethnicity are provided by the Jesuit provincial catalog of 1569, published in Egaña 1954, 283.

with so many women in history, we can know her primarily through the deeds of her sons. Both of her sons proved to be highly intelligent, learned, devout men, with a love of language (both were poets) and of the heavens (both were learned in astronomy). There is no doubt that many of their positive qualities came from their mother as well as from their father. In addition, Francisca taught her son Blas to speak fluent Quechua, her native tongue. Blas's first exposure to Andean legends and poetry certainly came from his mother.

Several scholars have speculated that Francisca Pérez was an Inca princess from the court of the emperor Atahuallpa (Esteve Barba 1968, xliii; González de la Rosa 1907, 190). Although there is no solid evidence, it seems almost certain that she was of Inca, rather than Chachapoyan, descent; she was quite possibly related to Cayo Tupac Rimachi, the former governor of Chachapoyas and the nephew of Huayna Capac. The language she taught to Blas was Quechua, an Inca tongue, not Chachapoyan, which suggests strongly that she was of Inca, not Chachapoyan, descent. Her son Blas was highly biased in favor of the Incas, at the expense of other native groups in South America.[17] Valera was also strongly partisan in favor of the Inca Atahuallpa, against Atahuallpa's half brother and rival for the throne, Huascar.[18] For example, in his *Vocabulario,* Valera wrote that Atahuallpa was the victim, first, of his brother Huascar's aggression and, later, of the "treachery and thousand lies" of Francisco Pizarro. Valera noted that the former emperor accepted Christian baptism and the Christian name *Juan* and died as a holy saint.

> He gained heaven and exchanged the kingdom on earth for that of eternal life. Some say that the king took *Don Francisco* as a name: it could well be that he took both names, but it is very certain that he had the name *Juan* and that he took this name out of respect for Doña Juanna, Queen Mother of the emperor Charles V. . . . He reigned three years, two in company with his brother and one alone, in such a way that our Lord was preserving the Incas and their king-

---

17. See, for example, Valera's discussion of Inca civil law and account of the spread of Inca rule under Pachacuti, cited by Garcilaso de la Vega ([1609] 1987, 261–64, 393–95).

18. See, for example, Valera's discussion of Atahuallpa cited by Anello Oliva ([1631] 1998, 107–8).

dom until this good Atahuallpa arrived, he who was destined for salvation and beloved and was carried off to heaven.[19]

It is possible that Valera might have learned about this version of Atahuallpa's life from his mother or her relatives, if she was in fact connected to Atahuallpa's royal family. Francisca left to her son a legacy of love for the Incas that would sustain him throughout his life.

Fray Jerónimo Valera, O.F.M.

Blas Valera's brother, Jerónimo, deserves special mention for the respected and powerful position he achieved among the Franciscans in Peru. His accomplishments are all the more remarkable given the discrimination against mestizos in the colonial church. The Franciscans did not even officially allow mestizos to enter their ranks in sixteenth-century Peru. That the friars not only accepted Jerónimo but also allowed him to become the head of their order in Peru attests to his outstanding personal qualities.

According to the seventeenth-century Franciscan chronicler Fray Diego de Córdoba y Salinas, Jerónimo was born in the small town of Nieva in the district of Chachapoyas. Although Córdoba y Salinas does not tell us the year of Jerónimo's birth, other evidence indicates that it was probably in the late 1550s (Córdoba y Salinas 1651, 257). As an infant or young child, Jerónimo traveled to Spain in the care of Catalina Ruiz and Isabel Bernal, returning to Peru in September 1559 (Bermudez Plata 1944, 324). As has been noted previously, his mother was absent from this trip, which suggests that she had died or had otherwise left Valera's household.

Jerónimo grew up in the household of his father's legitimate wife, Catalina Rodríguez de Aldana. There is no evidence that Luis and Catalina ever had any children of their own. Given the couple's

---

19. "Ganose el çielo y trocó el Reyno de la tierra por el de la Vida Eterna. Algunos diçen que el Rey tomó por nombre Don Françisco: bien pudo ser que tomase ambos nombres: más es muy çierto que tuvo nombre Juan y tomó este nombre por respecto de Doña Juanna Reyna madre del Emperador Carlos Quinto. . . . Reynó tres años; dos en compañía de su hermano; y uno solo, de manera que nuestro señor fue conservando los Incas y su Reyno hasta que llegasse este buen Atahuallpa que era electo y querido, y se lo llevó a la gloria" (from "Atahuallpa" in Valera's *Vocabulario*, quoted in Anello Oliva [1631] 1998, 138–39).

twenty-five-year separation from each other, the lack of offspring is not surprising. Growing up, Jerónimo would have been able to spend time with his older brother when Blas came home from school on vacation. When Blas became a Jesuit in 1568 at the age of twenty-four, Jerónimo would only have been about thirteen years old. Eventually, however, Jerónimo was sent to study at the Jesuit College of San Martín in Lima (Jerónimo Valera 1610, prologue). There, the two brothers would have had the opportunity to get to know each other again. In the late 1570s, Jerónimo petitioned the Jesuit General Mercurian in Rome for permission to follow in his brother's footsteps and become a Jesuit. On February 25, 1580, General Mercurian wrote to Blas, informing him that his brother could be welcomed into the Society.[20] Jerónimo must have been overjoyed at being allowed to become one of this very select group of men in the newly founded Society of Jesus. The increasing hostility to mestizos among the Jesuits in Peru at this time meant that it had not been certain that he would be admitted (Hyland 1994).

Three years later, however, in April of 1583, Blas was imprisoned by the Jesuits on mysterious charges (see chap. 8). Blas's imprisonment would last until 1594, when his superiors exiled him to Spain, where he would die in 1597. Jerónimo left the Jesuits at the time of his brother's troubles, transferring his allegiance to the Franciscans.

Jerónimo took the Franciscan habit in Lima on August 21, 1588 (Córdoba y Salinas 1651, 257–58). He taught theology in Lima for many years, specializing in the scholastic theology of "the Subtle Doctor," Duns Scotus. Twice he was chosen to be superior of the Franciscan house in Lima. He also sat as a judge for the Holy Office of the Inquisition, helping to determine the most difficult cases. In 1614, Fray Francisco de Herrera, commissioner general of the entire Franciscan order worldwide, elected Jerónimo to be the Peruvian provincial—that is, head of the Franciscans in Peru. This was an extraordinary honor for a man who was a mestizo; the Jesuits (since 1582), the Dominicans, and the Augustinians did not even accept mestizos into their orders at this time.

Prior to being chosen as provincial, Jerónimo composed a brief tract on the rights of the native Peruvians and the tribute services that

---

20. The letter is published in Egaña 1958, 168.

can be demanded from them (app. A). In 1599, the viceroy, Don Luis de Velasco, had presented a series of questions about the morality of Indian labor tribute to the Dominicans, Franciscans, and Jesuits in Lima;[21] Jerónimo was chosen by his confreres to draft the Franciscan response.

In his questionnaire, the viceroy made the following observations: (1) that it had already been determined that Indians must work in the mines; (2) that silver from the mines was essential for the defense of Christendom and for the health of the colony, because without silver, commerce would cease and the kingdom would become impoverished; and (3) that the flow of silver would cease if new mines were not put into production. Therefore, he asked whether it would be moral to assign Indians to the owners of newly discovered mines, in addition to the Indian labor already being used in the existing mines. If this increased tribute were to prove too burdensome on the native peoples, he continued, perhaps the natives' labor tribute of herding livestock, farming, construction, tending inns *(tambos)* and roads, and so forth could be reduced or even eliminated.

Jerónimo's answer to this begins with the observation that there is no doubt about the morality of sending Indians to work in the mines, because many learned men have already considered this question and found it just. However, writes Jerónimo, to increase the percentages of Indians laboring in the mines so that newly discovered mines could be exploited would be excessively harsh on the native population. He explains that the Indian population would be greatly diminished if their service in the mines were increased, harming not only the natives but the rest of the realm as well. Moreover, he adds, there is already sufficient silver in Peru for the defense of the faith and for commerce.

In response to the second part of the Viceroy's question, concerning native labor in agriculture and other work, Jerónimo is adamant that this tribute not be decreased. In fact, he points out that there is already a lack of Indians to work in the fields, in workshops, and on the roads and inns, a shortage that will increase as new Spaniards

---

21. Velasco's concerns over the morality of requiring natives to perform certain types of labor in the mercury mines of Huancavelica are examined by Guillermo Lohmann Villena (1999, 179–97).

arrive in Peru. This labor, he claims, is the most essential tribute of the Indians, for without it, there would be widespread food shortages and less trade. In Jerónimo's concern over this second type of native tribute service, we can see his care for the Franciscans' own financial interests, which would be harmed if there were fewer native Andeans to work in Franciscan fields and workshops. While Jerónimo's answer is fairly typical of his time, he seems not to have shared (or at least not to have expressed after having witnessed his brother's imprisonment) his older brother's radical pro-Indian sentiments. Much of Jerónimo's essay is devoted to arguing that it is a greater good for Indians to work in the fields than to labor in newly discovered mines; his positions are justified entirely by a long series of references to Gratian's *Decretum* (a twelfth-century compendium of canon law) and to books 3 and 5 of Aristotle's *Ethics*.

One sees the scholastic concern for Aristotle in Jerónimo's tract, an interest that would come to fruition in his later works, *Commentarii ac Quaestiones in Universam Aristotelis ac Subtilissimi Doctoris Ihoannis Duns Scoti Logicam* (Commentaries and questions of the most subtle doctor John Duns Scotus on the entire logic of Aristotle), published in Lima in 1610 (fig. 2). In his preface to the reader, the author states that he was almost afraid to write this book because of the "distressing voices of the critics in my ears," asking whether anything good can come out of Peru. He responds to these critics, however, by writing that God is powerful enough to raise sons of Abraham from Peruvian stones. His readers would have recognized this as a reference to a biblical passage in which John the Baptist berates the Pharisees for their pride in their pure Jewish ancestry, saying to them, "I tell you, God can raise up children of Abraham from these very stones" (Matthew 3:9 New American Bible). In other words, the gospel writer is stating that the true community of God has nothing to do with race or ancestry. Likewise, Jerónimo—whose mother was an Indian—is defending himself from critics by asserting that faithful Christians can arise from the children of Peruvian pagans, if God wills it. Only in 1610 did the Franciscans officially begin to allow mestizos into their order in Peru (Oleachea 1972); it is likely that Jerónimo was instrumental in this change of policy. The reconciliation of his pagan heritage with his Christian faith was clearly an important issue for Jerónimo, as it was for Blas.

COMMENTARII

AC QVAESTIONES

IN VNIVERSAM ARISTOTE-
LIS AC SVBTILISSIMI DOCTORIS IHOAN-
NIS DVNS SCOTI LOGICAM.

TOTVM HOC OPVS IN DVAS PARTES DISTRIBVTVM offertur:prima continet breue quóddam Logicæ Compendium qhod vulgo solet Summa seu Summulæ Dialecticæ nuncupari Quæstiones pro legomenales; prædicabilia Porphirij, & Aristotelis Anteprædicamenta,Prædicamenta & post Prædicamenta.

SECVNDA PARS LIBROS PERIHERMENIARVM SEV de interpretatione,libros priorum,Posteriorum,Topicorum & Elenchorum comprehendit.

AVCTORE R. P. F. HYERONIMO VALERA PERVANO ORDINIS Minorum Regularis obseruantiæ,Prouinciæ duodecim Apostolorum,Sacræ Theologiæ Lectorè iubilato & in Celeberrimo Limensi Conuentu S. Francisci Guardiano.

CVM PRIVILEGIO.

Limæ Apud Franciscum à Canto. Anno. M. DC. X.

Fig. 2. Title page of Jerónimo Valera's *Commentarii ac Questiones in Universam Aristotelis* (1610)

Despite his native ancestry, Father Jerónimo Valera was very well regarded by his fellow friars. Writing only twenty years after Jerónimo's death, Córdoba y Salinas has the highest praise for the mestizo friar.

> He was an excellent preacher, a learned writer and elegant Latinist, and a witty poet; a skillful astrologer and, in the summation of moral matters, a giant of wisdom, in whose heart the subtle Doctor Scotus had imprinted his teaching and humility. With scholasticism as his principle foundation, he was, without equal, the phoenix of theologians of his time. . . . He taught arts and theology in Lima for many years, where he poured out the genius of his learning, admired by the most learned for the great understanding [shown] in his writing. . . . he was born a learned man for the glory of his homeland, like a saint to acquire glorious triumphs. . . . Admiring his writing [one day], that great viceroy, and no minor theologian, the prince of Esquilache, exclaimed that he only wished for those in Spain to see Father Valera in order to give credit to Peru.[22]

According to Córdoba y Salinas (1651, 258), Jerónimo's book was a success in Europe, and the work's erudition and elegant writing led the general of the order to choose Jerónimo as official "author of the order," responsible for writing a history of the Franciscans and their missions around the world. Unfortunately, Jerónimo passed away before he could begin this monumental task. Córdoba y Salinas reports that Jerónimo died on Lazarus Friday (the fourth Friday of Lent) in 1625, "receiving all of the sacraments with marvelous acts of contrition and love of God." He was buried in the Franciscan monastery in Lima, where his tomb still exists.

---

22. "Era excelente Predicador, docto escritorio, elegante latino y agudo Poeta; curioso Astrologo, y en las materias morales epilogo gigante de sabiduria, en cuyo corazón selló el Doctor sutil Escoto su doctrina y humildad. Siendo lo escolastico su principal instituto, en que sin igual fue el Fenix de los Teologos de su tiempo. . . . Leyó muchos años Artes y Teologia en Lima, donde derramó los rayos de su dotrina, admirando los mas doctos en sus escritos la gran comprehension de las materias. . . . pues tambien nace un docto para las glorias de su Patria, como un santo para adquirirle gloriosos triunfos. . . . Admirando sus letras aquel gran Virrey, y no menor Teologo, el Principe de Esquilache, exclamó, que solo quisiera ver para credito del Perú, en las España, al Padre Valera" (Córdoba y Salinas 1651, 257–58).

THE JESUIT AND THE INCAS

A Boyhood in Chachapoyas

When Blas Valera was born in 1544, the Spaniards had been settled in Chachapoyas for only six years. As a youth, Blas saw firsthand how the conquistadors, including his father, created a European colony in the midst of sophisticated indigenous civilizations. Blas's boyhood would have been spent mainly at his father's estate in Quitaya. Spanish colonial estates of this kind were largely self-sufficient; an entire microeconomy encompassing several villages revolved around the Valera manor house. On the estate itself, of course, native laborers raised livestock and mined salt and gold for Blas's father. In Quitaya, Blas would have heard tales about the Incas from his mother and her relatives. His father also spent time recounting to Blas stories about the Spanish conquest of the Incas. For example, according to Garcilaso de la Vega, Blas wrote that his father had told him many times about the capture of Atahuallpa in the plaza of Cajamarca.

Periodic visits to the city of Chachapoyas would have brought Blas into contact with Spaniards, creoles, and other mestizo boys. He was surely friends with Alonso Camacho, a young mestizo whose father was one of the original settlers of Chachapoyas and sat on the town council with Luis Valera. Alonso, who was one year older than Blas, joined the Jesuits in Lima several years after Blas did.[23] Gonzalo Ruiz, the mestizo son of a wealthy Chachapoya resident, joined the Jesuits in Lima only several weeks after Blas; it seems likely that Blas and Gonzalo were companions from childhood.[24] Juan and Pedro de Añasco, two of the mestizo sons of Pedro de Añasco, another powerful Chachapoya *encomendero,* also joined the Jesuits a few years after Blas did.[25] In the small society of colonial elites in Chachapoyas, all these boys must have known each other well, visiting each other's houses and playing in the streets of Chachapoyas together.

In the city of Chachapoyas, Blas would also have gained his first exposure to the Mass and other Christian sacraments. The first secular priest in Chachapoyas was Father Hernando Gutierrez de Palacio. He was present in 1541 when the first Mercedarian friars settled in Chachapoyas. Father Palacio left in 1542, leaving the residents of the

---

23. See the Jesuit provincial catalog published in Egaña 1954, 513.
24. See the Jesuit provincial catalog published in Egaña 1954, 284.
25. See the Jesuit provincial catalog published in Egaña 1958, 141.

city without a parish priest. The *Libro del cabildo* tells us that after Palacio's departure, a priest named Diego Jaymes arrived in Chachapoyas. The *cabildo* assigned the vacant benefice to Jaymes in December 1542 (Harkness 1538–45, fol. 42a–b). Within a year, however, Palacios returned and reclaimed his parish. The *cabildo* then made Jaymes a sacristan to assist the priest. Blas was born the following year, in 1544, and Palacio, Jaymes, or one of the Mercedarian friars would have performed his baptism. Father Palacio remained in Chachapoyas until the early 1550s, when the benefice was granted to Pedro Palomar, a Spanish priest from Tiembla. Father Palomar arrived in Chachapoyas with his sixteen-year-old nephew Bautista Martínez in 1552, when Blas was twelve (Bermudez Plata 1944, 117).

Fathers Palacio, Jaymes, and Palomar were not the only Catholic priests in early Chachapoyas. Arriving in 1541, the Mercedarians built a monastery in the city.[26] The Mercedarians had been founded in 1218 by St. Peter Nolasco for the purpose of ransoming Christians captured and enslaved by the Moors. The ransoming of Christian slaves in North Africa was still an extremely important function of the order in the sixteenth century, but the Mercedarians had taken on additional duties. One of these was evangelization in the New World. In early colonial Peru, the Mercedarians were more involved in Indian missions than was any other order, except, perhaps, for the Franciscans (Hyland 1994, 251–66). In fact, the Mercedarians in Chachapoyas were soon followed by the Franciscans, who established a monastery there in the early 1550s (Barriga 1933, 174).

Toward the end of his life, Blas Valera praised the work of the Mercedarians, writing that they "do much [for the natives] with their sermons and confessions" (Blas Valera [1594] 1968, 188). About the Franciscans, he wrote, "there were not [among them] as many interpreters or men fluent in native tongues, but those who devoted themselves to the good of the natives did all that they ought" (185). For the most part, however, Valera had harsh criticisms of the early missionaries, especially for those who never learned the native languages. He also condemned the example set by many of the first conquistadors in

---

26. See the related letter signed by Luis Valera and the other members of the *cabildo* of Chachapoyas, "Carta del cabildo secular de la frontera de chachapoyas a Su Magestad encareciendo la necesidad que padece la religión de la Merced cuyo monasterio contaba doce años de fundación con gran provecho a los naturales" (Barriga 1933, 174–75).

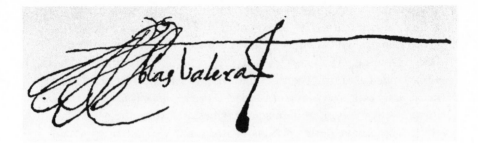

Fig. 3. Blas Valera's signature. (Reprinted from Toribio Polo 1907, 552.)

Peru; in this, he surely was reflecting in part on what he saw as a youth in Chachapoyas.

> The Spanish who succeeded [the Incas] in government did not care about [virtue] for a long time, occupied as they were with their disagreements and greed; and having to be the example of Christian virtue, [they] were the most decadent and wretched; and they counseled wives to leave their husbands, virgin daughters [to leave] their parents, and they gave [these women] over to public lewdness [i.e., prostitution], a thing that had not been seen in the [Inca] kingdom for over two thousand years.[27]

In the rough frontier society of early colonial Chachapoyas, Blas would have witnessed some of the abuse of native women about which he wrote.

Examining the family and early life of Blas Valera can give us insights into his development and later career. Until now, the details of his father's past, his brother's career, and his early life in Chachapoyas have been virtually unknown. Blas was the product of a dual heritage in a newly created frontier culture. On the one hand, his mother taught him respect for the great traditions of the Inca nobility. She must have spent many hours recounting to her son, in her native

---

27. ". . . los españoles que sucedieron [los Incas] en el gobierno, no trataban por mucho tiempo nada desto [de virtud], ocupados con sus desconciertos y codicias, y habiendo de ser el ejemplo de la virtud cristiana, fueron los más flacos y miserables, y dieron avilantez a que las casadas dejasen a sus maridos, las hijas virgines a sus padres y se diesen públicamente a deshonestidades, cosa que todo lo que antes precedió en más de dos mill años, no se había visto en el reino" (Blas Valera [1594] 1968, 182).

tongue, stories and poems about the Incas. On the other hand, Blas's father took care to give his sons the best education available in the colony. Blas's handwriting (fig. 3) is in fact remarkably similar to that of his father, and it is quite likely that, in the absence of other tutors, Luis taught his son to write—one can imagine little Blas at his father's knee while Luis showed him how to make his letters. From both parents, Blas received personal strength, courage, and intelligence, along with an abiding concern for the Andean past. Out of a remote city in one of the most rugged regions of the Peruvian viceroyalty, Blas and his brother, Jerónimo, arose to become two of the greatest thinkers and authors in early colonial South America.

CHAPTER THREE

". . . to go without subterfuge or excuse . . ."

Novitiate

On November 29, 1568, Blas Valera joined the Jesuits in Lima at the age of twenty-four. He had already studied the liberal arts and theology in Trujillo (Egaña 1958, 141), where he had devoted hours talking to the *amautas*—historians and storytellers—of Atahuallpa. From these men, he learned firsthand about the legends of the Inca's northern court in Quito (Garcilaso de la Vega [1594] 1968, 592–93). Although he could have returned to his father's estate in Chachapoyas after completing his studies in Trujillo, he chose instead to follow the path of a Jesuit missionary. For slightly more than the next three years, he would be a humble novice and student, studying and preparing for his eventual ordination as a priest in 1573.

When Valera was admitted to the Society, Jesuits had been in Lima for only a few months. The first Jesuits arrived in Peru on April 18, 1568, many years after the Mercedarians, Franciscans, and

---

". . . to go without subterfuge or excuse, as far as in us lies, to whatsoever provinces they may choose to send us—whether they are pleased to send us among the Turks or any other infidels, even those who live in the region called the Indies, or among any heretics whatever, or schismatics, or any of the faithful." This phrase is from the Jesuits' founding formula, which dates to 1550.

Dominicans. In fact, at this time, the Society of Jesus was less than thirty years old. The order's establishment is generally considered to date to September 27, 1540, when Pope Paul III approved St. Ignatius's first outline of the order *(Prima Formula Instituti)* and authorized the composition of detailed constitutions. St. Ignatius Loyola had founded the Society of Jesus after a lengthy period of spiritual searching and meditation while recuperating from a serious war injury. Unlike previous monastic and mendicant orders, the Jesuits were to be composed almost entirely of priests, who would no longer spend hours in the daily communal recitation of the psalms but would have unprecedented mobility to go wherever they were needed (Clancy 1976, 17–20; O'Malley 1995). This mobility was necessary for the Jesuits' missionary work, which was (and still is) a central purpose of the Society.[1] By the time the first seven Jesuits left for Peru in 1567,[2] the Society already had missions well established in the East Indies, Japan, Brazil, and the Congo.

The man in charge of the first Jesuits in Peru was Father Jerónimo Ruíz de Portillo, who would be provincial for the next seven years. Portillo was an energetic, outspoken man with a talent for public speaking. According to the seventeenth-century Jesuit chronicler Giovanni Anello Oliva ([1631] 1998, 203–10), Portillo's first sermon in Lima was a heartfelt exposition on the Jesuits' desire to foster the spiritual reformation of the colony. While Portillo spoke, there was a minor earthquake, which, Anello Oliva tells us, was popularly taken as a sign of the power behind the priest's words. It is quite possible that Valera was inspired to join the Jesuits after hearing this or another of Portillo's powerful homilies. Immediately upon arriving in Lima, Portillo began to solicit donations for the construction of the Jesuit house and church. Through the generosity of the citizens of Lima, the Jesuits soon possessed a residence for Society members, a college for Spanish and creole students, a separate novice house, and a church (Egaña 1958, 133). During construction, Portillo earned the nickname "the Bricklayer" because of his habit of spending his after-

---

1. Only in the late sixteenth and early seventeenth centuries did the Jesuits come to be seen as a symbol of the so-called Counter-Reformation. It is generally accepted today that the militant involvement of the early Jesuits in Catholic attempts to counter Protestantism has been greatly exaggerated. See O'Malley 1995.

2. The classic work on the Jesuits in Peru remains Vargas Ugarte 1963–65.

noons doing physical labor on the buildings, rather than working in his office. He would often go to say mass with the dust of his labor still clinging to him (Anello Oliva [1631] 1998, 203–10).

Once the buildings for the Jesuit house in Lima had been procured, Portillo immediately began to accept novices for the Society. The impossibility of staffing the Peruvian missions entirely from Europe, which lacked sufficient numbers of men to send to all of the Jesuits' overseas foundations, made it essential to train novices in Peru. In the annual letter to the Jesuit general dated January 21, 1569, Father Diego de Bracamonte explained why the provincial accepted novices in Peru.

> [Portillo] sees well that Your Paternity will not be able to send those that are needed for this new world; that even if all the Society from [Europe] were sent, it would not be the thousandth part of that which here [is needed].[3]

In the same letter, Bracamonte praised the new novices, singling out Blas Valera for special commendation.

> [Valera] is a great Latinist and poet and a great linguist in many languages here, which was what we greatly desired so that we would go learning the languages [spoken] here.[4]

Although the Dominicans, Franciscans, and Augustinians in Peru all refused to accept mestizos at this time (Oleachea 1972), the early Jesuits were committed to including mestizos among their novices in Lima. The famous José de Acosta later described why he and many of the other Jesuits in Peru were so eager to accept mestizos.

> [The mestizos] know very well the [natives'] language by having spoken it from infancy and can say in it what they wish; and, on the other hand, they are upright and solid in the Christian faith through having received it from their progenitors and having been raised in

---

3. ". . . bien ve que no le podrá V. P. enbiar los que acá son menester para este nuevo mundo, que aunque toda la Compañía de allá se la enbiase, no avría la miléssima parte de lo que acá ay que hazer" (Egaña 1954, 266).

4. ". . . gran latino y versista, y gran lengua en muchas lenguas de acá, que hera lo que mucho deseávamos para que los Nuestros vaian aprendiendo las lenguas de acá" (ibid., 252).

it. . . . And, without doubt, it is very useful to take as ministers of the word those mestizos that are found to be of sufficient virtue and tested for a long time and, moreover, do not lack [Christian] doctrine: and I believe it is certain that the labor and discourse of these men, who know not only the language but all other things of the Indians and have love for them, will be greatly advantageous. Therefore, if they are of good customs and tested for a long time, whatever other aspect [in their disfavor] must be postponed for the salvation of the Indians; and one must not be overscrupulous about their birth or hate or insult them (as some do) because they have been born of a Spanish father and an Indian mother. . . . Because is not God an accepter of all people?[5]

Acosta wrote the preceding lines in the late 1570s, after he had come to believe that the Society should no longer accept mestizos. In fact, he continued this passage by explaining that experience had proven mestizo Jesuits unfit for the Society because they could not give up their native customs. Nonetheless, the preceding selection reveals why the early Jesuits in Lima favored admitting mestizos. It was believed that mestizos' familiarity with Indian languages and customs would benefit the Jesuit missions to the natives. Blas Valera, Gonzalo Ruiz, Pedro de Añasco, and other mestizos would certainly play prominent roles in the early Jesuit missions in the Andes before the Society closed its doors to men of Indian descent in 1582.

The first novices received by the Jesuits in Lima were a diverse group of people. In addition to Valera, Gonzalo Ruiz and Juan Rodriguez were among the mestizos accepted during the Jesuits' first

---

5. ". . . porque saben muy bien el idioma por haberlo hablado desde la infancia, y pueden declarar en él lo que quieran, y por otra parte, son íntegros y sólidos en la fe cristiana por haberla recibido de sus progenitores y haber sido criados en ella. . . . Y, sin duda, es muy útil tomar a cuantos de éstos se hallaren que sean de suficiente virtud y probado por mucho tiempo, y además no faltos de doctrina, por ministros de la palabra; y creo cierto que con el trabajo y discurso de ellos, que no sólo conocen la lengua, sino las demás cosas de los indios y les tienen amor, si son fieles y diligentes han de ayudar y provechar mucho. Por tanto, si son de buenas costumbres y probados por mucho tiempo, cualquier otro respeto hay que posponerlo a la salud de los indios; y no hay que ser muy escrupulosos con sus natales, ni odiarlos o afrentarlos, como hacen algunos, porque han nacido de padre español y de madre india. . . . Porque no es Dios aceptador de personas?" (Acosta [1577] 1954, 517).

years in Peru.[6] The first group of novices also included prominent creoles, such as Martín Pizarro, a wealthy member of the Pizarro family (Anello Oliva [1631] 1998, 227). Spaniards, some powerful and others of more modest position, also became members of the Society. For example, Father Juan Toscano, dean of the cathedral chapter of Lima and one of the most important men in the colonial church, joined the Jesuits during their first year in Lima (ibid., 234–35). Another Spaniard, Brother Juan Gutiérrez, who became one of the most beloved members of the Society, also was a novice in Lima with Valera. Gutiérrez was a public scribe who, as an older man, converted to the Jesuit way of life when the fathers arrived in Lima. According to Anello Oliva, he was very holy and saintly, with a deep devotion to the Virgin of the Immaculate Conception. Although he was only a lay brother, all of the priests and other Jesuits eventually came to him for advice because of his wisdom (ibid., 235–38). His presence among this first group of novices must have been very helpful as these very different men strove to get along with one another.

The novices were secluded from the other Jesuits and required to undergo a rigorous program of study, service, and prayer. Valera and his companions were taught the liberal arts by Father Miguel de Fuentes, a picaresque character who would later run afoul of the Inquisition for seducing a convent of nuns. Yet Fuentes was also dedicated to the cause of justice for the native Peruvians and advocated the restitution of land and rights to the native Andeans (Pérez Fernández 1986). In addition to studying, the novices were expected to do a variety of menial tasks, which included jobs in the Jesuit residence, such as gardening and housecleaning, as well as work in the charity hospital for natives in Lima. In the Indian hospital, the novices were required to help in any way necessary, whether it was by spoon-feeding a patient or by emptying bedpans. These experiences must have come as a shock to novices who, like Valera, had grown up with servants ready to perform any disagreeable task. Menial work was meant to help the novices grow in humility and obedience, two of the central virtues of the religious life.

Central to Jesuit life was interior prayer. Although the famous

---

6. This information is from the provincial catalogs published by Egaña (1954, 284; 1981, 253). Juan and Pedro de Añasco, Valera's two mestizo friends from Chachapoyas, would not join the Society until 1572 (Egaña 1954, 513; 1958, 141).

Spiritual Exercises of St. Ignatius did not acquire final form until the Fifth General Council of 1593,[7] the Jesuit vocation stressed the interior experience of Christianity through prayer and repentance. This is seen in St. Ignatius's description of his *Spiritual Exercises*. The practitioner of the meditations therein is meant to be drawn into the internalization of the "true" Christian life. As Terence O'Reilly, S.J., has noted, "the words 'interno' and 'interior,' and their cognates, occur fifteen times in the work" (O'Reilly 1991, 108). Ignatius stated this principle in the text: "It is not knowing much that fills and satisfies the soul, but feeling and tasting things internally" (ibid.). Throughout the retreat, one is guided to pray for intense inner experiences, such as remorse, sorrow, compassion, and joy. Such experiences were, for the early Jesuits, the sign of the activity of divine grace in the human soul. Although vital aspects of the *Spiritual Exercises* were derived from the late medieval emphasis on internal spirituality, the Jesuit balance of the interior life with action in the outside world was a true innovation. Ignatian spirituality sought to form men capable of carrying the fruits of profound inward meditation into missions in the remotest reaches of the globe.

Blas Valera did well in his novitiate, impressing his teachers with his personality, humility, and language skills. In 1569, the author of the provincial catalog praised him.

> He is humble; he has a very stable personality and much practical wisdom; [we have] high expectations of him.[8]

In the same year, Father Bracamonte lauded Valera's linguistic and poetic abilities to the Jesuit general, St. Francis Borja. Valera's novitiate ended in early 1570, when he professed his first vows. Within a short time after his first profession, he was sent to be part of the Jesuit's first stable mission in South America—Huarochirí. Thus

---

7. The *Spiritual Exercises* is a coherent body of specific meditations intended to bring the retreatant to a closer union with Christ. The meditations are divided into four weeks, totaling approximately thirty days of contemplation. The theme of the first week is the malice of sin and the torments of hell and is meant to highlight the human need for redemption. The following weeks all focus on the person of Christ; the meditator is brought to contemplate the stages of Christ's earthly life (second week), his Passion and death on the cross (third week), and the joy and serenity of his resurrection (fourth week).

8. "Es humilde, tiene buen asiento y buena cordura, da buena espectación" (Egaña 1954, 284).

began Valera's career as a missionary, during which he would travel tirelessly throughout most of the Andes.

The Huarochirí Mission

Jesuit missionary activities in Peru soon expanded beyond evangelization centered in the Jesuit colleges in Lima and other cities of the viceroyalty. On February 8, 1570, Viceroy Toledo wrote to King Philip II to inform him that the Jesuits had agreed to take charge of the *doctrina* of Huarochirí, which had been abandoned by the Dominicans.[9] In his letter, Toledo explained that it was essential that the Jesuits accept *doctrinas*—as Indian parishes were known— because of the great shortage of priests to serve in them. In the archdiocese of Lima alone, the viceroy complained, there were more than forty rural *doctrinas* without any priests whatsoever.

In the Jesuit annual letter of 1571, Father Juan Gómez stated that Provincial Portillo had accepted Huarochirí because both Viceroy Toledo and the archbishop of Lima, the Dominican Jerónimo de Loaysa, had pressured the Society to do so. However, the letter continues, the Jesuits were also inspired to work in Huarochirí for another reason.

> There were in that *repartimiento* thirty thousand souls without priest or pastor to govern them. This *doctrina* has been forsaken by priests and religious because the land is very harsh and unhealthy, but we subordinated all of these things in exchange for assisting those souls redeemed by the blood of Jesus Christ.[10]

The province of Huarochirí, which is centered along the river valleys east of Lima, is roughly the size of Massachusetts. Within Huarochirí, there is a great diversity of ecozones, ranging from high alpine pastures to warm fertile valleys, where potatoes and maize are grown. Forests were plentiful throughout the region during the time of the Jesuit missions, although the slopes were later denuded of trees

---

9. The letter is published in Egaña 1954, 375–76.

10. ". . . estaban en aquel repartimiento treinta mil almas sin sacerdote ni pastor que las governase. A sido desamparada esta doctrina de clérigos y religiosos por ser tierra muy áspera y enferma, pero los Nuestros pospusieron todas estas cossas a trueque de acudir a aquellas almas redimidas por la sangre de Jesuchristo" (Egaña 1954, 396).

by Europeans searching for building materials and charcoal. Game, particularly mountain lions *(pumas)* and deer, abounded in the forests, where these animals were hunted for ritual purposes as well as for food. The wild vicuña and guanacos, smaller relatives to the llamas, were hunted in the high altitude plains known as the puna (Spalding 1984).

Early in the year 1570, seven Jesuits from Lima—four priests and three lay brothers—arrived in Huarochirí to begin the process of Christian evangelization. One of the lay brothers was Blas Valera, whose language skills were essential to the success of the mission. Upon their entrance into Huarochirí, the Jesuits settled in a house located roughly in the center of the *doctrina*. There, they organized a regular Jesuit residence, with Father Bracamonte as superior. The priests soon developed a cycle of visiting the countryside. Each priest, together with Blas or one of the other lay brothers, would spend fifteen to twenty days at a time journeying throughout the small settlements in the province. The two men would then remain in the Jesuit house for eight days before leaving again on another mission. On their missions, the fathers heard confessions, baptized children and adults, performed marriages, preached, and sought out and destroyed Andean religious objects. In addition to providing "spiritual refreshment and medicine"—as the destruction of native sacred objects was termed—the fathers also carried ordinary medicines, bread, fruit conserves, raisins, honey, sugar, and other gifts. These were distributed liberally by the missionaries to the poor and the sick whom they met on their travels.[11]

From the Jesuit house, the priests ran a school for native boys in which the children learned reading, writing, and Christian doctrine. The missionaries also ministered daily to those natives living in the vicinity of their house. One of their most important tasks was hearing the last confessions of dying Indians, who would be attended regardless of the hour and whether or not the native desired a Catholic priest at his or her deathbed. Between the difficult journeys through the countryside and the heavy work schedule at home, the Jesuits in Huarochirí endured a grueling schedule. Blas Valera, who was only

---

11. These details concerning the Jesuit mission in Huarochirí are taken from an anonymous Jesuit history written in 1600. See the original text in Mateos 1944a, 219–25.

twenty-six years old at the time, was in excellent health and could withstand the rigors of life in Huarochirí.[12] Two of his fellow Jesuits, Fathers Sebastián Amador and Hernan Sánchez, were not so fortunate and died within a year due to the physical hardships of the mission (Mateos 1944a, 224).

While in Huarochirí, the Jesuits placed a great emphasis on working with the native leaders, or *curacas,* in the missionary process. When the Jesuits first arrived in Huarochirí, the head *curaca* of Huarochirí, Don Sebastián de Quispe Ninavillca, was on the verge of being deposed by the other indigenous leaders. The Jesuits were instrumental in "restoring him to his state" (Mateos 1944a, 223). In the annual letter of 1571, Father Juan Gómez describes the manner in which Don Sebastián won the assistance of the Society.

> The principle *cazique* of this province, called Don Sebastián, has shown signs of wishing to amend his life: and thus one day he came to the fathers saying that he wanted to state his sins publicly, so that they could see who he has been. And thus, he said publicly that he had been for many years with concubines, for which he asked pardon from our Lord God; and he told the fathers to enter into his house and to throw out of there all of the women that they saw to be suspicious. With that, he moved many of his subjects to discover their hidden evils.[13]

After this episode, Don Sebastián became the Jesuits' faithful ally in exchange for the fathers' help in restoring his position. During the Jesuits' short time in Huarochirí, Don Sebastián and Valera apparently became friends and discussed their mutual Andean heritage together. In their conversations on religion, we know that Valera and

---

12. The Jesuit catalogs, which give brief descriptions of every member of the Society in Peru and were to be sent to the Jesuit general in Rome, emphasized that Valera was strong and in good health until the time of his imprisonment in 1583. For example, the catalog of 1576 notes that he was in good health—an important consideration in the days before modern medicine (Egaña 1954, 141).

13. ". . . el cazique mayor desta provincia, llamado don Sebastián, a mostrado señales de querer enmendar su vida; y ansí un día vino a los Padres diziendo que él quería públicamente dezir sus peccados, para que biesen quién abía sido; Y ansí, dixo públicamente que el abía muchos años amancebado, por lo qual pedía perdón a Dios nuestro Señor; y dixo a los Padres que entrasen en su cassa y que echasen della todas las muxeres que biesen ser sospechosas. Con lo qual mobió a muchos de los suyos a que descubriesen sus maldades escondidas" (Egaña 1954, 422).

Don Sebastián compared Christian and Andean ideas of sacrifice. They also theorized about the nature of the Andean gods, agreeing that a type of native supernatural being known as *huamincas* were identical to angels in Christian belief (Blas Valera [1594] 1968, 154, 155). In all likelihood, they passed many hours speculating about the relationship between Christianity and Andean paganism, but these reflections were not cited by Valera in his writings.

Don Sebastián's hold on power remained firm even after the Jesuits left, assisted, no doubt, by periodic campaigns to remove native pre-Christian religious objects. Apparently, he was careful to remove from the *doctrina* any alternative religious authority that might challenge his own power. A Quechua text written in Huarochirí in the early 1600s recalls the vigor with which Don Sebastián sought out and destroyed native religious objects, thereby destroying any religious cults that were not authorized by him.

> The Spanish arrived and took absolutely all [the huacas] from [the people]. Afterwards, of the few [religious] things that remained, he who in life was Don Sebastián had them all burned.[14]

During the time of the Jesuit mission in Huarochirí, Don Sebastián's conversion to Christianity inspired other native leaders to accept the new faith. In the annual letter of 1571, the Jesuits reported with delight that other *curacas* also had repented of their previous sins and accepted the Christian faith. For example, the author of the letter described how Don Alonso, a leader of the Indians of Huancayo, underwent a religious conversion, after which the Jesuits sent him to their house in Lima to perform a general confession. Because of Don Alonso's conversion, it was claimed, the entire population of Huancayo was inspired to confess ancient "miseries" and to embrace Christianity. For fifteen days, the letter reports, the native people of the town of Huancayo gathered en masse around the Jesuit house, confessing to their former beliefs and accepting instruction in Christianity (Egaña 1954, 423). Natives who were not of the *curaca* class were also reported to have experienced emotional conversions to Christianity. For example, the annual letter recounts the case of the

---

14. ". . . chay yna captinsi ñaca ñinchic yna vira cochacuna chayamuspa tucoy yman cactapas tucoy quechoporcan / huaquinin pochonincunactas quipampi huañoc don sebastian tucoyta rupachichircan" (*Huarochirí Manuscript* [ca. 1607] 1991, 200).

Indian Culquitacma, who said that he had pretended to be a Christian for thirty years without actually believing in the religion brought by the Spaniards. After hearing a sermon on the sacrament of baptism, however, he came to the fathers, confessed his sins, and eagerly accepted instruction in the faith. As part of the baptismal ceremony, the native catechists were dressed in white and formed part of a procession that, as it passed through the streets, supposedly inspired other Indians to convert (ibid., 421).

One of the Jesuits' most important converts was a man named Melchior, who became one of the fathers' most useful assistants in Huarochirí. Melchior appeared at the Jesuit house one day—having come from a nearby settlement—and, in a discussion with a Jesuit priest, began to reveal "the rites and ceremonies" of his people (Egaña 1954, 422). For example, he told of the black stones that he and his family worshiped, and he described how his people adored the sun when it rose, asking it for prosperity, health, and life. He then showed the priest the holy black stones—which he had carried with him—and demonstrated the forms and prayers of Andean worship.[15] After this, the priest instructed him in the Christian faith, placing a particular emphasis on the final judgment of all humans.

Upon hearing about the eternal torments that awaited those who had not lived according to God's commandments, Melchior began to sob and to beg for the remedy that would save him from hellfire. According to the written record of the event, the priest refused to answer for awhile, to make Melchior even more anxious and more desirous of his "spiritual medicine." The Indian implored the priest,

> Father, do not detain me any longer; tell me where my remedy is, such that even if it is at the ends of the earth I will go there immediately to obtain it![16]

The priest finally responded that Melchior should go to the Jesuit house in Lima to make a general confession and that the Lord would

---

15. These black stones are related to the modern *conopas*, which have been described thus: "At the lowest level [of Andean stone cults] were the conopas, usually quartz crystal or unusual pebbles, in which the family ancestors were said to reside. Conopas shaped like corn, potatoes and llamas were handed down from father to son and used to promote the fertility of crops and livestock" (Sharon 1978, 59).

16. "Padre, no me detengáis más, decidme dónde está mi remedio, que aunque sea al cabo del mundo y iré luego allá para alcanzarle!" (Egaña 1954, 422).

then help him. The record states that before Melchior left for Lima, he spent three hours on his knees before a crucifix in the Jesuit house, "crying bitterly and having a conversation with our Lord, so heartfelt that the brothers who were outside [were greatly] consoled and edified" (Egaña 1954, 422). Also according to the written record, after a ten-day sojourn in Lima, Melchior returned to Huarochirí to remain with the Jesuits (Egaña 1954, 422–23).

Melchior's tale reveals how central confession and penance were to the Jesuits' missionary enterprise. Melchior's confession and the anguish that he felt over his sins were the primary means by which he proved that he was a trustworthy Christian. The Jesuits believed that for Melchior, for the *curacas,* and for other converts, the sacrament of penance was the primary rite through which the natives could show themselves truly ready to enter the Christian life. Important converts, such as Melchior and Don Alonso, were sent to the Jesuit house in Lima to make their "general confession"—that is, a confession of the sins of one's entire life. The Jesuit author José de Acosta, who was Jesuit provincial in Peru in the late 1570s and early 1580s, emphasized the absolute necessity of confession for the Indians. Acosta argued that penance was the only sacrament with the power to save the Indians from eternal damnation: ". . . in these new towns of Indians there is nothing after the faith that must be inculcated with so much frequency and care, being the only hope that remains to [the Indians] of their salvation."[17] The emphasis on repentance and sorrow over sin was in keeping with the great importance placed by the Jesuits on the interior, emotional experience of Christianity. It was also in accordance with the major Catholic theologians of the fifteenth and sixteenth centuries, who considered confession to be the primary means of personal reform (Tentler 1977).

Blas Valera played a vital part in most of the conversions that occurred in Huarochirí while the Jesuits were there. Only three of the Jesuits in Huarochirí—Father Alonso de Barzana, Father Cristóbal Sanchez, and Valera himself—could speak Quechua, and of these three, only Valera was a native speaker. Valera therefore had a key role in translating in the mission. A later Jesuit author, Giovanni

---

17. ". . . en estos nuevos pueblos de indios nada hay después de la fe que se haya de inculcar con tanta frequencia y cuidado, siendo la única esperanza que les queda de su salvación" (Acosta [1577] 1954, 595).

Anello Oliva, described Valera's contribution to the mission in glowing terms.

> Because of being a mestizo—son of a Spanish father and his mother an Indian—he knew the language of the land with the perfection of the selfsame Indians, which was very important and of great utility for this ministry, because as the Indians saw that that missionary possessed as large a portion of their blood and nation as [he did of] the Spanish, they believed what he told them; they paid more attention to his words than to those of another; it seemed to them that if he did not believe [his words] to be true, he would not have preached them, nor, even less, would he, being of their lineage, deceive them.[18]

This must have been an exciting mission for Valera; in addition to his having an important role, his enthusiasm for native customs and his belief that the natives would be converted easily were shared by his fellow evangelists in the early days of the mission. According to the first report that the Jesuit fathers sent from Huarochirí, composed after they had been there for at least six months, the Jesuits expected the natives of the Andes to convert to Christianity with relative ease (Egaña 1954, 420–24).

Implicit in the idea that Andeans could be converted to Christianity quickly was the conviction that native customs and beliefs provided a solid basis for Christianity. Although the Jesuits in Huarochirí had no doubts that Andean religion was erroneous, they believed that the native customs had enough innate virtue to have prepared Andeans for Christianity. The Jesuits were not alone in their positive estimation of the spiritual maturity of the Andeans; influential churchmen, such as Bartolomé de las Casas and Domingo de Santo Tomás, had earlier argued that Andean traditions and language possessed a rationality that would enable Andeans to assent quickly to the Christian message (MacCormack 1991, 205–25, 240–48).

---

18. ". . . por ser mestiço hijo de padre español y su madre india sabía la lengua de la tierra con la perfección que los propios indios que importaron mucho y fueron de muy grande utilidad para este ministerio porque como los Indios veían que aquel religioso tenía tanta parte de su sangre y naçión como de la española davan crédito a lo que les deçía; pagávanselas sus palabras más que si fueran de otro: pareçiéndoles que si no entendiera si eran verdades no se las predicaría, ni menos quisiesse engañarlos, siendo de su linaje" (Anello Oliva [1631] 1998, 254). Much of this quote, however, was crossed out by the Jesuit censors of Anello Oliva's work.

Jesuit confidence in the readiness of Andean religious customs to be transformed into Christian ritual was demonstrated by the Corpus Christi celebrations organized by the fathers in Huarochirí. On May 25, 1570, the Jesuits oversaw Corpus Christi festivities that fully incorporated the dances, poetry, and costumes of indigenous Peruvian religious ceremonies. The first report of the Jesuits in this mission described their Corpus Christi celebrations.

> The feast of Corpus Christi was done in this *repartimiento* with much solemnity, and nine [Indian] boys dressed in crimson and green taffeta came out to [the feast]; and with a pleasing tune, they sang several songs in their language, in praise of the most sacred sacrament [i.e., the Eucharist], something that gave great pleasure to the Indians. After these songs, the Indians came out with their very pleasing dances. . . . Some came dressed in shirts of silver and others in shirts scattered with pieces of silver, and the most principle [of the Indians] bore shirts of gold; and all of them [wore] headpieces of silver . . . [with] a great quantity of feathers. The most singular of these dances was that of the nobles, who are called Incas, and the most noble of them recited lyrics, of four syllables each verse. . . . And asking where they took [the verses], they stated that the same [lyrics] that they anciently gave to the sun and to their king . . . were converted to the praise of Jesus Christ [by] taking material from that which they had heard preached [by the missionaries].[19]

The Jesuits demonstrated their optimism for the Andeans' conversion by allowing formerly non-Christian dances and ritual poetry in a Christian celebration. Clearly, at this early stage, the Jesuits did not see Andean customs as a deep threat to their missionary endeavors.

Despite their initial successes in Huarochirí, the Jesuits abandoned

---

19. ". . . se hizo en este repartimiento la fiesta de Corpus Christi con mucha solemnidad y salieron a ella nuebe niños vestidos de tafetán carmessí y berde; y con gracioso tono cantaron algunas conciones en su lengua, en loor del Santíssimo Sacramento, cosa que dió mucho gusto a los indios. Demás destas canciones, salieron los indios con sus danzas muy vistossas. . . . Venían algunos vestidos de camisetas de plata, y otros de camisetas sembradas de chapería de plata, y los más principales traían camisetas de oro; y todos ellos unas celadas de plata . . . [con] grande cantidad de plumas. La más singular destas danzas fué la de los nobles que se llaman ingas, y el más noble dellos decía la letra, de quatro silabas cada berso. . . . y preguntando de dónde lo sacaban, dezían que los mesmos que antiguamente daban al sol y a su Rey, éso a conbertían en loor de Jesuchristo tomando matheria de lo que oían predicar" (Egaña 1954, 425).

the mission early in 1572. Both Viceroy Toledo and the Council of the Indies were angered by the Jesuits' refusal to continue in Huarochirí. On March 20, 1574, Toledo wrote to the king to complain of the Jesuits' decision to leave Huarochirí and of their reluctance to accept any other *doctrina*. The viceroy concluded his epistle by suggesting that, because of the lack of missionaries in the highlands, any order that did not accept Indian *doctrinas* had no right to remain in the Indies.[20] In October of the previous year, Father Diego de Bracamonte, the former head of the Huarochirí mission, had been coldly received in Madrid by the president of the Council of the Indies, Juan de Ovando, because of the latter's anger over the abandonment of Huarochirí.[21]

Why did the Society leave their only permanent highland mission in Peru in 1572, risking the ire of the Spanish government? Part of the reason is the great physical hardships of the mission, which had resulted in the deaths of two of the seven members. Another answer to this question, however, can be found in a letter of April 19, 1572, from Father Bartolomé Hernández to Juan de Ovando. Although Hernández had not been in Huarochirí himself, he had spoken with those who had. Huarochirí had been left after only two years, he wrote, because the missionaries had not had any success in converting the natives.[22] The Indians, Hernández explained,

> for [the] most part are like the Moors of Granada, and most, or all, only have the name of Christian and the exterior ceremonies; and [they] internally have no concept of the things of our faith.[23]

The Jesuit missionaries eventually came to believe that although the natives may have professed to be Christians, they still retained many of their native beliefs. The Jesuit emphasis on interiority had made the fathers question native sincerity in the faith, even when the indigenous peoples complied with all of the external requirements of sixteenth-century Spanish Christianity. The Corpus Christi celebrations, in which the Jesuits had been so proud of the native participa-

---

20. The letter is published in Egaña 1954, 622.
21. The letter in which this is mentioned is published in Egaña 1954, 559.
22. Hernández's letter is published in Egaña 1954, 461–75.
23. ". . . por la mayor parte se están como los moros de Granada, y que los más, o todos, sólo tienen el nombre de christiano y las cerimonias exteriores; y que interiormente no tienen concepto de las cosas de nuestro fe" (Egaña 1954, 464).

tion with Andean songs and dances, may well have demonstrated to the missionaries how far the natives were from an ideal understanding of the faith. According to a cycle of native tales collected in Huarochirí in 1607, the people of the region fused the celebration of the body of Christ during Corpus Christi with the festival of a major fertility goddess *(huaca),* Chaupiñamca. Worshiped at the great temple in Mama, Chaupiñamca continued to receive homage from a large population of devotees in the region.

> Accordingly they, the Mama people, in order to celebrate her festival on the eve of Corpus Christi, used to bathe Chaupi Ñamca in a little maize beer. Additionally, some of them laid out all sorts of offerings for her, and worshipped her with guinea pigs or other such things, and all the people gathered together, both men and women, their curaca and their alcalde. They used to stay there all night long, staying awake till dawn, drinking and getting drunk. . . .
>
> After that they went out to the fields and simply did nothing at all. They just got drunk, drinking and boozing away and saying, "It's our mother's festival!"[24]

Although the combination of pre-Christian festivals with Christian feasts had been common when Christianity was introduced to Europe, such religious syncretism was unacceptable to the Jesuits. The Huarochirí mission was therefore abandoned partly out of frustration that the native peoples could only accept Christianity by viewing it through the prism of their former beliefs.

Blas Valera did not agree with his fellow Jesuits' negative assessment of the natives' inner experience of Christianity, and he would express his opinions in writing much later in life. For the time being, however, it appears that he was content to return to Lima after his mission in the highlands.

Santiago del Cercado

Valera's next assignment was to the Jesuit mission of Santiago del Cercado. During his time there, he was ordained to the priesthood. El

---

24. The translation is by Salomon and Urioste, from *Huarochirí Manuscript* [ca. 1607] 1991, 84. Frank Salomon's excellent introduction to that edition provides a thorough discussion of the *huaca* Chaupiñamca.

Cercado, as it was known, was a native *doctrina* located on the out-skirts of Lima. It had been assigned to the Jesuits in 1570, the same year the Society had been given charge of Huarochirí. Valera worked in El Cercado first as a lay brother—preaching to and teaching the Indians, as well as attending to their physical needs. In 1573, Valera was ordained a priest in the Lima diocese, making him the first mestizo Jesuit ever to receive holy orders.[25] As a priest, he ran El Cercado and said mass, heard confessions, and performed baptisms, marriages, and last rites.

The *doctrina* of Santiago del Cercado was created by Governor Lope Garcia de Castro in 1570. In the environs surrounding Lima, there were a multitude of tiny hamlets of native peoples. The governor's intention was to bring all of these native peoples together in one town, El Cercado, so that they could be instructed in Christianity and administered more efficiently. The process of forcing indigenous peoples to leave their dispersed settlements to live in towns was known as "reducing" the population. Creating "reductions" in order to govern natives more effectively was a priority of the Spanish colonial government at this time, when the process was occurring throughout the Andes. In creating El Cercado, Garcia de Castro was carrying out the will of the new viceroy, Francisco de Toledo. Although earlier viceroys also had advocated "reductions," Toledo initiated the most intensive program of resettlement of native populations, as part of his larger program of controlling the Andean population. In centralized towns, priests could offer regular instruction in the faith, rather than only seeing each scattered group of parishioners several times a year. The Catholic priests would also be able to discover the presence of pagan practices more easily if all of the natives were living together in one town. Moreover, living in a "rational" European-style town was thought to decrease sinfulness and aid the development of "reason." The Jesuit Father Bartolomé Hernández expressed this belief in 1572 to Juan de Ovando, president of the Council of the Indies.

In his letter to Juan de Ovando, Hernández argued that the Andean manner of living in a multitude of tiny, scattered settlements gave rise to evil customs that hindered conversion to Christianity. He advocated the consolidation of Andean hamlets into a smaller num-

---

25. This information is from a provincial catalog printed in Egaña 1954, 706.

ber of large towns; this, he claimed, would greatly enhance Christianization efforts. His arguments for these consolidations centered on the effect they would have in making the Indians live in a more "civilized" fashion. Demonstrating his European bias against indigenous lifestyles, Hernández claimed that the Indians currently lived as "savages ... gathering together and sleeping like pigs."[26] The manner in which the Andeans lived, he wrote, made the natives' internal conversion to Christianity impossible.

> First it is necessary that [the Indians] be men who live civilly in order to make them Christians. ... Your Lordship will see that a people who live with such bestial customs [are very] far from being able to receive the law of God, a law so discrete and sagacious and spiritual and conforming to natural law.[27]

The reasons for moving the scattered native peoples living around Lima into one settlement are given by Antonio López in an unpublished manuscript containing the deeds of property for El Cercado. López, who provided land and a house for the *doctrina,* explained that the reduction was necessary to make the Indians give up their "lazy vices and drunkenness." In his deed, he stated:

> Let it be known by all those who see this letter that I, Antonio López, local judge and resident of this city of the kings of these kingdoms of Peru, say that inasmuch as the very illustrious lord licentiate Lope Garçia de Castro of His Majesty's council and president of the royal audience of this aforesaid city and governor of these aforesaid realms; because he was informed that in this aforesaid city and its outlying areas there are many settlements of Indian men and women [scattered over] many parts where they reside and live; and because they are divided and apart, he has not been able to—nor can he—have with them a census so that they can be instructed and taught the things of our holy Catholic faith and so that they will live in a civilized manner as Our Majesty orders; because of this, they have lived and continue to live loosely and at their own discretion and will; and so that such a great impropriety

---

26. The letter can be found in Egaña 1954, 467.

27. "... primero es necesario que sean hombres que vivan políticamente para hazerlos christianos. ... y a gente que está hecha a vivir con costumbres tan bestiales bien verá Vuestra Señoría quean lexos está de ser capaz de recibir la ley de Dios, ley tan discreta y avisada y espiritual y tan conforme a la ley natural" (Egaña 1954, 467).

ceases and the tendency that the Indians have for their lazy vices and drunkenness [is brought to an end], he gave a provision for Alonso Manuel de Anaya, *corregidor,* and Diego de Porras Sagredo to gather together [the Indians] and reduce them to towns.[28]

When Valera entered the *doctrina* in 1572, El Cercado was still quite new. In El Cercado, the Jesuits owned a house, a church dedicated to St. Blaise, and a garden that provided fresh food for the priest and his assistant. A father and a lay brother resided permanently in the parish, sustained by the native parishioners' tribute of corn beer *(chicha),* which was sold for profit. The Jesuits said mass and preached to the natives on Sundays and on feast days. During the week, Valera and his fellow religious taught Christian doctrine and performed other sacraments, including baptism, marriage, and extreme unction (last rites). Jesuits from the Lima house often went to El Cercado to assist with preaching and hearing confessions.[29] Later in the sixteenth century, El Cercado would become famous for its prison for native men and women found guilty of "witchcraft"—the practice of their ancient Andean religious rituals (Anello Oliva [1631] 1998, 259–60). However, this house of detention had not yet been constructed during Valera's time in El Cercado.

According to a later account by Valera, El Cercado was a difficult mission in its early years. In his time there, the young mestizo was forced to see a great many of his parishioners perish from disease. Many of the natives who were relocated to El Cercado resisted being moved from their ancestral lands; their unhappiness at being in the *doctrina* must have tried the enthusiasm of the young Jesuit. About his first years in El Cercado, Valera later wrote:

---

28. "Sepan quantos desta carta vieren como yo antonio lópez, alguazil de canpo y morador en este ciudad de los Reyes destos Reinos del piru digo que por quanto wl muy ille senor licenciado lope garçia de castro del consejo de su magestad y presidente en la Real audiencia desta dicha ciudad y governador destos dichos Reinos porque fue ynformado que en esta dicha ciudad y termino della en diversas partes ay muchos Rancherias de yndios y yndias dondo estan y biben y que por estar dibididos y apartados no se a podido ni puede tener con ellos la quenta que para ser dotrinados y ensenados en las cosas de nuestra santa fee catolica conviene y para que biban en puliçia como su magestad manda por que a esta causa an bibido y biben sueltamente y a su discrecion y boluntad y para que cese tan gran ynconbiemente y el aparejo que tienen para sus viçios oçiosida del y borracheras dio una provision para que alonso manual de anaya, corregidor y diego de porres sagredo los untasen y reduzesen a pueblos" (Harkness 1568b).

29. On El Cercado, see Egaña 1954, 136–37; Anello Oliva [1631] 1998, 259–60.

Finally, [the Society] was given a harvest, which was to found the town of Santiago (which they call El Cercado), attached to Lima, and to gather together and to instruct [the Indians]. Upon doing this, an infinite [number of natives] died with the change of residence; those interested [in the project] took others, who did not rejoice over so much felicity.[30]

Resistance to being forced into the *doctrina* remained in many native groups. It is known, for example, that the native peoples from the area of St. Lazarus in Lima refused to reconcile themselves to their new home. In 1599, the native shrimp fishermen of St. Lazarus living in El Cercado wrote to King Philip III, asking to be returned to the parish of St. Lazarus, where they had lived in the time of the Incas.

Despite these difficulties, Valera believed that the natives of El Cercado eventually became model Christians. Given both a proper education in the faith and safety from abuse by the Spaniards, he argued, the Indian peoples of El Cercado excelled in acts of Christian piety and charity. Valera described in detail the daily acts of charity performed by the natives of the urban *doctrina*.

Finally, there remained a large number [of Indians], who up to now have persevered with so much virtue, honesty, and devotion that it is to be admired. Through their charity and work, without help from anyone, they have built the Church of San Blas,[31] which was later converted into a hospital; they have built the [Church] of Santiago, which in exquisiteness, beauty, and adornment exceeds many in Lima. The oratory of the altar of the tabernacle of the most holy sacrament [i.e., the Eucharist]; the fine vestments of the ministers who serve there; the music for the divine office, not only vocal but also of diverse instruments and of *vihuelas de arco;* the very illustrious and sumptuous ceremony with which the most holy sacrament

---

30. "Finalmente, dióse un corte, que fue fundar el pueblo de Santiago, que llaman el Cercado, pegado a Lima, y que estuviesen juntos y fuesen dotrinados por los de la Compañía. Hízose así, muriéronse infinitos con la mudanza de lugar, sacaron otros los interesados, que no holgaban de tanta felicidad" (Blas Valera [1594] 1968, 186).

31. It is possible that this name was chosen because Blas was the priest in El Cercado at the time. However, St. Blaise, considered a patron of diseases of the throat, was at the height of his popularity in the sixteenth century, at which time the custom of blessing the throat with candles on the feast of St. Blaise developed. It is possible, therefore, that he was selected as a patron for the *doctrina* church out of a concern for illness and that the church was named after him.

[is brought] to the sick Indians; the confraternity that, in [the Eucharist's] honor, has been instituted, in which are incorporated the confraternities of our Lady and of the true cross and of the souls in purgatory; the helpfulness and comfort [given] by this confraternity, [which provides] the curate and medicines and provisions and vegetables for the hospital, aid to the poor and to orphans, the sustenance of the priests who reside [in El Cercado] to teach them, the continual alms that they give (not only to their spiritual fathers, but also to those in the house of probation that is there)—all of these things come from the Indians and not from anyone else; apart from all [of these charities], these same Indians help with their alms the hospitals and confraternities and needs of the poor in Lima.[32]

Although his work in the *doctrina* of El Cercado was not without its difficulties, Valera clearly felt satisfied that his efforts had borne fruit in the souls of his native parishioners. One can imagine the joy he must have felt on seeing native musicians singing and playing the violin to accompany the divine office or on seeing the Indians process through the streets with great solemnity and pomp, carrying the Eucharist to the sick.

Later Missions

CUZCO

Sometime prior to 1576, Valera was transferred from El Cercado to Cuzco, the ancient Inca capital. The Jesuit house in Cuzco had been

---

32. ". . . finalmente, quedó buen número, que hasta ahora ha permanecido con tanta virtud, honestidad y devoción, que es para admirar. Ellos de su limosna y trabajo, sin ayuda de otro, han hecho la iglesia de San Blas, la cual despues se conmulto en hospital; han hecho la de Santiago, que en lindeza, hermosura y adorno excede a muchas de Lima. El oratorio del altar del sagrario del Santísimo Sacramento, los aderezos de los ministros que allí sirven, la música para los oficios divinos, no sólo de voces, sino de instrumentos diversos y de vihuelas de arco, el aparato tan ilustre y sumptuoso con que sale el Santísimo Sacramento para los indios enfermos, la cofradía que en su honor se ha instituido, en la cual están incorporado las Cofradías de Nuestra Señora y de la Vera-Cruz y de las ánimas del Purgatorio, la utilidad y comodidad desta cofradía, la cura y medicinas y provisión y recaudos del hospital, el socorro de los pobres y huérfanos, el sustento de los padres que allí residen para enseñarlos, las limosnas contínuas que allí hacen, no sólo a sus padres espirituales, sino a la casa de probación que allí está, todas estas cosas salen de los indios y no de otros; fuera de que estos mismos indios ayudan con sus limosnas a los hospitales y cofradías y necesidades de pobres de la ciudad de Lima" (Blas Valera [1594] 1968, 186).

founded in 1571. One of the founders of this house was Valera's fellow mestizo and Chachapoyan, Gonzalo Ruiz.[33] While Ruiz was in Cuzco, he was briefly the catechist to the rebel Inca ruler Tupac Amaru. The Inca leader had been captured in 1572 by the nephew of St. Ignatius Loyola and had been handed over to the Jesuits to be prepared spiritually for his execution. Ruiz's role was soon taken over by the Spanish nobleman and Jesuit Father Alonso de Barzana, who served as Tupac Amaru's confessor throughout the Inca's final days. Although the Inca was sentenced to death for rebellion against the Spanish Crown, Barzana pled on his knees before the viceroy for Tupac Amaru's life to be spared. Barzana's emotional appeal fell on deaf ears; however, his actions earned for him and for the Jesuits the goodwill of many of the Inca nobility in Cuzco (Mateos 1944a, 13–14).

Barzana was still present in Cuzco when Valera arrived at the Inca capital. The two men had worked together in Huarochirí, where, with Barzana's support, native Andean religious dances and poetry had played an important part in Christian celebrations. Barzana was a highly idealistic and saintly man, who would later spend the rest of his life in dangerous missions in what is now Argentina and Chile. He was motivated in his work by the conviction that the conversion of the native Americans to Christianity would bring about the Second Coming of Christ and the new millennium. A common belief in the sixteenth century was that the final resurrection would occur once all peoples of the world, including the Jews and the pagans, had been converted to Christianity.[34] The establishment of the Spanish and Portuguese empires and the subsequent spread of Christianity among the pagan peoples of the world were thus thought by Barzana and others to signal the end of the world and the beginning of the millennium. In a letter to St. Francis Borja, Barzana wrote that the time appeared ripe for the evangelization of the Americas. The conversion

---

33. See the documents published in Egaña 1958, 143.

34. This belief is based on an interpretation of certain biblical passages. For example, 1 Corinthians 15:28 NAB states, concerning the Second Coming: "When, finally, all has been subjected to the Son, he will then subject himself to the One who has made all things subject to him, so that God may be all in all." The author of the Book of Revelation describes heaven after the Resurrection thus: "I saw before me a huge crowd which no one could count from every nation and race, people and tongue" (Revelation 7:9). These and other passages have been taken to suggest that the Christian gospel must be preached to all nations before the Last Judgment and the end of the world.

of the American "gentiles," he stated, seemed a return to the days of the primitive church, when the apostles were able to spread Christianity with supernatural effectiveness. Barzana desired to preach to the gentiles in South America, he wrote, "where the greatest open door, the greatest light of understanding, is found."[35]

In Cuzco, Barzana, Valera, and the other Jesuits resided in a former Inca temple that had been known as Amaro Cancha (Enclosure of the Snake). This temple had once housed a sacred idol shaped as a metal serpent holding a scorpion in its mouth. According to Valera, the Jesuits had placed the tabernacle containing the Holy Eucharist on the altar that had once sheltered the snake idol (Blas Valera [1594] 1968, 158). In the city of Cuzco, Valera taught Latin and preached to and confessed natives.[36] He was also the spiritual advisor for the Nombre de Jesús confraternity, whose membership included many important Inca nobles. Every Wednesday and Friday, the confraternity met for "spiritual discussions" and communal prayer, led by the young mestizo Jesuit. It may have been at these meetings that Valera began to develop his radical views concerning the Inca and Christian religions. In a work written later in life, Valera referred to the records (quipus) of Cuzco and to discussions with Inca nobles in Cuzco on such matters as the nature of the Andean creator god, Illa Tecce; the development of idolatry in Peru; and the manner of Inca ritual sacrifice (Blas Valera [1594] 1968, 153–57). From the context of his citations, it appears that Valera's "spiritual discussions" with certain of the native elites were wide-ranging yet focused on the similarities between the ancient Andean faith and the Christian religion.

Although no list of the participants in the Nombre de Jesús confraternity has been found, we can surmise the names of three of the native members from Valera's writings. Valera notes that one member, Don Luis Inca, was a Cuzco nobleman who wrote two works in Quechua about native religion. Francisco Yutu Inca and Juan Huallpa Inca also appear to have belonged to this organization (Blas Valera [1594] 1968, 153–57). Interestingly, Juan Huallpa Inca had been in the court of the emperor Huayna Capac. There, the young Inca

---

35. This letter of 1566 from Barzana to St. Borja is published in Egaña 1954, 84–85.
36. This information is from the provincial catalog published in Egaña 1958, 140–41.

aristocrat had been responsible for the ruler's wardrobe, a position of considerable importance.[37]

In 1576, the Society decided to send Barzana and Valera to Potosí. In a letter written to General Mercurian on February 15, 1577, Acosta described the Indian protests to the departure of the two priests.[38] To detain Barzana in Cuzco, the "Indians of Cuzco" passed one day and night crying outside the Jesuit college and then marched through the streets, shouting and shedding more tears. Natives had similar processions through the streets, shouting and crying to voice their distress at Valera's impeding transfer. In addition, Acosta recounted:

> There came to the Father Visitor and to me an infinity of [Indians], bringing to us a written petition and asking us with great sentiment that we not take from them Father Valera, by whose means they knew God and were Christians; and not content with this, they went to the house of the *corregidor* of this city, and they gave such a cry that they made him come another turn with them and the other Spaniards about the same demand. ... the Father Visitor and I decided that the journey of Father Valera to Potosí, which was agreed on, would wait for now, at which the *corregidor* and the priests—and even more the Indians—have demonstrated great consolation and gratitude.[39]

The members of the Nombre de Jesús confraternity, along with many of the other "Indians of Cuzco," clearly did not want Valera to leave. His preaching in Quechua, his discussions about the affinities between Andean and Christian beliefs, and his legitimation of the

---

37. According to a report made in Cuzco on March 13, 1571, Juan Huallpa was "de casta de Ingas, que en tiempo de Guayna Capac fué 'veedor de su ropa, y costejador si la dicha ropa se hacia del largo y medida que era menester para el vestido del dicho Inga'" (Montesinos [1644] 1882, 211).

38. The letter is published in Egaña 1958, 269–70.

39. "... vinieron al Padre Visitador y a mí una infinidad dellos trayéndonos una petición escripta y pidiéndonos con mucho sentimiento, que no les quitasemos de aquí el Padre Valera, por cuyo medio conocían a Dios y heran christianos; y no contentos con esto, fueron a casa del corregidor desta cibdad, y tanta grita le dieron, que le hizieron venir otra buelta con ellos y con otros españoles sobre la misma demanda ... nos resumimos el Padre Visitador y yo, que la ida del Padre Valera a Potosi, que estava acordada, se quedase por aora; de lo qual han mostrado gran consuelo y agradecimiento el corregidor y los curas, y mucho más los indios" (Egaña 1958, 269–70).

Inca past (see chap. 5) had obviously affected them deeply. Clearly, the mestizo priest had inspired a deep love among the Inca elites in his confraternity; one can only speculate on the full range of what was discussed in their weekly meetings (fig. 4).

The description of Valera in the 1576 catalog reveals that the thirty-two-year-old Jesuit was in good standing with the Society at this time. The catalog stated that Valera had good health, good wits, and good judgment. It praised his knowledge of Quechua and of Latin and his work preaching to and confessing native peoples. It concluded by noting that he was humble and obedient, with a satisfactory prayer life and great love for his order (Egaña 1958, 141).

JULI

Valera's transfer from Cuzco was delayed, but by 1577, he was in the *doctrina* of Juli with Barzana, three other Jesuit priests, and three Jesuit brothers (Egaña 1958, 335). It is not clear how long he remained in Juli, but the experience must have been sobering. Although Juli eventually became a source of Jesuit pride as an ideal mission, the private letters of two of the first missionaries in Juli, as well as the confidential report of the Jesuit *visitator* Juan de la Plaza, reveal a mission initially fraught with disappointment and violence.[40] One of the Jesuit missionaries there, Diego Martínez, was moved to write that the "doubts and bitterness of the heart" occasioned by seeing both the natives' indifference to the faith and the Jesuits' violence against the Indians were so great that he and many others wished to leave the *doctrina*.[41] Martínez, incidentally, had originally been so pleased at being sent to Juli that he wrote on November 11, 1576: "I wouldn't change my luck with that of the king Don Philip. . . . [it would be] the greatest happiness to wander from village to village among the Indians, on foot, teaching prayers all the days of my life" (Egaña 1958, 275).

In November 1576, the Jesuits first entered the *doctrina* of Juli. Juli was located on the shores of Lake Titicaca, in the beautiful—but barren—high plains of the southern Andes. Apart from the urban *doc-*

---

40. For a more positive view of the Juli mission, see Burgaletta 1999, 45–50.

41. The pertinent letter from Martínez to the Jesuit provincial is published in Egaña 1958, 361–62.

Fig. 4. Jesuit church in Cuzco. (Photo courtesy of Brian S. Bauer.)

trina of El Cercado, Juli was the first *doctrina* accepted by the Society since the Jesuits' departure from Huarochirí. The *doctrina* of Juli had been administered formerly by the Dominicans from 1546 to 1573. However, the Dominicans were so abusive of the natives that the friars were forced out of Juli in 1573 by Viceroy Toledo. According to an inspection of the *doctrina* in 1567, the friars committed numerous abuses against the Indians. They illegally extracted food and labor from the native community, making a considerable profit. The friars also subjected the residents of Juli to physical cruelty—beatings, imprisonment, and even death—without trial and for trivial matters. The 1567 inspection also emphasized the friars' frequent sexual abuse of the native women. Furthermore, the Dominicans accepted bribes from the native leaders to allow non-Christian Andean rituals to be performed (Meicklejohn 1988). Dominican abuse of the native peoples in Juli left a legacy of hostility toward Christianity, which the Jesuits found difficult to overcome.

When Valera arrived in Juli in 1577, he entered a *doctrina* in which native resentment over Dominican mistreatment persisted. Juan de la Plaza, who inspected the Juli mission in 1577, reported, "the fruit [among the Indians in Juli] is not as great as anticipated, nor [are] the difficulties as little or as easy as they seem to those who do not experience them."[42] One of the primary difficulties experienced by the Jesuits in the Juli mission was the Indians' avoidance of mass and instruction in Christian doctrine. Plaza wrote to General Mercurian that on Sundays and feast days, when the natives were to gather in the plaza for sermons and mass, "many hide themselves and [are] absent . . . and go to work in the fields" (Egaña 1958, 336–37). In a letter written August 1, 1578, Father Diego Martínez informed Father Plaza that the missionaries still had great difficulties in making the Indians go to mass (ibid., 363). His complaints were echoed by another missionary in Juli, Father Andrés López, who wrote Plaza on August 6, 1578, reporting that most natives did not go to hear mass or Christian instruction of their own free will. For the people of Juli, López explained, attendance at mass and at sermons was viewed simply as

---

42. This quote is taken from Plaza's confidential report, published in Egaña 1958, 335.

another labor obligation *(mit'a)*, to be avoided if possible (ibid., 375–77).

The Jesuits' response to Andean unwillingness to be present for mass and for Christian teaching in Aymara and Quechua was to force the natives to attend on Sundays and feast days. Plaza reported to General Mercurian that Indian constables were placed on the streets of Juli on Sunday mornings to prevent natives from avoiding mass by fleeing into the countryside. Most of those who did go to mass and to hear sermons, Plaza wrote, went only because they were forced to do so. Plaza emphasized that the Jesuits were the only missionaries in Peru to rely on force to make the Indians be present at mass (Egaña 1958, 336–37). In 1578, Father Martínez wrote that the Jesuits were becoming "hateful to the Indians" because of the force used by the Jesuits in making the Indians attend instruction in Christian doctrine (ibid., 363).

Another manner in which the native peoples of Juli responded to the Jesuits was by avoiding the sacrament of confession unless actually forced to participate. According to Plaza, of the three thousand Indians whom the Jesuits in Juli confessed in 1577, fewer than one-third appeared voluntarily for the sacrament (Egaña 1958, 335). Faced with the natives' disinclination to confess in the Christian manner, the Jesuits responded with force. In his letter to the Jesuit general, Plaza described the methods used by the fathers to compel the Indians to go to confession. Most commonly, he wrote, Indians were imprisoned for living together without marriage; these Indians would not be released from jail until they confessed their "sins" and married their partner. Other Indians, Plaza continued, confessed only when the Jesuits called a family group *(ayllu)* to the Jesuit house; the fathers then refused to allow the family to go home until each member had privately confessed to his or her sins. Finally, Plaza stated, others confessed only on their deathbeds, after the priests had been told of their illness by the native constables.

Fathers Martínez and López also referred to the violence by which Indians were brought to confession. Martínez wrote,

> most of the people do not come voluntarily to confess, [but they come only because of] the violence of the native chiefs and assistants to the priests and, sometimes, [because of being] in prison and

[because of the Jesuits] bringing the [Indians] bound and having them locked up, which makes for a great deal of grumbling among those who have to confess.[43]

Martínez wrote further of the great difficulty for the confessor in not always knowing whether a native was confessing voluntarily or by force. He complained that it was extremely difficult to know how to hear the confession of someone who, as Martínez wrote, "comes with an ill will and against his desires" (Egaña 1958, 335).

In this atmosphere of violence and coercion, it is not surprising that the native peoples responded with sullen resistance to evangelization. In Juli, there was little attempt by the Jesuits to accommodate native customs, as there had been in Huarochirí. Instead, under the direction of José de Acosta, the Jesuits were unwilling to allow native cultural expressions in their secular or religious celebrations. There was no encouragement of native singing or dancing in Christian festivities in Juli. This is very apparent in the ceremonies that were organized in December 1576 in honor of a visit to Juli from Acosta, the Jesuit provincial in Peru at the time. At these festivities, the natives performed dances before processing to the church with crosses to hear mass. Significantly, in their dances, the Indians were dressed in European-style clothing and danced "Spanish-style"; there were no native costumes or dances.

The mission in Juli must have been an unpleasant experience for Valera, who had come to the *doctrina* right after his triumphs in Cuzco, where he was so deeply beloved by many of the natives of the city. Not only did the Jesuits in Juli coerce the natives with violence, but there was little optimism about the Andeans' potential for conversion to Christianity. Rather than attempting to build Christianity upon the natural virtues of Inca religion in the Andes, the Jesuits in Juli had come to see Andean customs and beliefs as a serious hindrance to the faith of Christ. The sixteenth-century emphasis on the interior experience of Christianity, which created much higher standards for native converts than had existed in preceding centuries,

---

43. ". . . el no venir lo más del pueblo de boluntad a confesarse, si no es con violencia de hilacatas y fiscales; y algunas vezes con cárcel, y traerlos atados y tenerlos encerrados, que haze regañar harto a los que an de confesar" (Egaña 1958, 362). In their use of punitive measures against the natives, the Indian leaders in Juli were acting on the orders of the Jesuit fathers.

meant that the Jesuits' disillusionment with the native potential for Christian evangelization would be experienced throughout the Peruvian church. Eventually, the conviction that the native peoples were not "truly" Christian would lead to episcopal campaigns in the seventeenth and eighteenth centuries to extirpate idolatry, as well as to modern notions that Andean peoples are "cryptopagans" even when they profess a belief in Christ.[44]

POTOSÍ

Sometime prior to 1579, Valera had been transferred to Potosí. Located in the south-central mountains of Bolivia, Potosí was the silver-mining center of colonial South America. The city was populated largely by native laborers who were forced to work in the silver mines as part of their ethnic groups' tribute to the colonial government. By the seventeenth century, with a population including tens of thousands of natives from all over the viceroyalty, Potosí was one of the largest cities in the world.

On February 25, 1580, General Mercurian wrote to Valera in Potosí, thanking him for "the account that Your Reverence wrote ... [about] the success of the gospel preaching in those kingdoms."[45] In this letter, the general also granted permission for Valera's brother Jerónimo to enter the Society, and he gave some advice concerning the native confraternity that Valera was attempting to found in Potosí.

While in Potosí, Valera continued his researches into Andean religion and the Inca past. It was in Potosí, apparently, that he befriended the Mercedarian writer Fray Melchior Hernández. According to one of Valera's later works, Hernández composed a text entitled *Anotaciones,* in which he discussed Inca religious history through the analysis of key Andean terms. In addition, Valera stated that Hernández also wrote a work on the interpretation of Inca prayers (Blas Valera [1594] 1968, 154). These two works by Hernández have since been lost; the only existing references to them are in Valera's text. Little is known of Hernández himself, save for several brief references in the

---

44. For the change in missionary attitudes toward the native potential for the Christian faith, see MacCormack 1985b. Two outstanding treatments of the campaigns to extirpate idolatry are Mills 1997 and Griffiths 1996.

45. "... la relación que V. R. escrive ... del sucesso de la predicación evangélica en essos Reinos." This letter is published in Egaña 1958, 812–13.

history of the Mercedarian order composed by the great Mercedarian playwright Tirso de Molina and a comment by the Mercedarian chronicler Martín de Murúa that Hernández had written a catechism in Quechua (Murúa [1613] 1987, 485). However, according to an unpublished document in the archive of the Spanish Inquisition, Hernández was in Potosí until early in 1580. In 1580, Hernández was brought before the tribunal of the Holy Office on charges of attempting to rape two Indian women and one mestiza during confession. The three women who testified against him were Catalina Paxna, Ana Paxna, and Juana de Manarion. According to their testimony, Hernández's impotence impeded the commission of his crimes. Catalina Paxna reported that Hernández first accused her of causing his impotence by witchcraft and then broke down crying before her, begging for her forgiveness. After a lengthy time in prison, Hernández was eventually acquitted of these crimes (AHN 1580b).[46] His superiors sent him next to Huamanga (Ayacucho) and then to Panama, where he spent the rest of his life as a missionary to the native Chiriquí people (Tirso de Molina [1639] 1974, 173, 349, 373). His ethnographic description of the native Panamanians, the *Memorial de Chiriquí,* survives as an imprint in the British Museum (Hernández [1606] 1996, 233–47).

The Inquisition material reveals that Hernández was in Potosí at the same time as Valera. The records of the Holy Office also state that the Mercedarian friar was a mestizo, like Valera. It seems likely that the two mestizo priests, who shared a mutual concern with explaining Andean religion in Christian terms, would have met to discuss their common interests. If Hernández had caught wind of his impending arrest, he might even have given his papers to Valera to save them from the prying eyes of the inquisitors. In his discussions of Andean religion throughout his *Relación de las costumbres antiguas de los naturales del Pirú* (Account of the ancient customs of the natives of Peru), Valera repeatedly cites Hernández's analyses of different Quechua terms. The Jesuit's references to Hernández's work cover a variety of topics, such as the nature of Punchao, the Inca sun god; the manner of *opacuna,* the Inca ritual of confession; and the existence of

---

46. For the belief that native women magically induced impotence in men to protect themselves from sexual abuse, see Behar 1989.

huamincas, the angelic messengers of the creator god Illa Tecce (Blas Valera [1594] 1968, 153, 154, 166). Hernández also apparently shared Valera's famous etymology of the name of Peru, claiming that it was taken from the name of the first king of Peru, Pirua Pácaric Manco Inca (ibid., 154; Montesinos [1644] 1930, 8–10). Valera was clearly influenced by Hernández, particularly in his method of using linguistic definitions to explain key concepts of Andean religious belief. Hernández's *Anotaciones* may well have inspired Valera's own *Vocabulario,* which was later used by the seventeenth-century chronicler of the Inca Giovanni Anello Oliva. Unfortunately, Valera's *Vocabulario,* like Hernández's work, has since been lost.

Return to Lima

Valera was recalled to Lima in 1582 to work on translating the Catholic catechism into Quechua for the Third Lima Council of Bishops. While Valera was in Lima, he also began offering free Quechua classes to any interested persons. In a 1583 petition prepared by two mestizo students, Hernán González and Juan Ruiz, three witnesses testified that they had observed Valera teaching Quechua in the Jesuit school in Lima. One of the witnesses who observed Valera's classes was Friar Blas de Atienza, a mestizo and the commander of the Mercedarian house in Lima. Friar Atienza testified that Valera's Quechua classes were available "to all priests and people who want to learn [Quechua]" and were offered free of charge: "[they] do not cost His Majesty nor any other person anything."[47] Diego de Porras Sagredo, a leading citizen of Lima who had been commissioned by Governor Castro to be in charge of founding El Cercado (Harkness 1568a, 1569), had attended Valera's Quechua classes. He, too, recounted that Valera taught Quechua in Lima "to everyone who wishes to go learn it . . . [and] for free."[48] Valera's language lessons were testified to as well by the writer Francisco Falcón, whose lost work, the *Apologia*

---

47. ". . . a todos los sacerdotes y personas que la quieren oyr . . . y sin que a su magestad ni a otra persona les cueste cosa alguna" (testimony of Friar Blas de Atienza, August 30, 1583, published in Barriga 1953, 272). The petition requested the archbishop to allow mestizos to be ordained; Friar Atienza's testimony was in response to a question concerning whether mestizo priests made ideal Quechua teachers.

48. ". . . a todas las personas que la quisieren ir a oír . . . gratis" (AGI 1583b).

pro Indis (Defense of the Indians) apparently influenced Valera's thought (AGI 1583c). Another leading citizen of Lima, Diego de Agüero, son of Captain Diego de Agüero, stated that he had heard about Valera's free language lessons.[49] In the same petition, Friar Alonso Díaz, another Mercedarian, noted that he had seen Valera working on his Aymara translation of the catechism in the Jesuit school.

The translation project would bring Valera into close contact with José de Acosta, the Jesuit provincial, with whom Valera would disagree on numerous issues. Although the two men shared a deep anger over Spanish abuses of the native Peruvians (see chap. 7), they held very different views on Andean culture and on the principles of translating Christian religious terms into Quechua. Unfortunately for Valera, his close contact with Acosta provided the provincial the chance to acquaint himself with many of Valera's ideas on the Incas and on language, some of which bordered on heresy (see chaps. 6 and 7). Acosta, who was deeply committed to evangelization in Quechua,[50] was in charge of the entire translation project. The Quechua translation was produced by a committee that included Juan de Balboa, a creole professor of Quechua at San Marcos; Dr. Alonso Martínez, a prebendary of Cuzco; the mestizo secular priest Father Francisco Carrasco; and Valera's fellow mestizo Jesuit Father Bartolomé de Santiago. Later, three other experts in Quechua were called in to assist with the translation. These experts were the Augustinian friar Juan de Almaraz, the Dominican friar Pedro Bedón, and Blas Valera (Barnes 1992, 71).

During his work on the catechism, Valera came to disagree with Acosta over the method of translation and the meanings of Quechua religious terms. In the remains of his work recorded by Garcilaso de la Vega and in the *Relación de las costumbres antiguas*, Valera argued that the Inca religion possessed an understanding of the true God and had native terms for Christian concepts. He provided several illustrations of these equivalent terms. For example, he claimed that *Illa Tecce* signified the "Light Eternal," or God as *principium rerum sine principium* (the beginning of things without beginning); that *huamin-*

---

49. "... ha oído este testigo decir por público y notorio" (AGI 1583a).

50. Acosta's commitment to Christian catechesis in Quechua is discussed in MacCormack 1994.

cas signified angels; that *tito* signified chastity; and that *huancaquilli* denoted the hermit (Blas Valera [1594] 1968, 153, 154, 169). However, a review of the finished catechism reveals that its translators scrupulously avoided using native religious terms; the Spanish religious term was virtually always preferred. Within the Quechua text of the catechism, for example, the Spanish words for God *(Dios)*, priest *(sacerdote)*, and hermit *(ermitaño)* were used, instead of the Quechua terms Valera provided *(Illa Tecce, villca,* and *huancaquilli).* As Enrique Bartra has noted (1967), Valera's views on the subject did not prevail in the Quechua catechism, although the Aymara translation does demonstrate Valera's theories of translation. Under Acosta, who was influenced by Polo de Ondegardo, the catechism attempted to wean Andean peoples completely from their ancient religion, rather than build their Christian faith on the virtues of the pagan past. In the effort to eradicate native beliefs from the hearts of the Andean peoples, all religious terms from the pre-Christian past were left out of the Quechua catechism. The implication, of course, was that Andean beliefs, values, and customs were too morally corrupt to have any place in a Christian culture.[51]

Acosta's conviction that Andean religion and customs were intrinsically degraded and had to be eliminated was amply expressed in his important missionary text *De Procuranda Indorum Salute* (On procuring the salvation of the Indians).[52] *De Procuranda* was one of the most widely read works on missiology in the sixteenth and seventeenth centuries. In this work, Acosta argued against those who believed that native peoples were mentally incapable of truly converting to Christianity and gaining salvation (Burgaleta 1999, 80–81, 91–96). Acosta maintained that natives were capable of salvation but were impeded in this by the bad example provided by corrupt priests and by the natives' own degraded customs. According to Acosta, the missionary's task was to wean the Indians from their "superstitious and sacrilegious rites" and the "habits of savage barbarism." These "savage customs" should then be replaced with Christian European

---

51. Louise Burkhart (1989) explores how the Spanish missionaries in Mexico reached similar conclusions. In Mexico, she argues, Nahua and Christian worldviews were so different that it was impossible for priests to translate Christian concepts in the Nahua language, which lacked terms for notions of sin, good and evil, and so on.

52. For a detailed discussion of *De Procuranda,* see MacCormack 1994.

mores and disciplines (Acosta [1577] 1954, 502–3). The Jesuit provincial stated that one of the greatest difficulties for the missionary in the Indies were the "bestial customs" of the Indians, which would try the missionary's patience (409–12). The Indians were unwilling to accept Christianity, he argued, not because of their "nature" or race, but because of their customs *(consuetudines)* and education. Christianity was inimical to natives because of their low level of morality, he wrote, which was due to customs similar to those of beasts. Experience, he emphasized, had confirmed that the Indians' moral viciousness was the result of living according to the customs of animals, rather than the habits of men (412–14). To procure the salvation of the Indians, Acosta wrote, the natives must first be taught to live as human beings before they can be taught the "celestial and the divine," that is, Christianity; their salvation depended entirely on whether they would learn to live as men (491–92). Therefore, the missionary's task had to include making the natives adopt more "human" customs. In Acosta's view, teaching Christianity in the Andes was useless without first extirpating the "pestiferous customs" of the Indians (497).

In *De Procuranda,* Acosta explained the relationship between the Indians' "bestial" customs and their general inability to become good Christians. He stated that although Andeans have the intelligence to be saved, their "lost" customs lead them to vices that they refuse to give up for the sake of Christianity: most significant among these vices were sexual lust and the observance of witchcraft and superstition (409–12). The Andeans' alleged sexual perversities figured large in Acosta's discussion of the immoral habits that resulted from corrupted customs. The Andean custom that Acosta, like many of his fellow missionaries in Peru, believed most essential to extirpate was the *taquis*—public rituals of drinking and dancing. During the *taquis,* "the worst obscenities and most unnatural crimes . . . are held in great honor by the Indians," the provincial claimed (496). The lure of these crimes was so great, Acosta continued, that they constituted "the most powerful enemy of the Christian religion" (496–97). The Jesuit concluded this section of his book with criticisms of missionaries who tolerated Andean forms of celebration among their flock, thereby making a "great mockery" of the Christian faith.

Acosta maintained that because Andean customs were so contrary to the gospel that Indians had great difficulty in accepting Christianity (607), the Christianity of most baptized Andeans was feigned (421). The experience of the Jesuit missionaries in Huarochirí and in Juli had convinced the Jesuit provincial that natives were insincere in their conversions to the new faith. For Acosta, it was not enough that the native people were brought to worship the Christian God with Christian rites in Christian churches; he complained that the Indians did not truly adore the Lord "in their hearts" and that their children and grandchildren likewise lacked an interior faith.

Valera was deeply opposed to Acosta's views on Andean custom, Andean religion, and the sincerity of the native peoples' conversion to Christianity. Concerning the religiosity of the natives of El Cercado, he wrote,

> Who will say that [their faith] is feigned or will attribute it to evil motives? What more can be done externally by the most ancient Christian worshiper?[53]

Valera taught his followers that there were actually few differences between Catholicism and Inca religion when it came to a true understanding of God; he did not see the practice of native customs as a hindrance to Christianity at all.

Not only did Acosta's beliefs about the evil nature of native culture affect missionary policy (as seen, for example, in the translation of the catechism), but by the 1580s, the Jesuit's increasing hostility toward native lifestyles was also reflected in the Peruvian Jesuits' attitude toward accepting mestizos into the Society. Most of the Jesuits of the time subscribed to a neo-Thomist view of culture, in which customs could be eradicated only after many generations of reeducation.[54] The Spanish neo-Thomists believed that external customs had a formative effect on the interior person. As Acosta wrote ([1577] 1954, 412–13), "custom . . . when entering from infancy itself through the senses, models the still tender and unpolished soul." Because mestizos were raised with many of the customs of their mothers, who had

---

53. ". . . quién dirá que es fingido, o quién lo echará a mala parte? Qué más pueden hacer en esto exterior los más antiguos devotos en la cristianidad?" (Blas Valera [1594] 1968, 186).

54. For a discussion of neo-Thomism and attitudes toward native American culture in sixteenth-century Spain, see Pagden 1982.

converted to Christianity only recently, the mestizos began to fall under suspicion.

In his meetings with Acosta over the translation of the catechism, Valera must have felt himself to be increasingly at odds with the head of the Jesuits in Peru. During the Advent season in 1582, something occurred that would have made Valera feel even more marginalized in his community. On December 14, 1582, the Jesuit fathers at the provincial congregation in Lima voted unanimously to exclude all mestizos from the Society. According to the text of this decision, they agreed to

> close the door to mestizos . . . because experience has shown at length that this class of people does not do well.[55]

Many of the fathers who had been originally enthusiastic about mestizo brothers, such as the first provincial in Peru, Jerónimo Ruiz del Portillo, voted in favor of the ban on mestizos. Although mestizos had been extremely helpful in missionary work, it was claimed that they had not proven themselves deserving of entrance into the Society. This was asserted despite the fact that the mestizo fathers Bartolomé de Santiago and Pedro de Añasco were lauded as two of the Jesuits "most famous in holiness" in all of Peru.[56]

In *De Procuranda,* Acosta explained in more detail why it was necessary to restrict mestizos from the priesthood.[57] He argued that

---

55. ". . . cerrar la puerta a mestizos . . . porque la experiencia ha mostrado a la larga no probar bien este género de gente." The text of this decision can be found in Egaña 1961, 205–6.

56. In the late sixteenth century, the Dominicans and Augustinians in Peru also refused to receive mestizos into their orders. The Franciscans officially denied their habit to mestizos, yet allowed some, such as Jerónimo Valera, into their order anyway. Early in the seventeenth century, the Franciscans changed their policies to allow mestizos—due, no doubt, to the influence of Jerónimo Valera, one of the leading Franciscans in Peru. The Mercedarians accepted mestizos throughout the sixteenth century, granting them positions of honor in the order. Contrary to current opinion, the episcopacy routinely ordained mestizos as priests in sixteenth- and seventeenth-century Peru, but only for Indian *doctrinas—ad titulum indorum.* For a discussion of the complex interplay among episcopal, mendicant, Jesuit, royal, and papal policies on mestizo ordination in sixteenth-century Peru, see Hyland 1994, 185–238; 1998a.

57. *De Procuranda,* which was composed in 1577, five years before the unanimous vote against mestizos, suggested that it might be possible to allow only a few of the most trustworthy mestizos to be priests. By 1582, however, Acosta was prepared to ban mestizos from the Jesuits forever.

mestizos should not be entrusted with the task of evangelization because of the "irregular customs" and "vices" that they absorbed from "having suckled Indian milk and having been raised among Indians" (Acosta [1577] 1954, 517). Acosta believed that Indian customs formed a highly durable whole that, when passed from mother to son, impeded the path of Christianity. The danger of retaining native customs, therefore, made mestizos poor candidates for the priesthood in the minds of Acosta and the other Spanish Jesuits in Peru. Acosta stated,

> Experience has shown that most of these [mestizos] impede the faith more with their corrupt customs than aid it with their skilled tongues. (518)

Mestizo priests, who might allow the performance of native rituals as part of Christian celebration, were clearly dangerous to the faith in Acosta's eyes.

The Jesuits' decision against allowing mestizos into the Society must have dealt Valera an emotional blow. However, several months later, Valera was to suffer a much more devastating event. In April 1583, Valera was charged with a mysterious crime. When the procurator for the Peruvian province, Father Andrés López, left for Europe on April 11, 1583, part of his mission was to explain to the Jesuit general why Valera ought to be dismissed from the Society. A letter to the general stated that this information had to be communicated personally because the Valera affair was considered too sensitive to commit to paper (Egaña 1961, 675).[58] According to an unpublished manuscript in the archives of the Spanish Inquisition, the Jesuits in Peru told others that Valera had been convicted by the Inquisition for sexual crimes. However, documents in the Inquisition archives make it clear that Valera was never in trouble with the Holy Office for any reason. Rather, Valera was imprisoned—and later exiled—by the Jesuits themselves, for a crime that they were loath to commit to paper (see chap. 8).

The nature of Valera's crime is suggested by the punishment,

---

58. It was common for institutions and individuals in the Spanish colonial world to be concerned over the possibility of their written words falling into the wrong hands. Many of the Spanish state papers, for example, were written in code so that foreign governments could not have easy access to these documents.

which included the provision that he never be allowed to teach grammar again. In his writings on grammar, Valera challenged the legality of the Spanish conquest of the Incas, a proposition that bordered on heresy in sixteenth-century Peru (see chaps. 6 and 7). Valera also used grammar extensively in his arguments concerning the similarities between the Inca and the Christian religions.

The full circumstances of Valera's crime and punishment are examined at length in chapter 8. It is worth noting that none of the other mestizo Jesuits in Peru were charged with any crime or punished in any way after the 1582 vote against mestizos. Here, it will suffice to say that from April 1583 until 1587, Valera was confined to a prison cell in the basement of the Jesuit house in Lima, where he was flogged weekly. During this time, his once-vigorous health appears to have broken down. After these four years of imprisonment, he was placed under house arrest in Lima for six years. He was not allowed to perform any of the "holy things" of a priest, to converse with outsiders, or to leave the house for any reason, and he was to do menial work within the house.[59] It is likely that he wrote his lengthy history of the West during his years of house arrest. In 1593, when Valera's imprisonment was finally to end, Acosta advised that Valera's continued presence in the colony posed a danger both to Valera and to Peru. Acosta therefore recommended that Valera be exiled to Spain (Egaña 1966, 819). By 1594, Valera was to complete the voyage to Spain, sailing from Quito to Havana and then to Spain (Egaña 1970, 646). Unfortunately, he became very ill, and his journey was delayed as he recuperated in Quito and then in Cartagena for almost two years.

In Quito, Valera would have enjoyed a more congenial atmosphere than that in the Jesuit house in Lima. One of the most prominent members of the Jesuit house in Quito was Father Onofre Esteban, a fellow Chachapoyan who labored tirelessly on behalf of the natives in Quito. The Jesuit house in Quito also was a second home for Quito's radical bishop Luis López de Sólis, who continually angered the *encomenderos* of Quito by his attempts to check their abuses of the native peoples (Carmona Moreno 1993; Lilly 1600). During his stay in Quito, Valera was able to compose his *Relación de los costumbres antiguas*

---

59. The letter outlining Valera's punishment is printed in Egaña 1966a, 302–3.

de los naturales del Pirú, which described the nature of Andean religion and the progress of Christian evangelization in Peru.[60] Also in Quito, Valera enjoyed the opportunity to speak with a Spanish Jesuit named Father Hernando Morillo. Morillo later reported to General Aquaviva that Valera denied any wrongdoing whatsoever, stating that all of the accusations against him were false.[61]

In May 1596, Valera finally arrived in Spain.[62] There, he was placed under the care of Father Cristóbal Mendez, the provincial of Andalusia, who was ordered to keep Valera imprisoned until further notice. On June 3, 1596, Mendez wrote to the head of the Jesuit order, General Aquaviva, saying that Valera appeared to have been reformed. The Andalusian provincial allowed Valera to teach humanities in Cádiz, and he requested of Aquaviva that Valera be permitted once more to hear confessions. The general's response was negative, however, and he strongly emphasized that Valera could not be allowed to teach grammar.[63]

During the long, harsh days of his imprisonment and house arrest, Valera courageously continued to write about the Incas. Using information gathered previously from native elites and other chroniclers, such as Francisco Falcón and Melchior Hernández, Valera wrote prolifically about the customs, religion, and language of his mother's people. Sadly, most of his writings have been lost, some of them burned in the fires set in Cádiz by English pirates. However, enough of his work remains to gain a picture of his complex vision of the Inca past, in which he defended the civil rule, morality, and religious beliefs of this great Andean people. The following chapters will review his writings and explore the richness and complexity of his thought on the Inca kings, the Andean faith, and the Quechua language.

---

60. Although the *Relación de las costumbres antiguas* is not dated, the date of its composition can be determined by the statement in the text that the Jesuits had two missions to Chachapoyas and that the last one was twelve years before the writing of the text. The Jesuits' first mission to Chachapoyas was in 1576; its second mission was in 1582. See Egaña 1961, 615 n. 29.

61. Morillo's letter to Acquaviva is published in Egaña 1970, 646.

62. This information is from a letter published in Egaña 1970, 840.

63. The documents are printed in Egaña 1974, 168–69.

CHAPTER FOUR

Valera's Writings and Sources

Valera's Writings

Valera's years of research resulted in at least four works. His first work, an account of the conversion of the Andean peoples to Christianity, was written by 1579. We know of this work, which is lost, because of a letter dated February 25, 1580, in which the Jesuit General Mercurian in Rome thanked Valera for sending his manuscript "about the success of the gospel preaching in those kingdoms."[1] It is likely that Valera wrote this work during his time in the Juli mission.

During the years of his imprisonment, Valera composed his magnum opus—a massive history of native American civilization written in Latin. Much of this work was burned in the English attack on Cádiz, but some charred fragments were recovered and brought to the mestizo chronicler Garcilaso de la Vega by the Jesuit Pedro Maldonado de Saavedra. Garcilaso translated these remnants of Valera's work for use in his own chronicle of the Incas, the *Comentarios reales*

---

1. ". . . del sucesso de la predicación evangélica en essos Reinos." The text of the letter is provided in Egaña 1958, 812–13.

de los Incas y historia general del Perú (Royal commentaries of the Incas and general history of Peru). About Valera, he stated:

[he] wrote a history of the Peruvian empire in very elegant Latin, and could have written it in many other languages, for he had that gift. But to the misfortune of my country, which did not deserve perhaps to be written about by so noble a hand, his papers were lost in the sack and destruction of Cádiz by the English in 1596, and he died soon after. I received the remains of the papers which were saved from the pillage, and they caused me great regret and grief at the loss of the rest, the importance of which can be deduced from what survived. What is missing is the greater and better part. (Garcilaso de la Vega [1609] 1987, 19)[2]

Throughout the *Comentarios reales,* Garcilaso provided extensive quotations from Valera on a wide variety of subjects. The topics covered by Garcilaso's translations of passages from Valera include the name of Peru; Inca religion and ideas of time; native Mexican and North American peoples; the advantages of Quechua, the language spread by the Incas; Quechua poetry and quipus (Andean knotted-string communication systems); the role of translation in Pizarro's encounter with the emperor Atahuallpa; and descriptions of plants and animals of South America. Garcilaso also quoted Valera at length in praise of Inca government and civilization and of individual Inca rulers, including Atahuallpa. In the *Comentarios reales,* Garcilaso emphasized that Valera strongly favored Atahuallpa, while Garcilaso's mother's family, of royal Inca blood, were partisans of Huascar, Atahuallpa's rival in the Inca civil war.

The extent of Garcilaso's indebtedness to Valera was the subject of a heated debate in the early twentieth century between two noted Peruvianists: José de la Riva Agüero and Manuel González de la Rosa. González de la Rosa (1907, 1908, 1909) maintained that virtu-

---

2. ". . . el Padre Blas Valera, que escrivía la historia de aquel Imperio en elegantíssimo latín, y pudiera escrevirla en muchas lenguas, porque tuvo don dellas; mas por la desdicha de aquella mi tierra, que no meresció que su república quedara escrita de tal mano, se perdieron sus papeles en la ruina y saco de Cáliz, que los ingleses hizieron año de mil y quinientos y noventa y seis, y él murió poco después. Yo huve del saco las reliquias que de sus papeles quedaron, para mayor dolor y lástima de los que se perdieron, que se sacan por los que se hallaron; quedaron tan destroçados que falta lo más y mejor" (Garcilaso de la Vega [1609] 1944a, 21).

ally all of the *Comentarios reales* had been written by Valera as a response to the chronicler Sarmiento de Gamboa's criticisms of the Inca Empire. Garcilaso, he continued, simply had plagiarized most of the Jesuit's work without due acknowledgment. Riva Agüero (1908, 1909, 1954) denied these charges against Garcilaso's integrity, in a scholarly polemic that brought new attention to the neglected Jesuit chronicler.

In the aftermath of this famous dispute, it has become clear that most of the *Comentarios reales* was written by Garcilaso himself and was not taken entirely from Valera's lost text. However, there are at least several sections of Garcilaso's work that were probably taken from Valera's great historical work without acknowledgment. There is no evidence that Garcilaso ever traveled through Chachapoyas, and it would have been difficult for him to have ascertained these facts in any other manner. Garcilaso's explanation of native Chachapoya religion, for example, in all likelihood derived from Valera. Likewise, his descriptions of the Inca campaigns in Chachapoyas, in which he provides accurate information about the geography of the Chachapoya region, probably came from Valera's work, although it is not acknowledged. Another passage that was likely taken from Valera without acknowledgment by Garcilaso concerns the observation of the equinox in Quito. Garcilaso is able to provide a highly accurate account of the sun's movement along the equator; here again, Garcilaso had never visited Quito and could not have obtained this knowledge easily (see Bauer and Dearborn 1995, 46–50).

While there are apparently occasional passages from Valera that Garcilaso used without citation, there are presumably sections from the remnants of the *Historia Occidentalis* that he chose not to quote. It seems likely that Garcilaso was selective in using sections from Valera's work, leaving significant material out of the *Comentarios reales*. After all, one sees Garcilaso being very sparing in his citations from many other chroniclers, such as José de Acosta and Pedro Cieza de León. On a darker note, however, two unpublished seventeenth-century texts accuse Garcilaso of falsifying the passages that he copied from Valera. Fernando de Montesinos, in his seventeenth-century *Memorias historiales i políticas del Perú* (Historical and political memoirs of Peru), suggested that Garcilaso invented Blas Valera's explanation for the name of Peru.[3] However, lacking any real evidence that Garcilaso was lying, Montesinos was forced to be content with a vague accusation. More seriously, Montesinos repeated a charge from his anonymous source that Garcilaso intentionally lied about the Inca quipus and about pre-Inca history, ignoring information that was sent to him from the Jesuits in Peru (USevilla 1644, book 1, chap. 4). Nonetheless, this accusation deals only with a very specific instance of Garcilaso's text (see chap. 6 in the present study). Given Garcilaso's careful citations from other authors, there is no reason to doubt the accuracy of Garcilaso's use of the remains of Valera's charred manuscript.

Another Jesuit, Alonso de Sandoval, apparently also had access to an original text of Valera's magnum opus, while he was preparing the second edition of *De Instauranda Aethiopum Salute* (On procuring the salvation of the Africans), published in 1647. According to Sandoval, Valera's great work was entitled *Historia Occidentalis* (History of the West) and contained at least five books. Sandoval (3.30) remarks, "Famous is the temple that Blas de Valera places in Titicaca," and he notes in the margin, "Valer. Hist. Occid. lib. 5. c. 4."[4] If one compares these words with Garcilaso's citations from Valera about Lake Titicaca, one can see that they refer to different aspects of the lake. Whereas Sandoval seems to allude to an actual description of the sun temple in Lake Titicaca by Valera, Garcilaso, citing Valera, refers to the physical properties of the lake and to the words of the native colonists in Copacabana about the wealth of the temple. Sandoval's citation is particularly important, however, because he reveals the title of Valera's book and gives us an idea of its length—at least five books, each containing multiple chapters.

Sandoval was born in Seville and arrived in Peru in 1577 at the age

---

3. ". . . a lo del otro autor que Garcilaso quiere se llame Blas Valera, digo que sea mui buena ora tal escritor peruano paso con que auiendo los ingleses cojidos los papeles deste autor en el saco de cadiz de 1596; ubiese deste saco Garcilaso las reliquias que de sus papeles quedaron como diçce el mesmo . . . ; al principio crei que los erejes quemaron los libros del Pe Blas Valera y que Garcilaso recurio sus çeniças, pero luego [illegible] y diçe que ubo las tales reliquias de un Pe de la Compañía. Yo estrañe la devoçion de los Herejes en repartir reliquias de lo saqueado, y en que si fueron por rescate, fuesen los redentores tan cortos que no le hiciesen de todas las obras del Pe Blas Valera" (USevilla 1644, book 1, chap. 5).

4. "Famoso es el templo que pone Blas de Valera en Titicaca" (Sandoval 1647, 458).

of one (Valtierra 1956). He studied at the College of San Martín in Lima, where he entered the Society of Jesus in 1593. The remainder of his life was spent primarily in Cartagena, where he devoted his life to administering to African slave populations, as well as to the indigenous populations in the region. His first edition of *De Instauranda Aethiopum Salute* was written during a stay in Lima from 1617 to 1619 and was published in 1627. This first edition does not contain the reference to Valera's manuscript. Sandoval must have encountered Valera's lost work sometime after 1620, when he was revising *De Instauranda*. During the years between 1620 and 1642, when the heavily revised second edition of *De Instauranda* was finished, Sandoval is known only to have visited the cities of Cartagena and Lima, where he must have seen a copy of the *Historia Occidentalis* that either had not been damaged in Cádiz or had been returned to the Jesuits by Garcilaso. It is quite possible that this manuscript still exists in South America; for now, however, this work has been lost, except for the fragments preserved by Garcilaso and Sandoval.

Valera also compiled a vocabulary in Spanish, which was used by Giovanni Anello Oliva in his seventeenth-century chronicles about the Incas. Anello Oliva referred to this work of Valera's as "an old handwritten vocabulary of Father Blas Valera that Father Diego de Torres Vasquez brought with him from Cádiz."[5] In his chronicle of Peru, written in 1631, Anello Oliva has high praise for Valera, stating that the earlier scholar was "very learned in the Quechua language and a great investigator of Peruvian antiquities and of the Incas."[6] Anello Oliva claims to have encountered Valera's manuscript in the Jesuit college in La Paz, where it was kept as a "hidden treasure."[7]

From the nature of Anello Oliva's citations of the *Vocabulario*, it appears that, with its lengthy descriptions, it was more akin to an encyclopedia than to a dictionary. Anello Oliva first refers to Valera's *Vocabulario* to support his thesis that there were many Peruvian kings before the Incas. He explains that, according to Valera, the thirty-ninth king of Peru was Capac Raymi Amauta, who governed

---

5. "... en un vocabulario antiguo de mano del Padre Blas de Valera, que traxo consigo el Padre [Diego] de Torres Vásquez desde Cádiz" (Anello Oliva [1631] 1998, 95).

6. "... muy inteligente de la lengua quichua y grande escudriñador de las antiguallas del Perú y de sus Incas" (ibid.).

7. "... tesoro escondido" (ibid.).

for forty years during the time of the fourth "sun" before Christ's birth. Furthermore, he adds, Valera's *Vocabulario* mentions three other pre-Inca kings of Peru—Capac Yupanqui Amauta, the forty-fifth king; Cuis Manco, the sixty-fourth king; and Capac Lluqui Yupanqui, the ninety-fifth ruler—along with "other kings distinct from those that I have recounted in the genealogy [of the Incas]."[8]

Two other entries in the *Vocabulario* are cited by Anello Oliva. One concerns the emperor Atahuallpa, whom the *Vocabulario* praises extravagantly. According to Valera's *Vocabulario*, Atahuallpa was the innocent victim of both his brother Huascar's aggression and Francisco Pizarro's treachery. From Anello Oliva's text ([1631] 1998, 138–39), we learn that Valera argued that Atahuallpa was one of the elect, preordained to salvation, and was now a Christian saint in heaven. Atahuallpa's full brother, Diego Titu Atauchi (not to be confused with Don Alonso Titu Atauchi), is the subject of Anello Oliva's final reference to the *Vocabulario* (141–42).[9] The entry referenced described how Titu Atauchi led an army against the Spanish after Atahuallpa's death, defeating the foreign invaders on the plains of Huamachuco. However, Valera explained, Titu Atauchi did not follow up this victory militarily, choosing instead to make a peace treaty with Francisco de Chaves, one of Pizarro's most trusted companions. Valera's text emphasized that Titu Atauchi and Francisco de Chaves were "great friends"; Chaves, of course, was a relative of Luis Valera, Blas's father. This alleged battle on the plains of Huamachuco between Titu Atauchi and the Spanish forces is described only by Valera (as cited by Anello Oliva) and Garcilaso; no other colonial document mentions it. Garcilaso presumably derived his knowledge of the engagement from Valera's *Historia Occidentalis*.

Although Anello Oliva's citations from the *Vocabulario* are relatively brief, they match some important aspects of Valera's writings as they are quoted by Garcilaso. The *Vocabulario*'s strong pro-Atahuallpa stance, in contrast to that of most other chroniclers, accords with Garcilaso's statements that Valera was a partisan of the

---

8. ". . . va nombrado en su Vocabulario otros reyes distinctos de los que tengo contados en la geneología" (ibid., 95–96).

9. Diego Tito Atauchi is not the Tito Atauchi (never baptized) who was one of Huascar's advisors and who was murdered along with Huascar. The son of the latter Tito Atauchi was named Alonso Tito Atauchi and was a well-known figure in colonial Cuzco.

northern emperor. Additionally, the *Vocabulario*'s statement that Capac Raymi Amauta reigned during the fourth "sun" before Christ's birth fits Valera's unique description of Peruvian ideas of time. According to Garcilaso ([1609] 1987, 83), Valera wrote that the Peruvians counted time in terms of multiyear periods known as "suns," the last of which began in A.D. 1043.

Yet despite Anello Oliva's description of the text and the similarities between the *Vocabulario* and Valera's thought as expressed by Garcilaso, Francisco de Mateos has questioned whether Valera was actually the author of this work or merely copied it for use in his historical researches. Mateos argues that Anello Oliva never expressly states that Valera was the author of the *Vocabulario;* rather, he interprets the chronicler's description of the *Vocabulario* as meaning that it was in Valera's hand. Moreover, after citing one of the fragments from the lost text, Anello Oliva refers to its composer as "the unknown author."[10] Mateos notes that the use of this phrase suggests that Anello Oliva did not believe Valera to have been the actual author of this text.

It is not at all clear, however, that the words cited by Mateos express Anello Oliva's thought; the questions surrounding Anello Oliva's manuscript are considerably more complicated than Mateos realized. In 1631, Anello Oliva completed his *Las vidas de varones insignes en sanctidad de la Compañía de Jesús de la provincia del Perú* (Lives of men famous in holiness from the Society of Jesus in Peru), begun around 1608. This work's first book, in which the citations from the *Vocabulario* are found, recounts pre-Inca and Inca history and provides a description of the Spanish conquest of Peru; the remaining three books narrate the lives of individual Jesuits in Peru based on personal recollections and interviews. Despite the many years of labor that Anello Oliva devoted to this work, the Jesuits never allowed it to be published. Only in 1898, after the last three books had been lost, was *Las vidas de los varones insignes* finally edited by Juan Pazos Varela and Luis Varela y Orbegoso, based on a manuscript (later destroyed by fire) in the Biblioteca Nacional in Lima. Yet it recently has been revealed that the manuscript that served as the basis of the 1898 edition had been heavily censored by

---

10. ". . . hasta aquí el auctor inçierta" (Mateos 1944c, 50–51).

the Jesuits in the seventeenth century. Anello Oliva's original manuscript, housed in the British Library, reveals that major portions of Anello Oliva's text, especially sections criticizing Spanish atrocities, were crossed out and do not appear in Anello Oliva's later manuscript, published in 1898 (see Gálvez Peña 1998). Additionally, Anello Oliva's original manuscript reveals other changes throughout the text, some of which concern Blas Valera.

If one examines the original manuscript of *Las vidas de varones insignes* (BL 1631),[11] one sees that Anello Oliva apparently knew that Valera was the author of the *Vocabulario* but that he vacillated over whether to state this. On folio 82a, Anello Oliva originally wrote,

> because in an old handwritten vocabulary that without doubt is by a person [who is] very learned in the Quechua language and a great investigator of the antiquities of Peru and of the Incas . . .[12]

The phrase "that without doubt is by a person,"[13] which refers to the author of the text, has been crossed out, and "by Father Blas de Valera"[14] has been written above it (fig. 5). Several pages later, referring to this same *Vocabulario*, Anello Oliva wrote,

> In the handwritten vocabulary that I cited above by an unknown author . . .[15]

Here, Anello Oliva again changed his mind, crossing out the words "by an unknown author"[16] and writing above them, "by Father Blas de Valera" (fig. 6).[17] Five pages later, Anello Oliva made a similar revision. Where he wrote, "the opinion of the unknown author,"[18] referring to the author of the *Vocabulario*, he simply crossed out the word "unknown," so that the text reads "the opinion of the author"

---

11. In the manuscript in the British Library, the title is *Varones insignes en sanctidad de la Compañía de Jesús de la provincia del Perú*.

12. ". . . porque en un vocabulario antiguo de mano que sin duda seria de persona muy inteligente de la lengua quechua y grande escudriñador de las antiguallas del Peru y de sus Incas . . ." (BL 1631, fol. 82a).

13. ". . . que sin duda seria de persona" (ibid.).

14. ". . . del Pe Blas de Valera" (ibid.).

15. "En el Vocabulario de mano que cite arriba de author inçierta . . ." (ibid., fol. 116b).

16. ". . . de author inçierta" (ibid.).

17. ". . . del Pe Blas de Valera" (ibid.).

18. ". . . la opinion del Author inçierto" (ibid., fol. 119b).

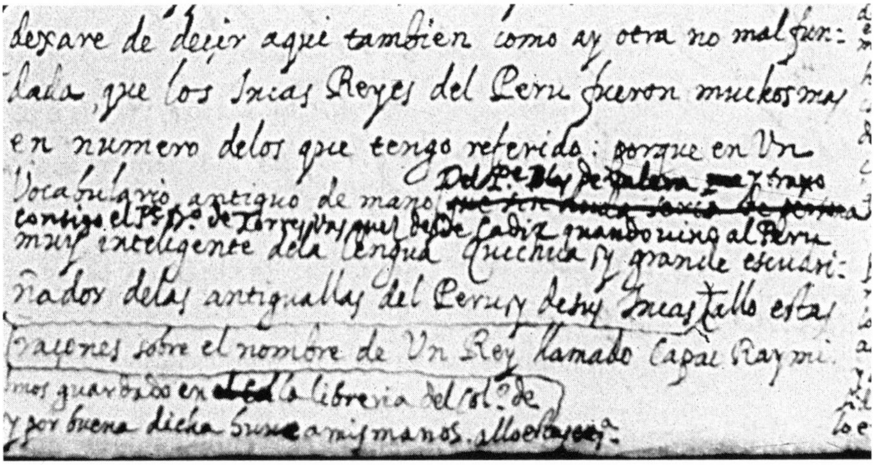
dexare de decir aqui tambien como ay otra no mal fun-
dada, que los Incas Reyes del Peru fueron muchos mas
en numero de los que tengo referido: porque en Un
Vocabulario antiguo de mano Del P.e Blas de Valera [illegible]
contigo el P.e D.o de Torres Vasquez desde Cadiz quando vino al Peru
muy inteligente de la lengua Quechua y grande escudriñador de las antiguallas del Peru y de sus Incas hallo estas
razones sobre el nombre de Un Rey llamado Capac Raymi.
[illegible] guardado en [illegible] la libreria del Col.o de
y por buena dicha [illegible] a mis manos. [illegible]

Fig. 5. Anello Oliva, Additional MS 25.327, fol. 82a. (By permission of the British Library.)

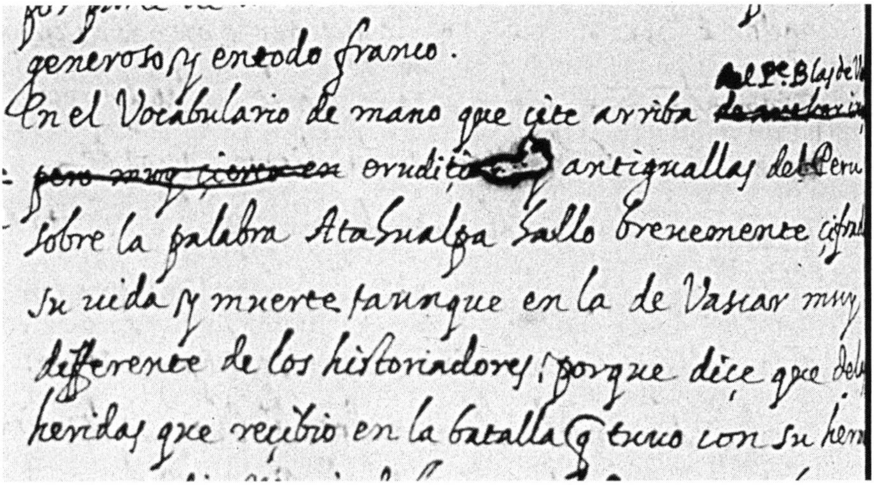
generoso y en todo franco.
En el Vocabulario de mano que cite arriba Del P.e Blas de V[illegible]
[illegible] erudito [illegible] antiguallas del Peru
sobre la palabra Atahualpa hallo brevemente cifra[illegible]
su vida y muerte aunque en la de Vascar muy
differente de los historiadores; porque dice que de l[illegible]
heridas que recibio en la batalla que tuvo con su herm[illegible]

Fig. 6. Anello Oliva, Additional MS 25.327, fol. 116a. (By permission of the British Library.)

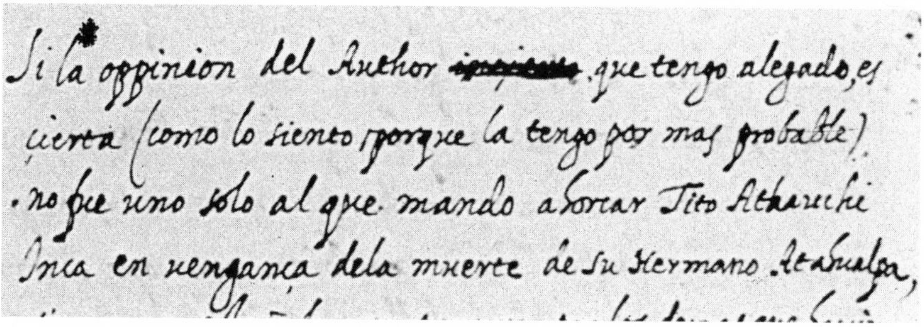

Fig. 7. Anello Oliva, Additional MS 25.327, fol. 120a. (By permission of the British Library.)

(fig. 7). But this phrase was published in the 1898 edition of Anello Oliva as "the opinion of the unknown author." Mateos, who considered the published phrase proof that Valera was not the author of the *Vocabulario,* did not know that the phrase had been altered by Anello Oliva in his original manuscript.

Anello Oliva was well aware of the reasons for Blas Valera's imprisonment and exile by the Jesuits in Peru (see chap. 8). Presumably because of the cloud that hung over Valera's name in the Society, Anello Oliva hesitated over whether to mention Valera as the author of this important text.[19] In fact, in a later section on the Jesuit mission in Huarochirí, Jesuit censors crossed out several lines praising Valera's work in the mission; these lines do not reappear in the approved version of the manuscript that served as the basis of the 1898 edition of *Las vidas de varones insignes.* These changes were part of a larger pattern of significant revisions in Anello Oliva's text.[20] Examining Anello Oliva's original manuscript reveals clearly that he did not believe that the author of the *Vocabulario* was unknown; rather, he knew Blas Valera to be the author of this extraordinary and provocative text.

---

19. Gálvez Peña also suggests that this may be a reason for Anello Oliva's initial hesitancy over describing Valera as the author of the *Vocabulario* (Gálvez Peña 1998, xvii).

20. See Gálvez Peña 1998, xli–liii; for a discussion of why the general refused to allow Anello Oliva's works to be published, see Millar Carvacho 1999.

The *Relación de las costumbres antiguas*

Although Valera's other original texts have been lost, one of his works, the *Relación de las costumbres antiguas de los naturales del Pirú* (Account of the ancient customs of the natives of Peru), still exists in a manuscript housed in the Biblioteca Nacional in Madrid (MS 3177). An examination of the original manuscript, with its distinctive title page, reveals this to have been a separate work in its own right. This work was composed in 1594, toward the end of the author's life, while he lay recuperating in Quito. Written in Spanish and in at least two different hands, the manuscript also contains two simple line drawings of the liturgical headgear *(huampar chucu)* of the Inca high priest of the sun *(vilahoma)*. The manuscript came to light in 1836, when it was found in the private collection of Böhl de Faber in Cádiz, the city where Valera was mortally injured and the home to Valera's now lost *Historia Occidentalis* and *Vocabulario*.

Most of the *Relación de las costumbres antiguas* is devoted to describing the religion of the Peruvian peoples prior to the Spanish conquest. Andean religious belief, ritual and sacrifices, temples and sacred places, and priests and priestesses *(aclla)* are discussed in detail. The author also includes sections on the natural abilities of the native peoples and on the civil customs of the Incas as expressed in their legal codes. Finally, the work concludes with an account of the successes of Christian missions in Peru, emphasizing the central role played by the Jesuits in spreading the gospel in the Andes. As in the *Historia Occidentalis,* the Incas are portrayed in the *Relación* in a very complimentary manner (see chap. 7), to the point that the Andean priestly hierarchy is described in nearly Christian terms. Much of the text appears aimed at discrediting Polo de Ondegardo's account of native religion, using arguments identical to the criticisms of Polo made by Valera in the *Historia Occidentalis* (Garcilaso de la Vega [1609] 1987, 92). Underlying the theological discourse in the *Relación* are the religious typologies of Marcus Terentius Varro, cited by Valera in one of the fragments preserved by Garcilaso (ibid., 81–83).

Though written anonymously, the *Relación* has been attributed to Valera by a majority of Andean scholars, including González de la Rosa (1907, 1908, 1909); Philip Means (1928); León Lopétegui (1942, 88); Francisco Loaysa (1945), who published an edition of the

Relación under the name of Blas Valera; Alfred Metraux (1962); Henrique Urbano (1992); and Fernández García (1990). The work was definitely written by a Jesuit,[21] and the first clue to the identity of the author as Valera is the unique information provided in the text about Blas's father, Luis. In a marginal note alongside the text, the author writes:

> The authors are all of those already stated, but particularly Francisco de Chaves, Jerezano, who was the great friend of Tito Atauchi, brother of King Atahuallpa; [Chaves] not only informed himself of a thousand things but saw with his own eyes that which here is told, and [he] wrote a copious account and left it in the power of his friend and relative Don Luis Valera, and he [i.e., Luis] gave it to Diego de Olivares.[22]

In no other chronicle is there any mention of a history written by Francisco de Chaves, nor is there any other record that Chaves was the friend and relative of Luis Valera, with whom Chaves left his history. Luis's son, Blas Valera, is by far the most likely source of this information. Moreover, this passage mentions the detail that Chaves was the "great friend" of Tito Atauchi, Atahuallpa's brother. This echoes Valera's statement in the *Vocabulario* that these two men were great friends; only these two works note this fact, which would have been known to Blas as Chaves's kinsman.

Even more than this information about Valera's father, the many correspondences between the *Relación* and Valera's other works have led scholars to conclude that Valera composed the anonymous text. As in the citations from Valera by Garcilaso and in the quotes from Valera by Anello Oliva, the author of this account is pro-Atahuallpa, referring to him repeatedly as king and stating that "the government of the Incas ceased with the death of Don Juan Atahuallpa."[23] Only a

---

21. Referring to the Society of Jesus, the author writes, "y en ninguna cosa se apartaron del espíritu y modo de proceder *nuestro*" (Blas Valera [1594] 1968, 188; italics mine).

22. "Autores son todos los ya dichos, pero en particular Francisco de Chaves, jerezano, que fue grande amigo de Tito Atauchi, hermano del rey Atahuallpa; el cual no sólo se informó de mill cosas, pero vio con sus ojos esto que aquí se dice, y hizo una relación copiosa y la dejó en poder de su amigo y deudo Don Luis Valera, y éste se la dio a Diego de Olivares" (Blas Valera [1594] 1968, 155).

23. "... el gobierno de los ingas cesaron con la muerte de Don Juan Atahuallpa" (ibid., 182).

Atahuallpa would have described him in this manner; agreement with Valera's *Vocabulario*, the author of the ers to the emperor's baptismal name as *Juan,* rather than mmonly used *Francisco.* An example of the similarities between the *Relación* and Valera's *Historia Occidentalis* can be found in their statements about human sacrifice in the Inca Empire. Valera as he is cited in the *Comentarios reales* and the author of the anonymous *Relación* are the only writers to argue that the Incas never practiced human sacrifice. Both texts concur that the chronicler Polo de Ondegardo was mistaken in his conclusion that the Incas ritually sacrificed humans; in the *Relación,* the author explains that this misunderstanding was due to Polo's inability to understand the Quechua metaphors used by his informants for animal sacrifices (Blas Valera [1594] 1968, 155–57; Garcilaso de la Vega [1609] 1987, 92).

Another intriguing coincidence between the *Relación* and the works of Valera is in the references to the pre-Inca kings of Peru. According to the *Relación,* the first ruler of Peru was Pirua Pácaric Manco (Blas Valera [1594] 1968, 153–154)—not the Inca Manco Capac, as is stated by other chroniclers. Among Pirua's successors, the text continues, was a ruler known as Pachacuti VII, the lord of Pacari Tampu (169–70). The text also states that the Inca emperor Yupanqui, who bore the name *Pachacuti,* was actually the ninth emperor to be so named (167). This highly unusual account of pre-Inca kings is found only in one other colonial manuscript, book 2 of the *Memorias historiales i políticas del Perú* by Fernando de Montesinos.[24] In the *Memorias historiales,* Montesinos presents a chronology of ninety-three pre-Inca rulers, beginning with Pirua Pácaric Manco and including eight pre-Inca kings who received the honorific title *Pachacuti.* Besides the *Relación,* only one other text includes any of the other royal names from Montesinos's pre-Inca chronology: Valera's *Vocabulario.* The kings Capac Raymi Amauta, Capac Yupanqui Amauta, and Cuis Manco, all mentioned by Valera in his *Vocabulario,* are also all part of Montesinos's history; Valera is the

---

24. I am currently preparing a critical edition of Montesinos's chronicle, for which no adequate edition presently exists. The existing editions of the *Memorias historiales* contain numerous transcription errors, misrepresent the Quechua words written in the text, have added editorial material that purports to be part of the original text, and ignore the significant differences among the separate manuscripts of the text.

only chronicler apart from Montesinos to adhere to this very unusual pre-Inca history of Peru.

The numerous correspondences between the *Relación* and Valera's other works extend to the sources used as well. The fragments of Valera saved by Garcilaso and the anonymous *Relación* share the same bibliography, including authors not mentioned by any other chronicler. Juan de Oliva, Falconio Aragonés, Diego de Olivares, and the Franciscan friar Marcos de Jofre are all writers whose works are mentioned by Valera in the remaining fragments of the *Historia Occidentalis* and also by the author of the *Relación*. Nowhere else are these four sources cited in the colonial literature, which suggests that Valera, who used these works in the *Historia Occidentalis,* authored the anonymous *Relación* also. Additionally, other sources cited in the *Relación,* such as the *curaca* of Huarochirí Don Sebastián de Quispe Ninavillca or the Christian Inca leader in Cuzco Juan Huallpa Inca, are individuals whom Valera would have met in the course of his missionary career. It is not surprising that Valera would cite such important native leaders in his work.

The noted Peruvianist Jiménez de la Espada, however, never accepted Valera as the author of the *Relación,* because he believed the text to postdate Valera's death. The author of the *Relación* describes the Jesuit foundation of Santiago del Cercado, which Jiménez de la Espada erroneously thought to have been founded in 1616 or 1617. But as the documents about El Cercado cited in chapter 3 reveal, this *doctrina* was actually founded in 1571. Valera was one of the first priests to serve there. The date of the manuscript can be determined by a statement in the text that the Jesuits had two missions to Chachapoyas and that the last one was twelve years ago. The Jesuits' first mission to Chachapoyas was in 1576, and the second was in 1582 (see Egaña 1961, 615 n. 29), giving a date of 1594 for the writing of the *Relación.* At this time, Valera was recuperating in Quito, and he presumably prepared the *Relación* as an epitome of some of the ideas in his much longer *Historia Occidentalis.*

Occasionally, other Jesuits are suggested as possible authors of the *Relación.* José Durand (1961) proposed that the Spaniard Luis López wrote the manuscript. Rejecting Valera as the author of the text on the very dubious grounds that a mestizo would have been psychologically unable to appreciate his Indian heritage, Durand posits that

López's other writings reveal him to have been the author. In fact, when the Lima Inquisition arrested López for the particularly brutal rape of Doña María Pizarro, the sister of the Jesuit brother Martín Pizarro, whom López despised,[25] the inquisitors found among his papers a manuscript criticizing the viceroy Francisco de Toledo. Among López's sixty points criticizing the viceroy are (1) that Spain lacks a valid title to the Indies and therefore the viceroy has no authority in Peru, (2) that the Spanish government in Peru demands excessive tribute from the Indians, (3) that Indian lands are taken by the Spanish, and (4) that the *reducciones,* such as Santiago del Cercado and Huarochirí, are "the cause of great evils" (López [1581] 1889). Because López is critical of Spanish policy in the Andes, Durand assumes that he must be the author of the *Relación.* However, many other aspects of López's letters contradict aspects of the anonymous text. For example, whereas the *Relación* praises the faith of Christian Indian converts very highly, López has nothing but disdain for the Christianity of the native Peruvians. He writes that the Indians are "so inconstant and [with] such evil customs in their idolatries, drinking, and concubines"[26] that it will need great perseverance to turn them from their evil habits. Elsewhere, he refers to Andean Indians as "vicious" and "embittered" (Egaña 1954, 324–36); it seems highly unlikely that he composed the *Relación,* which praises native culture as a firm foundation for the Christian faith.

One other scholar, Raúl Porras Barrenechea, suggested that the *Relación* was perhaps written by another Jesuit in Peru, although he considered it most likely that Valera was the author (Porras Barrenechea 1986, 462–64). Porras Barrenechea proposed three names of Jesuits whom he believed might have written the text: Alonso de Barzana, Bartolomé de Santiago, and Diego Martínez. All three Jesuits were known for their knowledge of native languages and culture and for their sympathetic work among the native Andeans. Upon closer examination, however, none of these Jesuits are suitable candidates as authors of the *Relación.* Alonso de Barzana, whose mission-

---

25. López's criticisms of his confreres, especially those born in Peru, whether mestizo or creole, run through many of his letters. For one of his criticisms of Martín Pizarro, see the letter published in Egaña 1954, 371–73.

26. ". . . tan inconstantes y tan mal acostumbrados en sus Idolatrias, beberes y amancebamientos" (letter by López, quoted in Egaña 1954, 361–71).

ary letters were published by the Jesuits and distributed throughout Europe, had a very distinctive literary style not found in the *Relación*. His Spanish was heavily sprinkled with Latin biblical quotations, and in all of his writings, he mentioned his conviction that the conversion of the Peruvian gentiles would bring about the Second Coming of Christ. It is unlikely that he would not have discussed this apocalyptic theme in an account of the conversion of the natives of Peru, were he the author. Bartolomé de Santiago, a mestizo from Arequipa whose widowed father was also a Jesuit, died in 1589 during an epidemic; he therefore could not have written a text composed in 1594 (see Hyland 1994, 104–6). Diego Martínez, a Spanish Jesuit who was rector of the Jesuit house in Juli for several years, certainly had the extensive knowledge of Quechua and native cultures possessed by the author of the *Relación*. However, by 1594, he had devoted many years to missionary work in Santa Cruz de la Sierra, particularly among the Gorgotoquis and Chiquitos (Egaña 1966a, 479, 605); were he the author of the *Relación,* one would expect him to discuss, at least briefly, the Jesuit missions in this area, rather than those in El Cercado, where he never served.

Although many Jesuits priests spent years working among the native peoples in Peru, learning to appreciate their languages and cultures, none fit the profile of the author of the *Relación* as well as Blas Valera. Not only does this work provide new biographical details about Valera's family, but it corresponds uniquely to Valera's other writings, the *Historia Occidentalis* and the *Vocabulario*. We are fortunate that this important manuscript was saved from the sack of Cádiz and is now preserved in the Biblioteca Nacional in Madrid.

The Circle of Sources

Blas Valera employed a variety of sources in his writings about the Incas. Because so much of his work has been lost, we cannot know the full extent of his familiarity with other written sources on native American history. However, from his remaining texts, we can glean a good deal of information about where he acquired his knowledge of the indigenous past. Valera's work provides the only record for several of his written Spanish sources, which have since disappeared. Moreover, Valera derived much of his information from the memories, quipus, and written texts of native elites from Quito to Lake Titicaca; all of this material has been lost as well, except for what is known through Valera's writings.

The Jesuit scholar used several well-known published works. For his descriptions of Mexican and Caribbean peoples, Valera had access to Francisco López de Gomara's *Istoria de la conquista de Mexico,* Peter Martyr d'Anghiera's *Decadas,* and Jéronimo Román y Zamora's *Repúblicas del mundo,* works cited repeatedly in Valera's discussions of New World civilizations outside of Peru (e.g., Blas Valera [1594] 1968, 154). Román y Zamora's *Repúblicas del mundo* appears to have served also as one of Valera's most important sources for information about the ancient world, including the Hebrews, Romans, Chaldeans, Syrians, and others. Garcilaso ([1609] 1987, 81) tells us that Valera was familiar as well with Bartolomé de las Casas's fierce manifesto against Spanish policy in the Indies, the *Brevísima relación de la destruyción de las Indias.* For his analysis of classical paganism, the Jesuit writer relied on the *Antiquitatum* of Marcus Terentius Varro (116–75 B.C.) as recorded in *De civitate Dei* (The city of God) by St. Augustine of Hippo. In fact, most of Valera's analysis of Andean religion is structured according to Varro's sophisticated typology of pagan religion (see chap. 7).

For his discussions about the language of the natives of Peru, the Jesuit chronicler claims to have had access to at least one of the works of Domingo de Santo Tomás, the Dominican grammarian who was an ardent defender of the Incas (Blas Valera [1594] 1968, 154). Valera also had an intimate knowledge of Polo de Ondegardo's *Tratado y averiguación sobre los errores y supersticiones de los Indios,* written in 1559. Polo de Ondegardo was a Spanish lawyer who had dedicated himself to uncovering the many pagan "errors and superstitions" of the native Andean peoples. His writings greatly influenced Valera's confrere José de Acosta, with whom Valera disagreed on numerous issues concerning native religious beliefs. In fact, Valera regarded Polo de Ondegardo's *Tratado* as superficial and often incorrect on many points of Inca religion; vituperative criticisms of Polo de Ondegardo's interpretations of Andean life can be found in at least two of Valera's texts (see Blas Valera [1594] 1968, 155–57, 160, 168, 173–74; Garcilaso de la Vega [1609] 1987, 92; Montesinos 1930 [1644], 39).

One of the most intriguing aspects of Valera's writings are his references to numerous works that are lost and known only through their citations by the Jesuit author. Of these lost works, one in particular seems to have influenced Valera's thought—the *Apologia pro Indis* (Defense of the Indians) by Francisco Falcón. According to Valera ([1594] 1968, 155), Falcón composed the *Apologia pro Indis* as a refutation of Polo de Ondegardo's descriptions of the Incas. The *Apologia* is cited five times by Valera, on matters of native Peruvian deities, sacrificial rites, liturgical prayers, and sacred temples. According to Valera, Falcón's work included a chapter entitled "De Praetoribus" (Concerning the leaders), in which Falcón argued that "among the gentiles there have not been kings more generous and clement than the Incas."[27] These citations are the only existing record of Falcón's *Apologia;* the work has disappeared without any other trace. Valera appears to have known Falcón in Lima, where the latter had testified that Blas was a good person who was very helpful to the Indians (AGI 1583c); it is likely that Valera had access to Falcón's writings.

The *Apologia* was not Falcón's only account of life during the days of the Inca Empire. Falcón was a peninsular attorney who strongly defended the former Inca government—especially on the matter of tribute payments—during the Second Lima Council of Bishops, in 1567 (Lohmann Villena 1970). In his lengthy report to the council, published in 1918 as *Representación hecha por el Lic. Falcón en concilio provincial, sobre los daños y molestias que se hacen a los Indios* (Account by Lic. Falcón in the provincial council of the harm and abuses done to the Indians). Falcón condemned the Spanish extraction of tribute from Andean peoples as unjust, illegal, and excessively harsh. Falcón's *Representación* apparently summarizes many of the arguments made in the longer *Apologia*.

In the *Representación*, Falcón begins by explaining that Spain has no legitimate title to rule in Peru because the colony was gained through an unjust war. While it would be impractical, he continues, to return the sovereignty of Peru to the Inca imperial line, Spain must grant broader powers to local native leaders *(curacas)* and return land, property, and grazing and water rights to the Indians. Falcón then argues that the tribute demanded of the native peoples is too

---

27. ". . . no ha habido entre gentiles reyes más benignos y clementes que los ingas" (Blas Valera [1594] 1968, 155).

high and should not exceed the levels it reached during the Inca period. At this point, he comes to the heart of his text, presenting a careful description of the political structure and economic functioning of the Inca state to demonstrate the low tributes and many benefits enjoyed by Inca citizens. What is remarkable about his depiction is how closely it parallels Valera's account, cited by Garcilaso, of the Inca government. Falcón portrays the Incas as a highly structured and harmonious state in which tribute was an exchange of labor for gifts between a grateful people and a beneficent ruler. Valera's very similar vision of the Incas apparently was derived from Falcón's lost *Apologia,* a much broader and more detailed text than the *Representación.* Although Falcón's work was lost, it has had an enduring influence through the citations of Valera in Garcilaso's *Comentarios reales.*

Another lost source utilized by Valera was the *Anotaciones de la lengua* by Padre Juan de Montoya, a fellow Jesuit. Montoya was one of the most learned men in the colony, having received a doctorate in theology from the Jesuit college in Rome, where he taught for several years before leaving for Peru.[28] During the Second Lima Council, Montoya was the official representative of the Jesuits, and he was presumably familiar with Falcón's presentation to the council. Possessing a gift for languages, Montoya was noted for his fluency in both Quechua and Aymara. It would not have been at all surprising for him to have compiled a work about Quechua to which Valera had access. He was known to have written a history of the different regions of Peru, which is unfortunately lost (Mateos 1944b, 49–50). Montoya resided in Juli during the period in which Valera was there, and it may have been in Juli that Valera had the opportunity to see Montoya's *Annotaciones de la lengua.*

Valera's citations from Friar Melchior Hernández's *Interpretación de las oraciones antiguas* and *Annotaciones* are the only known references to these two works. As I noted in chapter 3, Hernández was a Mercedarian friar in Potosí during the same period that Valera lived in the city. A mestizo fluent in Quechua, Hernández authored two other compositions: a catechism in Quechua that has been lost (Murúa [1613] 1987, 485) and an ethnographic description of the

---

28. See the report of Juan de la Plaza in Egaña 1958, 117.

native peoples of Panama, published in 1620 as the *Memorial del Chiriquí*. Valera's relative Francisco de Chaves wrote a "copious" account of the conquest of Peru by Pizarro, which Chaves gave to his friend and relative Luis Valera, Blas's father (Blas Valera [1594] 1968, 155). According to Blas, this text emphasized that human sacrifice, either of adults or of children, did not exist among the ancient Peruvians. Luis passed this text on to his fellow conquistador Diego de Olivares, whom Blas knew in Trujillo. Chaves's text, Valera continues, was in turn cited by Juan de Oliva in his *Annales* and by Diego Alvarez in his *De Titulis Regni Piruani* (Concerning the glories of the kingdom of Peru).

Very little is known about Diego Alvarez's *De Titulis Regni Piruani*. Alvarez was a Spanish attorney and a leading citizen and *encomendero* in Huánuco; he was also a close friend of Francisco Falcón (Lohmann Villena 1970, 143). According to Valera ([1594] 1968, 155), Alvarez was informed about native customs by the Indians of his *encomienda*. His book included at least one chapter on native sacrifices, "De Sacrificiis" (Concerning sacrifice). Little information exists about Valera's two lost Franciscan sources, Father Marcos Jofre and Father Mateo de los Angeles. Father Marcos Jofre was twice the provincial of the Franciscans in Peru. His work *Itinerario* contains a chapter on the methods of Indian sacrifice, "De Modo Sacrificandi Indorum." Valera (ibid.) states that Father Mateo de los Angeles, author of *De Ritibus Indorum* (On the rituals of the Indians), "died as a saint in Cassamarca," but no other data about this friar has yet been found. Juan de Oliva, author of the *Annales* (cited in both the *Historia Occidentalis* and the *Relación de las costumbres antiguas*) was a priest fluent in Quechua, about whom we know nothing else. Two additional sources for Valera were the writings of two other priests, Cristobal de Medina and Juan de Montalvo, who were both excellent Quechua speakers, according to Valera. *De Libertate Indorum Servanda* (On preserving the liberty of the Indians), by the doctor of canon and civil law Falconio Aragonés, rounds out the list of lost sources used by Valera (it is mentioned in both the *Historia Occidentalis* and the *Relación de las costumbres antiguas*).

Years ago, Lohmann Villena proposed that there was a core of pro-Indian writers in Peru in the 1560s and 1570s whose work is virtually unknown (Lohmann Villena 1970, 134). The investigations of the colonial scholars cited by Valera, from Falcón to Aragónes, form a substratum of writings about Andean people from the sixteenth century that are unknown by modern researchers. As long as these texts remain lost, we can know something of their contents only through the writings of Blas Valera, who sought relentlessly for new sources of Inca apologetics.

Another major source for Valera's work were discussions with native leaders from throughout the colony. The testimony of the "vassals of Atahuallpa"—former members of Atahuallpa's court—formed an important aspect of Valera's thought. Valera had contact with these men when he was at school in Trujillo. From them, the young mestizo learned their version of Inca history, including their story of how Atahuallpa was captured by Pizarro (Garcilaso de la Vega [1609] 1987, 678–88; Blas Valera [1594] 1968, 154–55).

The conversation and writings of the members of the Nombre de Jesús confraternity in Cuzco was another central influence on the Jesuit chronicler. In their weekly discussions, Valera and these men countered the critiques of Inca religion and government promoted by the official historians of Viceroy Toledo. Valera cites from several works prepared by these native Cuzco aristocrats. He claims to have access to two works by Don Luis Inca on Inca religion. The first of these works, Don Luis's *Relación,* is cited in support of Valera's statement that the ancient Peruvians originally worshiped only the sun, moon, and stars represented by idols, rather than the idols themselves (Blas Valera [1594] 1968, 155–57). The second work, known as the *Advertencias,* written by Don Luis in his own hand in Quechua, was referred to repeatedly by Valera in discussing Inca ritual sacrifice. Valera cited the quipus of two other Cuzco noblemen—Juan Huallpa Inca and Francisco Yutu Inca—on various aspects of ancient Andean belief. Juan Huallpa, the former "keeper of the wardrobe" for Huayna Capac, must have possessed invaluable recollections of Inca court life. All of these texts—the writings of Don Luis and the quipus of Juan Huallpa and Francisco Yutu—have disappeared. The only trace that remains of the ideas of these men is found in Valera's own works.

Valera's search for sources led him to consult native informants from throughout the Andes. The Jesuit scholar claimed to have spoken on matters of Andean history with *quipucamayoc*—historians and storytellers—in Quito, Cajamarca, Huamachuco, Pachacamac, Tarama, Sacsahuana, Chincha, Cuntisuyu, and Collasuyu (Blas Valera [1594] 1968, 154–60). Garcilaso ([1609] 1987, 127–28) tells us that Valera was told the "traditions of the verse and the fable" by Indians in charge of the "historical knots and beads" (quipus) in Cuzco. These particular quipus were allegedly the source of an Inca poem about the sky maiden and her relationship with the Creator. This poem, "Sumac ñusta," is the only surviving example of Valera's original Latin text of the *Historia Occidentalis* and is therefore worth examining here.

Sumac ñusta	Pulchra Nimpha	Beautiful nymph,
Torallaiquim	Frater tuus	Your brother
Puiñuyquita	Urnam tuam	Your urn
Paquir cayan	Nunc infringit	Now breaks,
Hina mantara	Cuius ictus	Whose blow
Cunuñunun	Tonat fulget	Thunders, crashes,
Illapantac	Fulminatque	And makes lightning fall.
Camri ñusta	Sed tu nympha	But you, nymph,
Unuquita	Tuam limpham	Your clean spring waters
Para munqui	Fundens pluis	Pouring out—you rain
Mai ñimpiri	Interdunque	And sometimes
Chichi munqui	Grandinem, seu	You send hail
Riti munqui	Nivem mittis	Or snow.
Pacharurac	Mundi factor	The maker of the world,
Pachacamac	Pachacamac	Pachacamac
Viracocha	Viracocha	Viracocha,
Cai hinapac	Ad hoc munus	For this office
Churasunqui	Te sufficit	Has provided you,
Camasunqui	Ac praefecit	Has appointed you.[29]

Valera presented both Quechua and Latin versions of this poem, and Garcilaso provided a nonliteral Spanish translation, which retained the original sense of the piece. It is worth noting that this poem is more than just a pleasant fable about a beautiful sky nymph. In these lines, Valera expresses his belief that the native Andeans understood that all phenomena, such as rain and hail, were derived

---

29. The Latin poem was translated into English by Dr. William Hyland. Valera's original Quechua and Latin can be found in Garcilaso de la Vega [1609] 1987, 128).

from the true God, the Creator. This is the same belief that is expressed in the *Relación de las costumbres antiguas;* in the beginning, the *Relación* states, all things, including the moon, sun, and stars, were servants of the one God, who had assigned different offices to each (Blas Valera [1594] 1968, 153–54).

Valera also cited oral testimony from native informants. In the *Relación de las costumbres antiguas,* Valera refers repeatedly to Don Sebastián de Quispe Ninavillca, whom he befriended while a member of the Jesuits' short-lived mission in Huarochirí. In the same text, he also mentions the Inca Diego Roca as a source. From Garcilaso ([1609] 1987 190), we know that Valera spoke to the Indian colonists *(mitimakuna)* on the settlement of Copacabana on the shores of Lake Titicaca, concerning the Inca temples; this probably occurred during his residence in Juli. Valera's writings about the Peruvian past were clearly the result of many years of exhaustive research using a great variety of native sources. In fact, among the colonial chroniclers of Peru, he is unique for the extent to which he interviewed a wide variety of native thinkers and leaders.

CHAPTER FIVE

". . . the age of our country and sequence of events . . ."

The *Historia Occidentalis*

Peruvian history was a major theme in Valera's writings. His *Historia Occidentalis* (History of the West) appears to have included accounts of the early origins of the native Americans, of the Peruvian dynasties before the Incas, and of the Inca rulers themselves. Throughout the remaining fragments of this work is material pertaining to the history of the Western Hemisphere prior to the time of the Incas. Although most of Valera's writings about the pre-Inca peoples have been lost, portions of his history of American migration and the pre-Inca dynasties of Peru survive in his *Relación de las costumbres antiguas,* as well as in the works of Garcilaso, Montesinos, and Anello Oliva.

Valera vehemently rejected the notion that the American Indians were the descendants of the lost tribes of Israel, a common theory in the sixteenth century (Garcilaso de la Vega [1609] 1987, 411).[1] In the

---

Citing St. Augustine.

1. Various writers, such as Ortelius, Arias Montano, and Antonio Montesinos, had proposed that the inhabitants of the Americas originated from one of the descendents of Noah. See Alcina Franch 1971 and Pricot 1962.

few sections that remain of Valera's work on this subject, he apparently speculated that the peoples of the Americas originated from the ancient Chaldeans, who once lived on the Plain of Sennaar in the Persian Gulf. The chronicler wrote that the religion of the natives of "greater Florida"[2] and the Caribbean islands was derived from the practices of the Chaldeans, who worshiped only natural features, such as lakes, springs, or stars (Garcilaso de la Vega [1609] 1987, 83). Likewise, he claimed that the faith of the first Peruvians was modeled on that of the Chaldeans (ibid.; Blas Valera [1594] 1968, 153–54). The Chaldeans were renowned in biblical history for founding the city of Ur, from whence came Abraham, the father of the Hebrew nation. They were believed to have descended directly from Noah, and they became famous as learned astrologers, priests, and magicians. By linking the ancient Peruvians to the Chaldeans, Valera was placing the peoples of the New World into the framework of biblical history.

Valera considered the Chaldeans to be the ultimate ancestors of the peoples of Peru, "greater Florida" (meaning all that was known of North America), and the Caribbean. It seems, however, that he viewed the Mexican natives, whom he called "this race of terrible and cruel men,"[3] as a very separate people. In his writings, he argued that the Mexicans had spread southward from Mexico and had peopled Central America and the tropical forests of South America (Garcilaso de la Vega [1609] 1987, 34). He believed that the natives of lowland South America, whom he would have seen as a young boy, were descended from the Mexicans. These people, known in Quechua as Antis, were described by him in the most unflattering terms, as was typical among the Inca elite.

> Those who live in the Antis eat human flesh; they are fiercer than tigers, have neither god nor law, nor know what virtue is. They have no idols nor likenesses of them. They worship the Devil when he represents himself in the form of some animal or serpent and speaks to them. If they make a prisoner in war or otherwise and know that he is a plebeian of low rank, they quarter him and give the quarters to their friends and servants to eat or to sell in the meat market. But if he is of noble rank, the chiefs foregather with their wives and chil-

2. ". . . la gran Florida" (Garcilaso de la Vega [1609] 1944a, 79).
3. ". . . generación de hombres tan terribles y crueles" (ibid., 33).

dren, and, like the ministers of the devil, strip him, tie him alive to a stake, and cut him to pieces with flint knives and razors, not so as to dismember him, but to remove the meat from the fleshiest parts, the calves, thighs, buttocks, and fleshy parts of the arms. Men, women and children sprinkle themselves with the blood, and they all devour the flesh very rapidly, without cooking it or roasting it thoroughly or even chewing it. They swallow it in mouthfuls so that the wretched victim sees himself eaten alive by others and buried in their bellies. (Garcilaso de la Vega [1609] 1987, 33–34)[4]

Similarly, Valera's description of the rites of ancient Mexico emphasized the alleged cruelty and savagery of these people (ibid., 81–83). The Mexican pyramid builders served an important function in the author's polemics. The Mexicans' demonic nature, as Valera described it, further highlighted the Incas' own moral virtue and holiness. It was also a subject on which he departed sharply from Las Casas, who regarded the Mexicans as models of natural virtue. Unfortunately, not enough of Valera's writings remain to determine whether he believed the Mexicans to have been close descendants of Noah who had declined sharply or an entirely distinct race from the ancient Peruvians.

The Pre-Inca Kings

One of the most extraordinary aspects of Valera's history is that he narrates the lives of some ninety-three pre-Inca native kings, beginning with the reign of Pirua Pácaric Manco, who lived millenniums before Christ. No other native account of the Andes presents anything similar to Valera's long pre-Inca history. For many years, the

---

4. "Los que viven el los Antis comen carne humana, son más fieros que tigres, no tienen dios ni ley, ni saben que cosa es virtud; tampoco tienen ídolos ni semejanza dellos; adoran al demonio cuando se les representa en figura de algún animal o de alguna serpiente y les habla. Si cautivan alguno en la guerra o de cualquiera otra suerte, sabiendo que es hombre plebeyo y baxo, lo hazen cuartos y se los dan a sus amigos y criados para que se los coman o los vendan en la carnecería. Pero si es hombre noble, se juntan los más principales con sus mujeres y hijos, y, como ministros del diablo, le desnudan, y vivo le atan a un palos, y, con cuchillos y navajas de pedernal, le cortan a pedaços, no desmembrándole, sino quitándole la carne de las partes donde hay más cantidad della, de las pantorrillas, muslos y assentaderas y molledos de los braços, y con la sangre se rocían los varones y las mujeres y hijos, y entre todos comen la carne muy apriessa, sin dexarla bien cozer ni assar ni aún mascar; trágansela a bocados, de manera que el pobre paciente se ve vivo comido de otros y enterrado en sus vientres" (ibid., 32–33).

source of Valera's account, which is presented most fully in Montesinos's *Memorias historiales i políticas del Perú,* has perplexed
scholars. However, in book 1 of Montesinos's manuscript, Montesinos explains that the history of this line of kings beginning with
Pirua comes from another manuscript whose author had interviewed
historians from the time of Atahuallpa. Concerning this chronology
of pre-Inca rulers, Montesinos writes,

> the author already cited says that, questioning the *amautas* and his-
> torians who came from the era of Atahuallpa, last Peruvian king,
> with whom he consulted . . . they told him about this tradition.[5]

Valera, of course, had access to the historical traditions of
Atahuallpa's court; Garcilaso, after citing Valera's praise of
Atahuallpa, "so great a man," writes that Valera learned about the
northern emperor "in the kingdom of Quito from the vassals of
Atahuallpa himself" (Garcilaso de la Vega [1609] 1987, 592–93).[6]

However, before examining Valera's distinctive view of Peruvian
history, one must first understand his method for reckoning time in
the ancient past. In his description of pre-Inca history, Valera discussed time in terms of "suns" and *pachacutis,* claiming that this
method was indigenous to the New World. Garcilaso tells us that
Valera "divided the periods, ages and provinces so as to show clearly
the customs of each tribe" (Garcilaso de la Vega [1609] 1987, 33).[7] In
a quote from Valera in the *Comentarios reales,* Garcilaso wrote:

> This manner of counting the age of the world in Suns was common
> to the Indians of Mexico and Peru. According to their count, the
> years of the last Sun are counted from the year 1043 A.D. (ibid., 83)[8]

---

5. ". . . diçe el autor ia citado que preguntando a los Amautas i Historiadores que
alcanzó del tiempo de Atahualpa ultimo Rey Peruano, con quienes consultó . . . le dijeron
sobre esta tradicion" (USevilla 1644, book 1, chap. 4).

6. ". . . de tan gran varón. . . . Hasta aquí es del padre Blas Valera, el cual recibió esta
relación en el reino de Quito de los mismos vasallos de Atahuallpa" (Garcilaso [1609]
1944b, 265).

7. "El Padre Blas Valera . . . llevava la misma intención que nosotros . . . que era dividir
los tiempos, las edades y las provincias para que se entendieran mejor las costumbres que
cada nación tenía" (Garcilaso de la Vega [1609] 1944a, 32).

8. "Esta manera de contar por soles la edad del mundo fue cosa común y usada entre
los de México y del Perú. Y según la cuenta dellos, los años del último sol se cuentan desde
el año del Señor de mil y cuarenta y tres" (Garcilaso de la Vega [1609] 1944a, 78–79).

This method of reckoning time is explained in more detail in the *Memorias historiales*. According to this text, the ancient Peruvians divided time into thousand-year intervals, called a *Capac-huata* or *Intip-huata*, "great year of the sun." Each millennium was further divided into two five-hundred-year periods known as *pachacutis* (Montesinos [1644] 1930, 38–39). Events occurring in the thousands of years before the Incas, a period for which Valera provides lists of rulers going back to the original inhabitants of Peru, are dated according to this system of "suns" and *pachacutis*. For example, Montesinos states that the Americas were first populated by Chaldeans at the dawn of the second "sun" after Creation (5); this would imply that the descendants of Noah first arrived in Peru two thousand years after the creation of the world. Forty-three years before the completion of the fourth "sun" after Creation, the account continues, Christ was born in Bethlehem; this corresponds to the second year of the reign of the Peruvian king Manco Capac, the third Peruvian king to bear that name (62). Once one is able to tie the system of "suns" to the birth of Christ (A.D. 1), one can calculate for the entire line of pre-Inca kings in Montesinos absolute dates that correspond to Valera's pre-Inca chronology. The final completed age of the last "sun" in Montesinos's genealogy of kings corresponds to the date A.D. 1043 (70–71); this, in turn, agrees with Valera's account in Garcilaso and reveals that Montesinos's anonymous source was using the same system as Valera.

Valera's history of pre-Inca kings is a radical departure from traditional Inca historiography. Other chroniclers of native Peruvian history, such as Cieza de León and Garcilaso, provide a list of twelve or thirteen Inca rulers descended from the first Inca, Manco Capac, who was said to be the divine child of the sun. The pre-Inca period is described generally as a time of constant warfare and barbarism. The native chronicler Guaman Poma organized pre-Inca history into four successive ages, with the fifth age corresponding to Inca rule (see Duviols 1989). However, nothing like Valera's account of ninety-three pre-Inca rulers, reaching back to the first inhabitants of Peru, exists elsewhere in the chronicles.

According to the description of Peruvian history found in Montesinos, the first inhabitants of Peru arrived around 2957 B.C., the time of the beginning of the second "sun" after Creation. The first king was known as Pirua Pácaric Manco, and he worshiped the creator god Illa Tecce. In the unpublished first book of Montesinos's text, it is explained that the first king's real name was Tupa Ayar Uchu Manco and that he was called Pirua as a metaphor for the abundance of food he provided.

> In the Quechua and Aymara languages, this name, *Pirhua* or *Pirua,* is metaphorical. It is understood to mean the barns or granaries that the Indians build to store their grain or something that serves the common sustenance. They gave this name to the Creator . . . [because] in the same way that they had stored all of their sustenance, so too all was in the Creator, without anything lacking. It is from here that, this king having carried to Cuzco from elsewhere seeds and everything necessary for human sustenance, they applied to him such a supreme name.[9]

In his *Relación de las costumbres antiguas,* Valera recounts that the first inhabitant of the Andes was a king named Pirua Pácaric Manco, who adored the creator god Illa Tecce. *Pirua,* Valera's text continues, was the word for storehouses and granaries and was a metaphor for the richness of the land and its first king (Blas Valera [1594] 1968, 153–54). It is worth noting that these are the only two chronicles to mention Pirua as the first king or to claim that the name of Peru was a metaphor for abundance.

After describing the first king, Pirua, Montesinos recounts the history of ninety-two subsequent rulers (USevilla 1644). These pre-Inca rulers pass through cycles of decline and renewal and suffer such traumas as invasions by giants and pestilence. The thirty-seventh king, Capac Raymi Amauta, was responsible for discovering the solstices (Montesinos [1644] 1930, 57). Therefore, Montesinos writes, the major solstice in the month of December bore Capac Raymi's name. This legend of King Capac Raymi matches precisely—word for word—the story of Capac Raymi recorded by Anello Oliva, who

---

9. "En las lenguas Quichoa y Aimara es metafórico este nombre Pirhua, ó Pirua. Entiendese por las trojes, ó alhóndigas, que hacen los Yndios para guardar los granos, ó cosa que sirve al comun sustento. Diéronle este nombre al Criador . . . y al modo que ellos tenían guardado el sustento todo, así todo estaba en el Criador sin faltar nada. De aquí es, que habiendo traído aquel Rey de otra parte las semillas al Cuzco, y todo lo necesario al humano sustento, le aplicaron tan soberano nombre" (Yale [ca. 1645] ca. 1860, book 1, chap. 4).

quoted the account directly from Valera's *Vocabulario*. Anello Oliva's citation from Valera's manuscript states that King Capac Raymi Amauta discovered the solstices, which were then named in his memory.

> [Capac Raymi Amauta] was a very wise philosopher. He governed forty years during the fourth sun before the birth of the Lord; he discovered the solstices and called them Raymi in his name.[10]

It must be emphasized that these are the only two accounts of this legend; no other chronicle admits to the existence of a king named Capac Raymi Amauta or credits him with discovering the solstices. Valera's *Vocabulario* also provided Anello Oliva with the names of two other pre-Inca rulers mentioned by Montesinos: Capac Yupanqui Amauta and Cuis Manco; likewise, these names occur only in the histories of Valera and Montesinos.

Another extraordinary aspect of Montesinos's work is that he claims that there were eight pre-Inca rulers bearing the honorific title *Pachacuti*. This accords with Valera's account in the *Relación de las costumbres antiguas,* in which the Jesuit scholar asserts that the Inca ruler Pachacuti was the ninth king of that name (Blas Valera [1594] 1968, 167, 169). In addition, Valera, in his *Relación,* reveals that King Pachacuti VII, the "lord of Pacari Tampu," restored the empire in Cuzco after the devastations of war and disease (169–70). Montesinos describes Pachacuti VII in similar terms, writing that this ruler tried to revitalize the kingdom after it had been ravaged by pestilence and war (Montesinos [1644] 1930, 67–68). Montesinos adds that Pachacuti VII also built a university at Pacari Tampu; this might have led to his being known as the lord of this site. Again, Montesinos and Valera are the only two chroniclers even to hint at the existence of rulers known as Pachacuti prior to the Inca Pachacutec; moreover, their account of Pachacuti VII is remarkably similar.

Because of the congruences between the historiographies of Valera

---

10. ". . . fue muy sabio philosopho: este governó quarenta años en tiempo del quarto Sol antes del naçimiento de Señor: halló los solstiçios y llamolos Raymi de su nombre" (Anello Oliva [1631] 1998, 95). Montesinos describes Capac Raymi Amauta using the exact same words: "fue muy sabio filossofo. Este gouernó quarenta años en tiempo del quarto sol antes del nacimiento del Señor, halló los Solsticios y llamolos Raymi de su nombre" (Montesinos [1644] 1930, 57).

and Montesinos, it is generally assumed that Valera was the primary source of Montesinos's history (e.g., Markham 1920). Valera is the only chronicler besides Montesinos to note the existence of Pirua, Capac Raymi Amauta, Capac Yupanqui Amauta, Cuis Manco, and Pachacuti VII and IX. No other chronicler mentions any of the pre-Inca rulers in Montesinos's chronology or even suggests the possibility of such a lengthy line. Montesinos's method of reckoning time in terms of "suns" and *pachacuti* is unique to Valera, as he is cited in Garcilaso; this also implies a correspondence between Valera and Montesinos's lost source.

Yet, despite the similarities between Valera's historiography and that of Montesinos, it is unlikely that Valera authored the anonymous text that served as Montesinos's source. One finds significant discrepancies between the works of the two authors. For example, whereas Valera vehemently denies that the Incas ever practiced human sacrifice, Montesinos's text admits that the Incas and other Peruvian kings did sacrifice boys and girls on occasion. The numbers of the rulers are slightly different as well. In Valera's *Vocabulario,* Capac Yupanqui Amauta is listed as the forty-third king of Peru and Cuis (Cayo) Manco as the sixty-forth ruler. However, in Montesinos's history, Capac Yupanqui Amauta is the forty-sixth king, while Cuis (Cayo) Manco is the sixty-second emperor. Moreover, Montesinos (USevilla 1644, book 1, chap. 4) reveals that the anonymous author who was his source criticized Garcilaso's *Comentarios reales.* Garcilaso's work was not published until 1609, thereby making it impossible for Valera, who died in 1597, to have written the work on which Montesinos based his native history. It appears that Valera and Montesinos's source shared the same historical tradition, without necessarily having influenced each other.

Montesinos himself stated that his history came from a manuscript "about Peru and its emperors" that he purchased at an auction in Lima. The author of the manuscript, he wrote, was a longtime resident of Quito who had assisted Bishop López de Solís with his investigation of the Indians of his diocese (USevilla 1644, book 1, chap. 4). López de Solís was bishop of Quito from 1594 to 1606, during which time he fought ardently for the rights of the native peoples (Carmona Moreno 1993). In fact, it is quite possible that Solís knew Valera personally from the Third Lima Council of Bishops, where the future bishop was an official theologian. In Quito, Solís maintained close ties to the Jesuits, much to the outrage of the diocesan clergy and other religious communities. The bishop justified his favoritism of the Jesuits—ordering, for example, that the diocesan seminary be run by Jesuits rather than by diocesan clergy—by testifying that "[the Jesuits] are such faithful and useful assistants to the prelates in this diocese, . . . as is seen in particular in the great fruit that they bear among the Indians in this diocese."[11] During his visitation of his diocese in 1596, two Jesuits, Onofre Esteban and Juan Vasquez, translated for the bishop in his interactions with the native Andeans. Incidentally, both Esteban and Vasquez knew Valera; Esteban, a fellow Chachapoyan, even wrote to General Aquaviva asking whether Valera had arrived safely in Spain after the latter's exile to Europe. It is quite possible that either Esteban or Vasquez may have composed the anonymous manuscript about Peru used by Montesinos.

Another likely author, however, is Diego Lobato de Sosa Yarucpalla, a mestizo born in Quito around 1538.[12] Lobato's mother, Doña Isabel Yarucpalla, was one of the principal wives of Atahuallpa; she later became the companion of Captain Juan Lobato in Quito (Hartmann 1986; Godoy Aguirre 1997). Lobato eventually was ordained a priest, and he served for a long time as a sacristan in the Cathedral of Quito. He is known to have worked as a translator on various occasions and to have written a *Historia de los Incas* (History of the Incas), which has been lost. Moreover, Lobato was still alive in 1614 (Godoy Aguirre 1997, 93), so he could have seen and commented on the *Comentarios reales*.

In any event, it seems clear that Montesinos's history of Peruvian kings, a chronology shared with Valera, came from the northern Andes—specifically, from the Quito region.[13] Certainly, the author of this history demonstrates a much greater familiarity with place-names

---

11. ". . . los dhos padres son en este obispado tan fieles y provechosos coadjutores de los prelados . . . como se be en particular en el gran fruto que en los yndios deste obispado [hay]" (Lilly 1600, fol. 89a).

12. I am indebted to Dr. Frank Salomon for the suggestion (personal communication, 2001) that Diego Lobato de Sosa Yarucpalla was the author of Montesinos's anonymous source.

13. For an alternative understanding of Montesinos, see Hiltunen 1999; for a review of Hiltunen's work, see Hyland 2001.

and events in what is now modern-day Ecuador than with those in the rest of Tahuantinsuyu.[14] An analysis of the orthography of Montesinos's original manuscript reveals that place-names south of modern-day Ecuador are frequently quite corrupt and altered. Also, the narrative gives precedence to events occurring within the Quito region, particularly during the Inca period.

For Valera, this lengthy narrative about the ninety-three pre-Inca kings of Peru may have helped to support his arguments about the legitimacy of the Inca Empire. Although Valera believed that the Incas were morally superior to their predecessors, he appears to have viewed the Incas as a renewal of the Peruvian kingdoms, not as a completely new dynasty. An important component of Spanish theory on natural lords concerned the longevity of a pagan empire; the longer a pagan empire had existed, the more legitimate were its rulers. Therefore, Valera had a compelling interest in expressing a view of Andean history that accentuated the longevity of its empires.

He also appears to have had an interest in the religious content of this narrative, particularly in its stories concerning Pirua Pácaric Manco and his worship of the creator god Illa Tecce. Unfortunately, because we have only fragments of Valera's own version of this long account of kings, it is impossible to determine with certainty how he related it to the rise of the Incas. Given his extremely high estimation of the Incas, however, it is likely that he shared Montesinos's view that the pre-Inca kings eventually fell into moral decay and idolatry, from which they were lifted by the Incas, acting in obedience to God's will.

Civilization and Prosperity

Valera was an unabashed apologist for the Incas. His praise for his mother's people emphasized, in particular, the civil order, learning, and high moral standards of the Inca Empire. In his estimation of Inca rule, he was undoubtedly influenced heavily by Falcón—who considered the Incas to have been the "most benign and clement" rulers (Blas Valera [1594] 1968, 155)—in addition to other lost sources (e.g.,

---

14. The corruption of the indigenous place-names outside of Ecuador in the text can be seen only by viewing the original manuscripts; all of the edited versions of Montesinos's work have "corrected" place-names.

Hernández's *Anotaciones de la lengua* and Don Luis Inca's *Advertencias)* and numerous *quipucamayocs* throughout the empire. More importantly, Valera was told about the Incas by his mother's relatives, as well as by the chronicle of his father's close friend Francisco de Chaves. Many of Valera's tributes to the Incas are familiar to students of the Andes through Garcilaso's lengthy quotes from the Jesuit. But despite Garcilaso's dependence on Valera for a variety of important points about the Incas, the views of the two men are far from identical. Valera's work, in particular, is unique among the chroniclers for revealing the distinctive view of history espoused by Atahuallpa's *amauta,* or historians. In the years after the Spanish conquest, some of these men still lived in Quito and Trujillo, where they were interviewed by Valera.

One of the most important aspects of Valera's thought, as he developed it through discussions with native elites, is that he answered many of the prevailing criticisms of the Inca Empire current in Peru in the mid–sixteenth century. Francisco de Toledo had been appointed viceroy of Peru in 1568, and a primary goal of his administration was to show the illegitimacy of the Inca Empire. To this end, Toledo sponsored historians who depicted Inca rule as tyrannical and short-lived. As Sabine MacCormack has shown (1985a, 421–45), Toledo had compelling political reasons for deprecating the nature of Inca government. When Toledo assumed control of the viceroyalty, a legitimate heir to the Inca throne had been established in the independent neo-Inca state of Vilcabamba, northwest of Cuzco. While Toledo eventually would bring about the military defeat of Vilcabamba, he was equally interested in ideologically discrediting any continuance of Inca rule. Also at stake, of course, was the broader issue of the justice of the Spanish conquest of the Inca. Influential Spanish theologians, such as Francisco de Vitoria, had expressed grave doubts about the legitimacy of European domination in Peru. Vitoria, for example, argued that there were relatively few justifications for a Christian prince to declare war against a pagan kingdom.[15] However, one possible justification, according to Vitoria,

---

15. For a discussion of Vitoria and the justification of conquest, see MacCormack 2000. For example, Vitoria concludes that a Christian kingdom is justified in conquering a nation that practices human sacrifice.

was if the pagan government could be proven to be tyrannical and abusive of its citizens.

Toledo therefore sponsored investigations into the Inca past throughout the provinces under his jurisdiction. He also selected an official historian, Sarmiento de Gamboa, to create a highly negative image of the Inca Empire. Sabine MacCormack (1985a, 429) writes:

> Sarmiento . . . was not interested in the greatness of the Incas; rather, his aim was to highlight sources of conflict within the Inca society and between the Incas and their subjects. Thus, where others would comment on the organizational skills of the Incas as a factor which held their far-flung empire together, Sarmiento stressed that the Incas ruled by fear. . . . Sarmiento was able to conclude that the Incas had been tyrants who ruled without the consent of their subjects, and that the debate questioning the legitimacy of the conquest of Peru and Spanish dominion there was entirely misplaced.

Valera, writing in the 1570s and 1580s, responded to the official judgments against the Incas by stressing the empire's moral and intellectual superiority. A theme repeated by Valera is that the Incas brought civilization to the Andes. Garcilaso quotes the following from Valera.

> The Indians of Peru . . . [u]ntil that time [of the Incas] had lived for many centuries in utter sloth and barbarism, with no teaching of laws or any other polity. But thenceforward they educated their children, communicated with one another, made clothing for themselves, not only to meet the requirements of decency, but also with some attempt at elegance and taste, cultivated their fields with industry and in company with one another, began to appoint judges, conversed politely, constructed buildings, both for private and for public and common use, and did many other praiseworthy things of the same kind. They very readily embraced the laws laid down by their princes who were guided by the light of nature, and observed them very faithfully. (Garcilaso de la Vega [1609] 1987, 261–62)[16]

---

16. "Los indios del Perú. . . . Desde aquel tiempo criaron sus hijos con doctrina, comunicáronse unos con otros, hizieron de vestir para sí, no sólo con honestidad, mas también con algún atavío y ornato; cultivaron los campos con industria y en compañía unos de otros; dieron en tener juezes, hablaron cortesanamente, edificaron casas, assí particulares

According to the Jesuit chronicler, it was through law and education that the Incas were able to raise the other Andean peoples out of their alleged barbarism. Laws concerning work, expenditures, and domestic behavior enabled the non-Inca to live more civilly in the Inca view, according to Valera, who noted that the Incas also insisted on educating the children of conquered local chiefs in order to "civilize" them.

> They also carried off the leading chief and all his children to Cuzco, where they were treated with kindness and favor so that by frequenting the court they would learn not only its laws, customs, and correct speech, but also the rites, ceremonies and superstitions of the Incas. This done, the curaca was restored to his former dignity and authority, and the Inca, as king, ordered the vassals to serve and obey him as their natural lord. (Garcilaso de la Vega [1609] 1987, 265)[17]

One of the most important aspects of Inca education in Cuzco and throughout the empire was the use of the Quechua language, which was spread through the Andes by the Inca rulers. Valera considered Quechua a key aspect of Inca cultural superiority to their neighboring peoples.

> In addition to [Quechua's] use in commerce and negotiations, and other spiritual and temporal affairs, it makes [men and women] keener in understanding and more tractable and ingenious in what they learn, turning them from savages into civilized and conversible men. Thus the Puquinas, Collas, Urus, Yuncas and other rude and wild tribes, who speak even their own languages ill, seem to cast off their roughness and savagery when they learn the language of Cuzco, and begin to aspire to a more civilized and courtly life, while

---

como públicas y comunes; hizieron otras muchas cosas deste jaez, dignas de loor. Abraçaron muy de buena gana las leyes que sus Príncipes, enseñados con la lumbre natural, ordenaron, y las guardaron muy cumplidamente" (Garcilaso de la Vega [1609] 1944a, 244).

17. "También llevavan al Cozco al cacique principal y a todos sus hijos, para los acariciar y regalar, y para que ellos, frecuentando la corte, aprendiessen, no solamente las leyes y costumbres y la propriedad de la lengua, mas también sus ritos, ceremonias y supersticiones; lo cual hecho, restituía al curaca en su antigua dignidad y señorío, y, como Rey, madava a los vassallos le sirviessen y obedesciessen como a señor natural" (Garcilaso de la Vega [1609] 1944a, 247).

their minds rise to higher things. (Garcilaso de la Vega [1609] 1987, 410)[18]

For Blas Valera, the Incas did more than bring a higher level of learning and civilization to the Andes, however. Valera tells us that the Incas were excellent administrators who were able to forge together a bureaucracy capable of bringing great prosperity to the land. When the Incas conquered a new territory, Valera writes, they appointed governors and officials for every kind of duty, to ensure the smooth functioning of the state. In his section on Inca administration, the Jesuit scholar comments:

> Governors and officials were selected by the Inca, and given their appropriate place in the hierarchy for all matters concerning the government of the empire and the payment of tribute, so that their rights and duties were evident and generally understood, and no one could be deceived. There were shepherds of various ranks to whom the royal and ordinary flocks were entrusted; and they tended them with great care and fidelity so that no sheep were ever missing, for they diligently warded off wild beasts; and thieves were unknown, so that they all slept securely. There were guards and accountants of various degrees for the fields and estates; and also stewards and administrators and inspecting judges. It was the duty of all of them to see that their village as a whole and each inhabitant in particular never lacked anything that was needful, and if there was want of anything to report it immediately to the governors, the curacas, and the ruler himself so that steps could be taken to supply it. This they did with wonderful care, especially the Inca, who earnestly desired that his people should not look upon him as a king, but rather as the head of a family and a diligent guardian. (Garcilaso de la Vega [1609] 1987, 268)[19]

---

18. ". . . demás del provecho que les causa en sus comercios, tratos y contratos y en otros aprovechamientos temporales y bienes spirituales, les haze más agudos de entendamiento y más dóciles y más ingeniosos para lo que quisieren aprender, y de bárbaros los trueca en hombres políticos y más urbanos. Y assí los indios Puquinas, Collas, Urus, Yuncas y otras nasciones, que son rudos y torpes, y por su rudeza aun sus proprias lenguas las hablan mal, cuando alcançan a saber la lengua de Cozco paresce que echan de sí su rudeza y torpeza que tenían y que aspiran a cosas políticas y cortesanas y sus ingenios pretenden subir a cosas más altas" (Garcilaso [1609] 1944b, 95).

19. "Otros governadores y ministros nombrava el Inca, subordenados de menores a mayores, para todas las cosas del govierno y tributos del Imperio, para que, por su cuenta

According to Valera, therefore, the Inca emperor and his officials had a personal responsibility to ensure that each individual in the empire had enough food and clothing for survival. The prosperity necessary to provide for everyone was achieved by careful scrutiny of the people's domestic and public labor. Valera writes:

> There were in fact certain judges appointed to inspect temples, public places and buildings, and private houses, and they were called *llacta-camayu*. These officials, either in person or through deputies, frequently visited the houses to see that both husband and wife carefully and diligently kept the household and family in proper order and attended to the obedience, occupations, and needs of the children. The diligence of the couple was assessed by the adornment, cleanliness, and tidiness of the house, furniture, and clothes, and even the pottery and other domestic utensils. Those who were regarded as careful and neat were rewarded with public commendations, while the careless were flogged on the arms and legs or punished in such other ways as the law established. Because of this all that was necessary for human consumption was so abundant that it was practically given away for nothing, even things which today are greatly prized. (Garcilaso de la Vega [1609] 1987, 263–64)[20]

---

y razón, las tuviessen de manifiesto, para que ninguno pudiesse ser engañado. Tenían pastores mayores y menores, a los cuales entregavan todo el ganado real y común, y lo guardavan con distinción y gran fidelidad, de manera que no faltava una oveja, porque tenían cuidado de ahuyentar las fieras, y no tenían ladrones, porque no los havía, y assí todos dormían seguros. Havía guardas y veedores mayores y menores, de los campos y heredades. Havía mayordomos y administradores, y juezes, visitadores. El oficio de todos ellos era que a su pueblo, en común ni en particular, no faltasse cosa alguna de necessario, y haviendo necessidad (de cualquiera cosa que fuesse), luego, al punto, davan cuenta della a los governadores y a los curacas y al mismo Rey, para que la proveyessen, lo cual ellos hazían maravillosamente, principalmente el Inca, que en este particular en ninguna manera quería que los suyos lo tuviessen por Rey, sino por padre de familias y tutor muy diligente" (Garcilaso de la Vega [1609] 1944a, 250).

20. "Porque havía ciertos juezes que tenían cargo de visitar los templos, los lugares y edificios públicos y las casas particulares: llamávanse llactacamayu. Éstos, por sí o por sus ministros, visitavan a menudo las casas para ver el cuidado y diligencia que assí el varón como la mujer tenía acerca de su casa y familia, y la obediencia, solicitud y ocupación de los hijos. Coligían y sacavan la diligencia dellos del ornamento, atavío y limpieza y buen aliño de su casa, de sus alhajas, vestidos, hasta los vasos y todas las demás cosas caseras. Y a los que hallavan aliñosos premiavan con loarlos en público, y a los desaliñados castigavan con açotes en braços y piernas o con otras penas que la ley mandava. De cuya causa havía tanta abundancia de las cosas necessarias para la vida humana, que casi se davan de balde, y aun las que hoy tanto estiman" (Garcilaso de la Vega [1609] 1944a, 246).

In other words, the Incas ensured prosperity in their empire by closely controlling and encouraging production at a household level. If the domestic family unit could function efficiently, with each individual busy at productive tasks, the empire as a whole would enjoy a surplus of goods. Valera emphasizes that everyone in the state was assigned useful tasks; for example, "the aged and infirm who were incapable of heavy duties [had to] occupy themselves with some useful exercise such as collecting brushwood or straw or catching lice; . . . the task for the blind was to clean cotton of the seeds and bits it has" (Garcilaso de la Vega [1609] 1987, 268).[21]

While the state officials saw to it that the people were kept busy throughout the year, the actual tribute that was demanded from the people was quite small, the chronicler continues.

> Concerning the subject of the tribute levied and collected by the Inca kings of Peru from their vassals, this was so moderate that when one realizes what it consisted of and how much it was, it can truthfully be affirmed that none of the kings of the ancients, nor the great Ceasars who were called Augustus and Pius can be compared with the Inca kings in this respect. For properly speaking it seems that they did not receive taxes and tributes from their subjects, but rather that they paid their subjects or merely imposed taxes for their benefit, such was their liberality toward their vassals. (Garcilaso de la Vega [1609] 1987, 272)[22]

So generous were the Inca rulers to their subjects, Valera states, that the tribute paid was quite minor when compared to what was received from the state. One of the most important aspects of the Inca Empire, as Valera portrays it, is that there was no want or hunger of

---

21. ". . . que los viejos y viejas y los impedidos para los trabajos mayores se ocupassen en algún exercicio provechoso para ellos, siquiera en coger seroxa y paxa, y en despiojarse . . . el oficio proprio de los ciegos era de limpiar el algodón de la semilla o granillos que tiene dentro de sí" (Garcilaso de la Vega [1609] 1944a, 250).

22. "Viniendo a los tributos que los Incas Reyes del Perú imponían y cobravan de sus vassallos, eran tan moderados que, si se consideran las cosas que eran y la cantidad dellas, se podrá afirmar con verdad que ninguno de todos los Reyes antiguos, ni los grandes Césares que se llamaron Augustos y Píos, se pueden comparar con los Reyes Incas. Porque cierto, bien mirado, paresce que no recebían pechos ni tributos de sus vasallos, sino que ellos los pagavan a los vasallos o los imponían para el provecho de los mismos vasallos, según los gastavan en el beneficio dellos mismos" (Garcilaso de la Vega [1609] 1944a, 254).

any kind throughout the land. This is especially poignant when we remember the miserable conditions of the Andean people at the time when Valera was writing, when hunger, disease, and premature death were continually present in the native households. During the period of Inca rule, the needy, the orphaned, and the infirm were all assured of receiving whatever goods they might need. Valera praised the generosity of the Inca kings.

> The burden of the tributes imposed by the kings was so light that what we are about to say may well appear to the reader to have been written in jest. Yet, not content or satisfied with these things, the Incas distributed all that was needful for clothes and food with abundant liberality and gave away many other gifts not only to lords and nobles but also to taxpayers and the poor. They might therefore more properly be called diligent fathers of families or careful stewards than kings, and this gave rise to the title *Cápac Titu* which the Indians applied to them. *Cápac* is "a prince powerful in wealth and greatness" and *titu* means "a liberal, magnanimous prince, august demi-god." This is also the reason why the kings of Peru were so beloved by their vassals that even today the Indians, though converted to Christianity, do not forget them, but rather call upon them in turn by their names with weeping and wailing and cries and shouts, whenever they are in trouble or in need. We do not read of any ancient king of Asia, Africa or Europe having shown himself so careful, affable, beneficent, free and liberal toward his natural subjects as were the Inca kings toward theirs. (Garcilaso de la Vega [1609] 1987, 266)[23]

---

23. "La carga de los tributos que a sus vasallos imponían aquellos Reyes era tan liviana que parescerá cosa de burla lo que adelante diremos, a los que lo leyeren. Empero, los Incas, no contentos ni satisfechos con todas estas cosas, distribuían con grandíssima largueza las cosas necessarias para el comer y el vestir, sin otros muchos dones, no solamente a los señores y a los nobles, mas también a los pecheros y a los pobres, de tal manera que con más razón se podrían llamar diligentes padres de familias o cuidadosos mayordomos, que no Reyes, de donde nació el renombre Cápac Titu con que los indios les solían llamar: Cápac, lo mismo es que Príncipe poderoso en riquezas y grandezas, y Titu significa Príncipe liberal, magnánimo, medio Dios, augusto. De aquí también nasció que aquellos Reyes del Perú, por haver sido tales, fuessen tan amados y queridos de sus vassallos que hoy los indios, con ser ya cristianos, no pueden olvidarlos, antes en sus trabajos y necessidades, con llantos y gemidos, a vozes y alaridos los llaman uno a uno por sus nombres; porque no se lee que ninguno de los Reyes antiguos de Asia, África y Europa haya sido para sus naturales vassallos tan cuidadoso, tan apazible, tan provechoso, franco y liberal, como lo fueron los Reyes Incas para con los suyos" (Garcilaso de la Vega [1609] 1944a, 248–49).

The preceding quotations from Valera, all of which appear in Garcilaso's *Comentarios reales,* deeply influenced the thought of Garcilaso and of later chroniclers. By the early seventeenth century, when Garcilaso wrote his defense of Inca civilization, the colonial government's need to justify Spanish dominion had receded. After 1600, therefore, it became commonplace for writers to extol the many virtues of the Inca state, particularly after the publication of the highly influential *Comentarios reales.* Valera was the predecessor of the later pro-Inca historiography, providing a vital bridge between the seventeenth-century writers and the initial, pre-Toledo accounts of the Spanish conquest. His vision of the Inca Empire as a closely controlled state in which the details of daily life were monitored by the government may seem distasteful to modern readers.[24] However, it is by no means clear that such a state would have been abhorrent to a Spaniard of the late sixteenth century. The degree of control that Valera claimed for the Inca Empire would have seemed enviable to a European monarch of his day and was being attempted in Spain itself.[25] Moreover, for someone who had witnessed the hunger, poverty, and mortality of the Andean people under Spanish colonial rule,[26] as had Valera, the vision of an Inca past of plenty and order would have been greatly compelling.

The Wisdom of the Inca Kings

One of the hallmarks of a great empire, in Valera's view, was that it should be governed by great kings. This opinion was not unique to Valera, of course; in fact, seeing the character of the ruler as a metaphor for the nature of the realm seems to be a common attribute of monarchy (see Hocart 1970; Gose 1996). In keeping with his idealized picture of the Inca Empire, Valera (in the fragments that remain of his work) depicted the Inca kings as heroic and wise leaders. Unfortunately, Valera's complete account of the Inca kings no longer exists;

---

24. The actual degree of control exercised by the Inca government has been a matter of debate among scholars. See Rowe 1982 and Murra 1975 for an introduction to the issue.

25. For examples of the Spanish government's attempts to regulate the daily lives and worship of the Spanish peasants, see Christian 1989.

26. For a discussion of the demographic catastrophe occurring to the Andean peoples in the sixteenth century, see Cook 1981.

however, we can glimpse insights into his understanding of the Inca kings in his *Relación de las costumbres antiguas,* as well as in the works of Garcilaso and Anello Oliva. These texts retain selections from Valera's writings on five of the Inca rulers, all of whom he praised for governing in accordance with reason and natural law. It is likely that Valera's original list of rulers contained more kings than did the lists of other chroniclers. Both Garcilaso and Anello Oliva state that Valera claimed that the Inca dynasty had lasted for nearly six hundred years, rather than the three hundred or four hundred years assigned to it by other sixteenth-century writers (Garcilaso de la Vega [1609] 1987, 67; Anello Oliva [1631] 1998, 19).

The first Inca ruler for whom we have Valera's description is Inca Roca, considered by imperial tradition to have been the sixth Inca king. Valera claimed that the name *Roca* signified "prudent and astute prince" (Garcilaso de la Vega [1609] 1987, 103),[27] and he portrayed Inca Roca as a wise lawgiver and a patron of learning. According to the chronicler, Inca Roca founded the schools in Cuzco that would serve to spread learning through the empire. In these academies, the Inca princes, young men of royal blood, and all of the high local nobility in the land were educated by the most learned men *(amauta)* of the kingdom.

> [They] attained the knowledge of how to govern and became more civilized and better skilled in the art of war. They learnt about the times and seasons of the year and could record and read history from the knots. They learned to speak with elegance and taste, and to bring up their children and govern their houses. They were taught poetry, music, philosophy, and astrology, or such little as was known of these sciences. The masters were called *amautas,* "philosophers" or "wise men," and were held in high veneration. (Garcilaso de la Vega [1609] 1987, 227)[28]

---

27. "Príncipe prudente y maduro . . ." (Garcilaso de la Vega [1609] 1944a, 99).

28. ". . . alcançassen el don de saber governar y se hiziessen más urbanos y fuessen de mayor industria para el arte militar; para conocer los tiempos y los años y saber por los ñudos las historias y dar cuenta dellas; para que supiessen hablar con ornamento y elegancia y supiessen criar sus hijos, governar sus casas. Enseñávanles poesía, música, filosofía y astrología, esso poco que de cada sciencia alcançaron. A los maestros llamavan amautas, que es tanto como filósofos y sabios, los cuales eran tenidos en suma veneración" (Garcilaso de la Vega [1609] 1944a, 214).

Valera's list of the subjects studied sounds very similar to the education of a Spanish nobleman during the Renaissance.

In addition to his importance as a patron of learning, Inca Roca was also a just, if stern, lawgiver, according to Valera. He instituted the death penalty for criminals convicted of theft, murder, adultery, or arson. Valera also wrote that he restricted higher learning to the nobility out of the fear that the populace, if educated, "would grow overweening and overthrow the republic" (Garcilaso de la Vega [1609] 1987, 226).[29] This latter point clearly reflects the Inca concern for a stable social hierarchy, although it may express as well the class attitudes learned by Valera in colonial Peru.

Valera's depiction of Inca Roca stands in great contrast to that of Sarmiento, Viceroy Toledo's handpicked historian. Sarmiento describes Inca Roca as a victorious general who, however, was given to idleness and pleasure. Apart from his victories in war, which he won with great violence and cruelty, his primary accomplishment was the division of Cuzco into Hanan (Upper) and Hurin (Lower). Sarmiento has nothing to say about Inca Roca as a lover of learning or as a lawgiver (Sarmiento de Gamboa [1572] 1972, 70–72).

The Jesuit chronicler has less to say about the next emperor whom he mentions, Inca Viracocha, the grandson of Inca Roca. According to the fragments quoted by Garcilaso, Valera wrote that Viracocha cautioned the Incas against bringing up their children too harshly, as "this Inca was reared so harshly and out of favor with his father" (Garcilaso de la Vega [1609] 1987, 308).[30] In the *Relación de las costumbres antiguas,* Valera adds that Viracocha was troubled by great wars caused by the priests, who incited people to rebel. The most serious war fought by Viracocha, the chronicler writes, was that against Hantahuaylla and the warriors of Chincha, who nearly defeated the Inca nation (Blas Valera [1594] 1968, 167). Here, Valera is referring to a watershed event in Inca history, when the Chancas attempted to invade Inca Cuzco. In this war, Prince Viracocha successfully defended the city, while his father, Yahuar Huacac, fled. After his victory, Viracocha was able to depose his father and take over the Inca

---

29. "... porque no se ensoberveciessen y amenguassen la república" (Garcilaso de la Vega [1609] 1944a, 214).

30. "... como este Inca se crió con tanta aspereza y disfavor de su padre" (Garcilaso de la Vega [1609] 1944a, 288).

government (see Garcilaso de la Vega [1609] 1987, 276–309). Valera alleged that Christ himself had appeared to the young prince, inspiring him to victory and demonstrating as well that the Inca victories were due to divine providence (Sansevero 1750, 247). According to Inca legend, Hancohualla (also known as Ancovilca), the defeated Chanca war chief, fled with his people into the jungles near Chachapoyas and there founded the opulent kingdom later known as El Dorado. As a boy, Valera would have seen many expeditions leave from his hometown in search of this mysterious land of gold.

Valera's claim that Inca Viracocha fought and defeated the Chancas is almost unique. Only Garcilaso follows Valera in this; most other colonial writers state that Inca Viracocha's son, Pachacuti, led the war against the Chancas, inspired by a vision of the sun god. In fact, according to most chroniclers, Inca Viracocha fled from the Chanca attack, leaving his son to defend the abandoned city of Cuzco against the enemy. Sarmiento, for example, claims that Viracocha cowardly left Cuzco undefended against the Chanca, fleeing for his life to Caquia Xaquixahuana, where he lived until his death several years later (Sarmiento de Gamboa [1572] 1972, 84–86).

The next Inca, known as Pachacuti, was traditionally considered to have been the greatest of all Inca rulers. Except for the matter of the Chanca war, Valera's description of Pachacuti, recorded by Garcilaso (who refers to him as Pachacutec), certainly accords with the legendary view of Pachacuti as the ideal king.

> On the death of Viracocha Inca . . . he was succeeded by his son, the great Titu, known as Manco Capac, a name he used until his father gave him the title of Pachacutec, "reformer of the world." He later justified this title by his distinguished words and deeds, to such an extent that his earlier names were forgotten and he was never called by them. He governed his empire with such industry, prudence, and fortitude in both peace and war that he not only extended the boundaries of all four parts of the kingdom they call Tahuantinsuyu, but also issued many laws and statutes, which have been very willingly confirmed by our Catholic kings, apart from such as refer to the worship of idols and to illicit marriages. (Garcilaso de la Vega [1609] 1987, 393)[31]

---

31. "Muerto Viracocha Inca, y adorado por los indios entre sus dioses, sucedió su hijo, el Gran Titu, por sobrenombre Manco Capac; llamóse assí hasta que su padre le dió el

Valera took pains to emphasize Pachacuti's support of learning, which the Jesuit considered to be the primary sign of an enlightened ruler.

> More than anything else, this Inca enriched, extended, and honored the schools founded by Inca Roca in Cuzco. He increased the number of instructors and tutors, bade all the lords of vassals, the captains, and their children, and the Indians at large, whatever their occupation, whether soldiers or those of inferior rank, use the language of Cuzco. . . . And that so useful a law should not have been made in vain, he appointed masters of great learning in Indian lore to teach the sons of the princes and nobility, not only those in Cuzco, but in all the rest of the provinces of his kingdom. (Garcilaso de la Vega [1609] 1987, 393)[32]

As a Jesuit steeped in the Ignatian belief that education was the cornerstone of a reformed society, capable of living in harmony with divine law, Valera emphasized the Inca's devotion of knowledge and learning to demonstrate the king's true greatness.

In addition, Valera remarked favorably on the emperor's many legal reforms, which amounted to a virtual reorganization of the Inca state.

> In short, this king, with the approval of his councils, approved many laws, regulations, and statutes, and privileges and usages for many provinces and regions, to the advantage of the natives. He suppressed many others as being contrary to the peace and to his

nombre Pachacutec, que es reformador del mundo. El cual nombre confirmó él después con sus esclarescidos hechos y dichos, de tal manera que de todo punto se olvidaron los nombre primeros para llamarle por ellos. Éste governó su Imperio con tanta industria, prudencia y fortaleza, assí en paz como en guerra, que no solamente lo aumentó en las cuatro partes del reino, que llamaron Tahuantinsuyu, mas también hizo muchos estatutos y leyes, las cuales todos confirmaron muy de grado nuestros católicos Reyes, sacando las que pertenescían a la honra de los ídolos y a los matrimonios no lícitos" (Garcilaso [1609] 1944b, 80–81).

32. "Este Inca, ante todas cosas, ennoblesció y amplió con grandes honras y favores las escuelas que el Rey Inca Roca fundó en el Cozco; aumentó el número de los preceptores y maestros; mandó que todos los señores de vassallos, los cápitanes y sus hijos, y universalmente todos los indios, de cualquiera oficio que fuessen, los soldados y los inferiores a ellos, usassen la lengua del Cozco, y que no se diesse govierno, dignidad ni señorío sino al que la supiesse muy bien. Y por que ley tan provechosa no se huviesse hecho de balde, señaló maestros muy sabios de las cosas de los indios, para los hijos de los príncipes y de la gente noble, no solamente para los del Cozco, mas también para todas las provincias de su reino" (Garcilaso [1609] 1944b, 81).

royal majesty and authority. (Garcilaso de la Vega [1609] 1987, 395–96)[33]

Pachacuti legislated sumptuary laws, commanded frugality, and suppressed idleness by assigning labor to all members of the empire, including the blind, the lame, and the mute, Valera continued. So that the people would not be oppressed by constant toil, Pachachuti ordered holidays, markets, and fairs to be held at certain times of the year. He also defined land boundaries and fixed tribute payments.[34] He confirmed some laws of previous Incas, while he reformed others, including those against "blasphemers, patricides, fratricides, murderers, traitors to the Inca, adulterers (male and female), those guilty of removing daughters from their homes or violating maidens or touching the chosen virgins, robbers of any object whatever, those guilty of unnatural crimes or incest of parents with children, and incendiaries" (Garcilaso de la Vega [1609] 1987, 396).[35] He introduced laws reforming the observance of religious rituals, and he attempted to break the power of the imperial priesthood by imprisoning many priests. Pachacutec's wisdom as a lawgiver was, for the Jesuit chronicler, an essential component in creating an ordered, peaceful society. To Valera, education and law were the underpinnings of a kingdom that conformed to an idea of natural law, and he therefore emphasized these attributes of the Inca rulers.

Finally, portions of Valera's comments on two of the remaining Inca emperors, Topa Inca Yupanqui and Inca Atahuallpa, have been

---

33. "En suma, este Rey, con parescer de sus Consejos, aprovó muchas leyes, derechos y estatutos, fueros y costumbres de muchas provincias y regiones, porque eran en provecho de los naturales; otras muchas quitó, que eran contrarias a la paz común y al señorío y majestad real" (Garcilaso [1609] 1944b, 83).

34. These aspects of Pachacuti's legislation—the sumptuary laws, the suppression of idleness, the organization of markets, the definition of boundaries, and the ordering of tribute payments—are also recorded by the chronicler Juan de Betanzos, whose primary informants were Cuxirimay Ocllo, a former wife of Atahuallpa, and her family. See Betanzos [1551] 1996, 98–106.

35. ". . . contra los blasfemos, patricidas, fratricidas, homocidas, contra los traidores al Inca, contra los adúlteros, assí hombres como mujeres, contra los que sacavan las hijas de casa de sus padres, contra los que violavan las donzellas, contra los que se atrevían a tocar los escogidas, contra los ladrones, de cualquiera cosa que fuesse el hurto, contra el nefando y contra los incendiarios" (Garcilaso [1609] 1944b, 83). Valera's list of the laws of Pachacuti as recorded by Garcilaso are very similar to his list of imperial laws in the *Relación de las costumbres antiguas* (Blas Valera [1594] 1968, 177–80).

preserved. Concerning Topa Inca Yupanqui, Pachacuti's heir, the chronicler wrote that he continued his father's policies of limiting the power of the priesthood by giving priestly office to men who did not come from powerful families. He also allowed for women priestesses to assist in imperial rituals and to hear the confessions of women; this was done to further erode the power of the traditional priestly cults. Before the time of Topa Inca Yupanqui, Valera asserted, no females except for the sacred virgins *(aclla)* were allowed to hold these offices (Blas Valera [1594] 1968, 167).

The grandson of Topa Inca Yupanqui was the Inca Atahuallpa, who was possibly a kinsman to Valera. Unlike most of the other six-teenth-century chroniclers of the Incas, Valera was strongly partisan in favor of Atahuallpa. After the death of the Inca Huayna Capac, Atahuallpa's father, Atahuallpa and his half brother Huascar fought a bloody five-year civil war for control of the empire. Huascar's power was centered in the Inca capital of Cuzco, whereas Atahuallpa's base was the northern city of Quito, close to the territory where Valera was raised. Atahuallpa triumphed in this war, and he was still savoring his victories when he was captured by Francisco Pizarro and his men, who eventually executed him. Virtually all of the sixteenth-century chroni-clers of the Incas portray Atahuallpa as an illegitimate usurper with no right to inherit the realm. In addition, it is generally stated that while Atahuallpa was imprisoned by the Spaniards, he ordered the vicious massacre of Huascar, along with thousands of Huascar's family in Cuzco (e.g., Garcilaso de la Vega [1609] 1987, 613–24).

Valera's descriptions of Atahuallpa differ greatly from the histo-ries offered by other chroniclers of the time. Garcilaso, who certainly had no affection for the man he considered a cruel usurper, empha-sized how highly Valera had praised Atahuallpa (Garcilaso de la Vega [1609] 1987, 592–93). According to Anello Oliva, quoting from Valera's *Vocabulario*, the mestizo historian asserted that Huayna Capac had divided the kingdom equally between his two sons, Atahuallpa and Huascar. Huascar, enraged at the division, made war on his brother and eventually died from wounds received in battle. Valera wrote:

> Atahuallpa—the last Inca king of Peru, who was tyranically and unjustly killed by the tyrant Francisco Pizarro. . . . King Atahuallpa was the son of Huayna Capac and the younger brother of Huascar

Inca; upon the father's death, the kingdom was divided between these two brothers, and although the division was by the father's will, nonetheless Huascar Inca . . . made war on his brother; and Huascar was vanquished in a certain battle and died in Cuzco of his wounds.[36]

In addition, Anello Oliva states, Valera argued that Atahuallpa was defeated by Pizarro only through lies and trickery, not through open battle. According to Garcilaso ([1609] 1987, 681–84), Valera claimed that Atahuallpa opposed conversion to Christianity and submission to Charles V only because Christianity was poorly explained to him. Claiming to have heard the true account of the conquest from the vassals of Atahuallpa, Valera maintained that the Spanish presentation of the Christian gospel to Atahuallpa was hopelessly garbled by the inadequacies of the translator, Felipillo. Had Atahuallpa been informed truly of the doctrines of the Christian faith, Valera reasoned, the emperor would have submitted to Christianity, and Pizarro would have possessed no legitimate excuse for warring upon the Andean ruler.[37] Moreover, Valera added, Atahuallpa had been inspired by God and by the sight of the cross to cede his kingdom peacefully to the Spanish, just as "the presence of Queen Esther had transformed into servitude the angry spirit of King Asuero" (Garcilaso de la Vega [1609] 1987, 687). Again, however, the inadequacies of Felipillo's translations led to misunderstandings between Pizarro and the Inca ruler, and the opportunity was lost for a serene transfer of power in which Atahuallpa would have become a vassal of Emperor Charles V.

Atahuallpa's receptivity to the gospel was proven by the ruler's eventual embrace of Christianity, a faith that, Valera affirmed, differed little from the Inca religion. While imprisoned by the Spanish, Valera explained, Atahuallpa underwent a sincere conversion to

---

36. "Atahualpa el ultimo Rei Ynca del Peru a quien tiranica i injustamente mato el tirano Francisco Piçarro. . . . El Rei Atahuallpa era hijo de Guayna Capac y hermano menor de Vascar Ynca, muerto el padre se dividio el Reino entre estos dos hermanos y aunque la division fue por testamento del padre, con todo Vascas Ynca . . . movio guerra al hermano y en çierta batalla fue vençido Vascar y murio en el Cuxco de las heridas" (Anello Oliva [1631] 1998, 138–39).

37. Margarita Zamora (1988) has demonstrated how this issue of Felipillo's translation is one of the most important themes of Garcilaso's work. However, she does not credit Valera with the development of this idea, despite Garcilaso's acknowledgments.

Christianity, and upon his death, he was transported directly to heaven as a saint.

> Then Pizarro entered the mountains, and being received in peace in Cajamarca, he used treachery and, saying a thousand lies, incited his companions so that in the time of greatest carelessness he seized the king; with an armed hand he captured him, promising him life if he would give a ransom; he gave a very handsome ransom; Pizarro took it and took the life of the king, who was much more fortunate than his murderers, because in the middle of his afflictions, he believed in our Lord, Jesus Christ, and was baptized, and taking the name *Don Juan,* he died with great lamentations at the hand of the tyrant and his executioner. . . . His death was in the year 1533; he reigned three years, two in the company of his brother and one alone, in the manner in which our Lord was preserving the Incas and his reign until this good Atahuallpa arrived, who was among the elect and beloved and was carried with him to heaven; and the Inca Empire came to an end.[38]

Once again, we see the very heroic nature of the emperor in Valera's writings. In his depiction, Atahuallpa is a saint, unjustly warred upon by his brother Huascar and tricked and lied to by Pizarro. The ruler's conversion to Christianity and his glorious entrance into heaven are signs that he—the living symbol of his empire—was among Christ's elect, preordained to convert and to receive the fullness of God's grace. Valera also stated categorically that the Inca Empire ended with Atahuallpa's death; he did not recognize the legitimacy of the later emperors crowned during the Spanish rule (see also Blas Valera [1594] 1968, 182).

Valera's descriptions of the Inca kings are highly laudatory, praising these men as sources of virtue and wisdom for their people. Valera

---

38. ". . . entonçes entro Piçarro en al sierra y siendo reçibido de paz en Caxamarca el usso de traiçion y diçiendo mil mentiras inçito a sus compañeros a que en tiempo del mayor descuido prediessen al Rey con mano armada prendieronle, prometieronle la vida con que diesse el rescate, dio el rescate muy rico, tomolo Piçarro y quito al Rey la vida el qual fue mas dichoso que sis matadores por que en medio de sus afiçiones creyo en Jesu-Christo nuestro Señor y baptizandose y poniendose por nombre Don Juan murio con grandes lagrimas a manos del tirano y su verdugo. . . . Fue su muerte el año de 1533 reino tres años, dos en compañia de su hermano y uno solo de manera que nuestro Señor fue conseruando los Yncas y su Reino hasta que llegasse este buen Atahuallpa que era electo y querido y se lo lleuo consigo a la gloria y cesso el Ymperio Yncano" (Anello Oliva [1631] 1998, 107–8).

considers the Inca rulers as models of natural virtue and wisdom, like the Jewish kings of the Old Testament. In fact, he attributes long lists of proverbs to the emperors, particularly to Pachacuti. These proverbs undoubtedly are intended to echo the Solomonic proverbs of the Old Testament and to implicitly compare the Inca kings to the ancient biblical rulers. The Inca Empire, in Valera's view, was a well-ordered land of plenty, where justice and law were assured to all citizens. Centers of higher learning flourished in the capital under the guidance of the *amauta*—wise men who taught poetry, music, philosophy, astrology, and how to "speak with elegance and taste." Although other chroniclers would commend the rule of the Incas, none surpassed Valera in praising the manifold virtues of Tahuantinsuyu and its noble kings; moreover, none were so eloquent in defending the cause of Atahuallpa, the victor in the Inca civil war and the last Inca king.

CHAPTER SIX

". . . the terminology of all matters, human and divine . . ."

For Blas Valera, the heart of Inca cultural superiority lay with the virtues inherent in the Inca language, Quechua. Following the humanist traditions of Acosta, Domingo de Santo Tomás, and others, Valera viewed language as one of the ultimate measures of a civilization's worth. In this chapter, I first examine Valera's arguments about the superiority of Quechua over other vernacular tongues. Then, I analyze Valera's assertions about Andean writing, concluding with a consideration of Valera's contribution to our understanding of Inca writing systems.

The Superiority of Quechua

According to the humanist ideals developed in the Renaissance, the art of language was central to civilized life. Throughout the sixteenth century, rhetoric and grammar were the most highly esteemed of the *studia humanitatis*—or the humanities, as we would say today. Grammar, of course, referred primarily to the study of the language

---

Citing St. Augustine.

of classical authors, such as Cicero, whose writings were free from the so-called impurities of medieval Latin. The study of Latin and Greek became the hallmark of a humanist education, the type of education that Valera enjoyed. Humanists believed that the knowledge of classical Latin texts would lead one to a more cultivated, harmonious, and virtuous existence. DeLamar Jensen writes:

> [the humanists] studied these ancient writings as models for reviving the language and broadening the context and horizons of literature. In the writings of Cicero and others, they found the same breadth of outlook that they esteemed in their own interpretation of life, which helped them to justify their belief in human dignity, the universality of truth, and the beauty of earthly things. (Jensen 1992, 122)

Implicit in the humanist point of view was a belief in the hierarchy of languages, with Latin, Greek, and Hebrew enjoying a privileged position with respect to the vernacular tongues (see Rafael 1993, 26–30). It was believed that the ancient languages of Hebrew and Greek possessed a particularly close relationship with divine truth because these were the original languages of the Bible. Study of these two tongues in the Renaissance and the early modern period facilitated the development of definitive biblical and patristic texts. It was also thought that learning Hebrew and Greek led to moral and cognitive virtues in their own right. However, many humanists considered Latin—in particular, the Latin of the classical Age of Augustus (31 B.C.–A.D. 14)—to be the truest and noblest tongue, "the only language worthy of true glory" (Martines 1979, 318). The sacred language of the church within Catholic countries, Latin often was regarded in a manner that seems mystical to us today. Not only was Latin a sacred tongue, but many humanists maintained that its use led its speakers to higher spiritual and intellectual levels. Although Castilian gained new prestige in Spain in the sixteenth century with the flowering of a vernacular literature and the publication of Antonio de Nebrija's *Gramática de la lengua castellana* (1492), Latin "was thought to stand in such close relation to God's own language that it still functioned as the special medium for framing God's laws and for conducting the liturgy" (Rafael 1993, 28).

Within Catholic Europe in the sixteenth century, however, there was considerable debate over the proper relationship between Latin and the vernacular languages. In Italy, this controversy, which formed one of the chief intellectual issues of the day, was known as the *questione della lingua*. This debate questioned whether classical Latin or the Italian vernacular—and if the vernacular, which of the Italian dialects—was the most suitable for literary endeavors. One of the more important strands of this discussion was the arguments of Calmeta (Vincenzo Colli) and Mario Equicola, who held that the most aristocratic and courtly vernacular tongue, high above the dialects of the plebeians, equaled Latin in merit (Martines 1979, 319). These views would be echoed later by Valera, who not only considered Quechua to be the equal of Latin but, in his writings, almost exclusively referred to Quechua as "the royal tongue," "the courtly tongue," and "the language of the Inca court."

In his writing on language, Valera was influenced by the work of the Dominican friar Domingo de Santo Tomás. Santo Tomás was responsible for one of the earliest grammars of Quechua. In the prologue to his grammar, he argued that the rationality and complexity of the Quechua language proved the civilized nature of those who spoke it. Words and language, he stated, best revealed a people's intelligence and civility. Quechua was a civilized tongue, he claimed, because it could be organized according to the same "rules and precepts" as Latin; it was not a barbaric language lacking moods, tenses, cases, rules, and all sense of order. The order and regularity of the Quechua language, Santo Tomás concluded, showed that the Andean peoples were not barbarians but a civilized nation deserving "to be treated with the mildness and liberty" of His Majesty's vassals in Europe (Santo Tomás [1560] 1891, v–viii).

While Valera follows Santo Tomás in using language as a measure of the Andeans' civility, he considers Quechua to be more than merely the equal of Castilian. Valera states quite plainly that Quechua was equal to Latin as a sacred tongue and was superior to the European or other Amerindian vernaculars. "The courtly language," he writes, referring to Quechua, "has this noteworthy property, that it has the same value to the Peruvian Indians as Latin to us" (Garcilaso de la Vega [1609] 1987, 410).[1] The Jesuit author commends Quechua for both

---

1. ". . . la lengua cortesana tiene este don particular . . . que a los indios del Perú les es de tanto provecho como a nosotros la lengua latina" (Garcilaso [1609] 1944b, 95).

its practical and its spiritual and intellectual advantages. These advantages, he adds, were well known to the Incas, who spread the language throughout the Andes with the intent of raising the levels of unity and civilization within the empire (Garcilaso de la Vega [1609] 1987, 404).

One of the primary practical purposes of imposing one language—Quechua—in the Andes, Valera continues, is that it led to a greater feeling of unity among the many different native peoples in Peru. "The use of the same or similar words almost always helps to reconcile men and unite them with bonds of genuine friendship," he tells us (Garcilaso de la Vega [1609] 1987, 407).[2] Because the Incas spread the "courtly language of Cuzco" among their subjects, "the Incas governed their whole empire in peace and quiet, and the vassals of various tribes behaved like brothers, for they all spoke the same language" (Garcilaso de la Vega [1609] 1987, 406).[3] Valera laments that, unfortunately, the unity created by the Incas' promotion of Quechua had fallen away under Spanish rule. Because the Inca government no longer had the authority to require people to learn Quechua and because the colonial Spanish government lacked the will to spread Quechua, a multiplicity of local languages had reappeared in Peru. Valera writes:

> It is also worthy of note that the multiplicity and confusion of tongues the Inca tried so carefully to resolve has reappeared so that at the present day there are more different languages among the Indians than there were in the time of the last emperor, Huayna Capac. Because of this the like-mindedness that the Incas tried to inculcate among the Indians by means of a common tongue now scarcely exists, despite the fact that they are Christians. (Garcilaso de la Vega [1609] 1987, 407)[4]

---

2. ". . . porque la semejança y conformidad de las palabras casi siempre suelen reconciliar y traer a verdadera unión y amistad a los hombres" (Garcilaso [1609] 1944b, 92).

3. "Con este concierto regían y governavan los Incas en paz y quietud todo su Imperio, y los vasallos de diversas nasciones se havían como hermanos, porque todos hablavan una lengua" (Garcilaso [1609] 1944b, 91).

4. "También es de notar que aquella confusión y multitud de lenguas que los Incas, con tanto cuidado, procuraron quitar, ha buelto a nascer de nuevo, de tal manera que el día de hoy se hallan entre los indios más diferencias de lenguajes que había en tiempo de Huaina Capac, último Emperador dellos. De donde ha nascido que la concordia de los ánimos que los Incas pretendían que huviera en aquellos gentiles por la conformidad de un lenguaje, ahora, en estos tiempos, casi no lo hay, con ser ya fieles" (Garcilaso [1609] 1944b, 92).

Another ill effect of the multitude of tongues, Valera continues, is that it greatly hinders Christian evangelization. Christian evangelization can only occur, he argues, when one language, Quechua, has been spread throughout Peru. Priests simply cannot learn the great number of languages needed to spread the gospel throughout the highlands. "It is indeed humanly speaking impossible," he tells us, "that the Peruvian Indians shall be instructed in the faith and in good manners so long as this confusion of tongues endures, unless the priests can learn all the languages of the empire, which is impossible. Nevertheless, a knowledge of the speech of Cuzco [i.e., Quechua], however imperfect, is of great use" (Garcilaso de la Vega [1609] 1987, 407).[5] Moreover, he continues, Quechua is extraordinarily easy to learn, for both natives and Europeans, because of its rational grammatical principles and its small vocabulary. He recounts:

> Many who have tried to learn the general language of Peru bear witness to how quickly and easily it can be picked up, and I have known many priests who have become proficient in it with average pains. . . . [One] priest, desiring to benefit the souls of the Indians, promised to learn it with all care and diligence, and after receiving some rules and advice from [a] Jesuit, worked so hard at it that six months later, he could hear the confessions of the Indians and preach to them, to his own immense delight and their great benefit. (Garcilaso de la Vega [1609] 1987, 408–9)[6]

In his enumeration of Quechua's practical advantages, Valera never loses sight of the intellectual and spiritual benefits of the "courtly tongue." Learning Quechua, he says, "turns savages into civilized and conversible men" (Garcilaso de la Vega [1609] 1987,

---

5. ". . . por lo cual (humanamente hablando) es imposible que los indios del Perú, mientras durare esta confusión de lenguas, puedan ser bien instruídos en la fe y en las buenas costumbres, si no es que los sacerdotes sepan todas las lenguas de aquel Imperio, que es imposible; y con saber sola la del Cozco, como quiera que la sepan, pueden aprovechar mucho" (Garcilaso [1609] 1944b, 92).

6. "La facilidad de aprenderse en breve tiempo y con poco travajo la lengua general del Perú la testifican muchos que la han procurado saber, y yo conoscí muchos sacerdotes que, con mediana diligençia, se hizieron diestros en ella. . . . [Un] sacerdote, con el desseo que tenía de aprovechar las ánimas de los indios, prometió de aprenderla con todo cuidado y diligencia, y haviendo recebido del religiosso algunas reglas y avisos para estudiarla, trabajó de manera que, passados seis meses, pudo oír las confisiones de los indios y predicarles con suma alegría suya y gran provecho de los indios" (Garcilaso [1609] 1944b, 93–94).

410).[7] Repeatedly, Valera tells us that learning "the royal tongue," Quechua, increases both intelligence and civility.

> All the Indians who . . . still retain the language of Cuzco are more civilized and intelligent than the rest. (Garcilaso de la Vega [1609] 1987, 404)[8]

> . . . the common Indians [who] . . . learn to speak the tongue of Cuzco fluently . . . seem themselves nobler, more cultured and of better understanding. (Garcilaso de la Vega [1609] 1987, 409–10)[9]

> [Quechua] makes [the Indians] keener in understanding and more tractable and ingenious in what they learn. . . . Thus the Puquinas, Collas, Urus, Yuncas, and other rude and wild tribes, who speak even their own languages ill, seem to cast off their roughness and savagery when they learn the language of Cuzco, and begin to aspire to a more civilized and courtly life, while their minds rise to higher things. Moreover, they grow better adapted to receive the doctrine of the Catholic Faith, and of course preachers who know this tongue well take pleasure in standing up to discuss higher things, . . . for just as the Indians who speak this tongue are of keener and more capacious intelligence, so also the language itself has greater scope and a wider variety of elegant ornaments. (Garcilaso de la Vega [1609] 1987, 409–10)[10]

Valera clearly holds an elevated view of Quechua, imbuing it with many of the attributes commonly assigned to Latin in the sixteenth century. His readers in the sixteenth century would have understood that his praise of Quechua held profound implications concerning the

---

7. ". . . de bárbaros los trueca en hombres políticos y más urbanos" (Garcilaso [1609] 1944b, 95).

8. ". . . todos los indios que . . . retienen hasta ahora la lengua del Cozco, son más urbanos y de ingenios más capaces, lo cual no tienen los demás" (Garcilaso [1609] 1944b, 89).

9. " . . . los indios vulgares que . . . hablan muy despiertamente la lengua del Cozco . . . parescen más nobles, más adornados y más capaces en su entendimientos" (Garcilaso [1609] 1944b, 94).

10. ". . . les haze más agudos de entendimiento y más dóciles y más ingeniosos para lo que quisieren aprender . . . y assí los indios Puquinas, Collas, Urus, Yuncas y otras nasciones, que son rudos y torpes, y por su rudeza aun sus proprias lenguas las hablan mal, cuando alcançan a saber la lengua del Cozco paresce que echan de sí la rudeza y torpeza que tenían y que aspiran a cosas políticas y cortesanas y sus ingenios pretenden subir a cosas más altas" (Garcilaso [1609] 1944b, 95).

degree of "civilization" in the Inca Empire; to compare "the language of Cuzco" to Latin was to suggest that the Incas possessed the highest degree of culture possible, equal to that of the ancient world.

Valera makes it quite clear that Quechua is an appropriate vehicle for the most sublime facets of Christian doctrine. In the text just cited, the Jesuit author states that the language is well adapted to discussing the "higher things" of the Catholic faith. At one point in his writings, Valera quotes a Spanish priest asking, "Is it possible that divine words, so sweet and mysterious, can be explained in so barbarous a tongue [as Quechua]?" (Garcilaso de la Vega [1609] 1987, 409).[11] As one would expect, Valera's response is in the affirmative. However, in the late sixteenth century, there was a growing belief among European and colonial theologians that native languages possessed no words that were equivalent to basic Christian concepts, such as "God," "angel," "church," "chastity," and so on (Rafael 1993, 23–83). This lack of translatability was seen as a mark of the alleged spiritual inferiority of native tongues. As chapter 7 examines in detail, Valera completely opposed this view. Instead, he maintained that Quechua religious terms embodied Christian religious concepts as expressed in Latin, as well as in Hebrew and Greek. For example, he states that in the Quechua term for God, *Illa Tecce*, *Illa* is the equivalent of *El* (God) in Hebrew, *Theos* (God) in Greek, and *Deus* (God) in Latin, while *Tecce* denotes the classical formulation of God as *principium rerum sine principio* (the beginning of things without beginning). The lofty property of being able to contain sacred Christian truths, it should be noted, is not accorded by Valera to any other native tongue. Valera's arguments place Quechua firmly in the constellation of sacred languages, along with Latin, Greek, and Hebrew.

Valera contends, moreover, that the Incas, as promulgators of Quechua, were responding to God's call, to prepare the way for Christianity. The Inca's spread of Quechua has a deeply religious significance in Valera's writings. By imposing Quechua, he tells us, the Incas were guided by divine providence and by "natural law" to lay the ground for Christianization. "Among the many means which the Divine Majesty has used to prepare and summon these barbarous

11. "Es posible que en una lengua tan bárbara se puedan declarar hablar las palabras divinas, tan dulces y misteriosas?" (Garcilaso [1609] 1944b, 94).

and wild peoples [i.e., the Uriquillas and Chirihuanas] to the preaching of the gospel, we must mention the care and diligence taken by the Inca kings," he writes, "in indoctrinating their vassals with the light of natural law so that all should speak one tongue" (Garcilaso de la Vega [1609] 1987, 410).[12] The clear implication of Valera's words is that the Incas, having the guidance of divine providence to spread Quechua, merited a central role in Andean Christianity, one in which the holy aspects of their faith and culture would be kept alive.

Quipus as Writing Systems

A central aspect of the Spanish evaluation of language in the sixteenth century was whether the language could be written. José de Acosta, Valera's Jesuit superior, ranked non-Christian societies according to the type of writing system used; for example, he considered the Chinese to have possessed a greater civilization than the ancient Mexicans because he believed Chinese characters to comprise a more complete writing system than Aztec hieroglyphics. The Incas, whom he thought lacked any writing system, were therefore inferior to the Aztecs in Acosta's typology of non-Christian civilizations (Alcina Franch 1987, 23–39). This type of criticism of the Incas would have been anathema to Valera, who viewed the Incas as morally and culturally superior to the ancient Mexicans and every other non-Christian nation. It is not surprising, therefore, that Valera's citations from quipus suggest that these Andean communication cords encoded narratives and poems of such complexity that they must have equaled writing. For example, he tells us that the Indians "in charge of the historical knots and beads" explained to him how "the knots and beads of some ancient annals in threads of different colors" preserved "Sumac ñusta," a Quechua poem about the sky maiden (Garcilaso de la Vega [1609] 1987, 127).[13] Other quipus cited by Valera, such as

---

12. "Y cierto que entre otros muchos de que la Divina Majestad quiso usar para llamar y disponer esta gente bárbara y ferina a la predicación de su Evangelio, fue el cuidado y diligencia que los Reyes Incas tuvieron de doctrinar estos sus vassallos con la lumbre de la ley natural y con que todos hablassen un lenguaje" (Garcilaso [1609] 1944b, 95).

13. ". . . los indios contadores, que tenían cargo de los ñudos y cuentas historiales . . . los ñudos y cuentas de unos anales antiguos, que estavan en hilos de diversas colores" (Garcilaso [1609] 1944a, 122).

those belonging to Francisco Yutu Inca and Juan Huallpa Inca, allegedly contained Inca legends and other complex material, which suggests that Valera believed the Inca quipus capable of recording information in a manner equal to writing.

Used throughout the Inca Empire, quipus were systems of knotted and colored cords, consisting of a main cord from which hung colored woolen threads called pendant threads (see fig. 8). The position and number of knots tied on the pendant threads provided numerical information based on the decimal system. The kind of knot used indicated the number, and its position along the string indicated whether it was a unit of one, ten, one hundred, or higher. Different colors of string were used to indicate the category being recorded—for example, people, llamas, or corn. Most quipus were used for recording numerical information relevant to Inca accounting (see Ascher and Ascher 1981).

A special, tax-exempt class of individuals known as *quipucamayoc* were skilled in the use of quipus. Most *quipucamayoc* appear to have labored primarily as accountants. These individuals went out among the local tribes and kept records of the exchange of goods and services in each locality. *Quipucamayoc* worked closely with local *curacas* to determine the people needed for labor tribute, as well as the quantity of goods used and produced. These officials also were responsible for keeping precise census data for all of Tahuantinsuyu.

However, Spanish accounts tell us that quipus were used to record myths and legends as well. Recent research by Gary Urton (1994, 1998) has demonstrated that Inca quipus encoded semantic units in addition to numerical information (see also Salomon 2001). Until Urton's work, however, it had been believed that nonnumerical information, such as stories and poems, could be recorded on quipus only through memorization; that is, the quipus functioned as an individual's memory aid for learning memorized histories, traditions, and poems. According to this view, one *quipucamayoc* could not read the quipus of another without first being told orally about their contents.

One of the most important sources for the belief that quipus were primarily mnemonic were some of Garcilaso de la Vega's comments about the quipus. In his *Comentarios reales,* he appears to argue that quipus—even those recording historical events—served not as actual writing systems but only as mnemonic devices.

Fig. 8. Quipu. (Courtesy of the Peabody Museum of Natural History, Yale University. Photo by William Sacco.)

These men [i.e., the *quipucamayoc*] recorded on their knots all the tribute brought annually to the Inca, specifying everything by kind, species, and quality. They recorded the number of men who went to the wars, how many died in them, and how many were born and died every year, month by month. In short they may be said to have recorded on their knots everything that could be counted, even mentioning battles and fights, all the embassies that had come to visit the Inca, and all the speeches and arguments the king had uttered. But the purpose of the embassies or the contents of the speeches, or any other descriptive matter could not be recorded on the knots, consisting as it did of continuous spoken or written prose, which cannot be expressed by means of knots, since these can give only numbers and not words. . . . Such speeches were preserved by the quipucamayus by memory in a summarized form of a few words: they were committed to memory and taught by tradition to their successors and descendants from father to son. (Garcilaso de la Vega [1609] 1987, 331–32)[14]

14. "Estos assentavan por sus ñudos todo el tributo que davan cada año al Inca, poniendo cada cosa por sus géneros, especies y calidades. Assentavan la gente que iva a la

Garcilaso states quite clearly that quipus merely assisted the recollection of memorized histories; they were only "perishable expedients," he writes, for they could not serve "as letters that perpetuate the memory of events" beyond the lives of their authors. The chronicler does mention that the creators of the quipus had to "study constantly the signs and cyphers in the knots so as to preserve in their memories" historical traditions, suggesting that the quipus may have encoded semantic elements; however, he himself seems to overlook this point when he writes that "descriptive material could not be recorded on the knots"[15] (Garcilaso de la Vega [1609] 1987, 331).

In an unpublished and overlooked section of the *Memorias historiales,* Montesinos claims that Garcilaso lied about the Peruvian quipus. Montesinos's anonymous source stated that Garcilaso "created a false account of these quipus, which they used in place of letters."[16] Garcilaso erred, Montesinos explains, because he refused to acknowledge the distinctive quipus used for recording historical traditions. These special quipus, he adds, could be read in their own right, without verbal assistance from the quipus' creators. Based on discourse 2, chapter 1, in his anonymous source—"treating the *amautas* and Indian historians and the difference in the quipus that they used for the tradition . . . of the Peruvian kings"[17]—Montesinos writes:

---

guerra, la que moría en ella, los que nascían y fallescían cada año, por sus meses. En suma, dezimos que escrivían en aquellos ñudos todas las cosas que consistían en cuenta de números, hasta poner las batallas y recuentos que se davan, hasta dezir cuántas embaxadas havían traído al Inca y cuántas pláticas y razonamientos havía hecho el Rey. Pero lo que contenía la embaxada, ni las palabras de razonamiento ni otro sucesso historial, no podían dezirlo por los ñudos, porque consiste en oración ordenada de viva voz o por escrito, la cual no se puede referir por ñudos, porque el ñudo dize el número, mas no la palabra. . . . Las cuales pláticas tomavan los indios quipucamayus de memoria, en suma, en breves palabras, y las encomendavan a la memoria, y por tradición las enseñavan a los sucessores, de padres a hijos y descendientes" (Garcilaso [1609] 1944b, 25).

15. ". . . eran remedios perescederos, porque las letras son las que perpetúan los hechos"; "estudiavan perpetualmente en las señales y cifras que en los ñudos havía, para conservar en la memoria la tradición que de aquellos hechos famosos ténían"; "ni otro sucesso historial, no podían dezirlo por los ñudos" (Garcilaso [1609] 1944b, 25–26).

16. ". . . formó la falsa relación destos Quipos, que usaron en lugar de letras" (Yale [ca. 1645] ca. 1860, book 1, chap. 4).

17. ". . . tratando de los Amautas e istoriadores indios y de la diferencia de los quipos de que usaban para tradición de los sucesos y hechos de los reis Peruanos" (USevilla 1644, book 1, chap. 4).

But because Garcilaso Ynga did not have knowledge of . . . the quipus that the *amautas,* or Indian historians, used and of the [quipus']
difference for the tradition and knowledge of the Peruvian kings,
because for this it was necessary to send him some of these quipus,
whose information was contained in themselves, he created a false
account . . . of these quipus, which they used in place of letters . . .
there were a great number [of these quipus] in Peru and especially in
Quito.[18]

In an earlier, slightly different unpublished version of the same chapter, Montesinos wrote:

Because Garcilaso did not have the information about this, says the
author of the manuscript in discourse 2, chapter 1, treating the
amautas and Indian historians and the difference of the quipus that
they used for the tradition of the events and deeds of the Peruvian
kings . . . ; he knows that in that year many of those quipus were
sent so that Garcilaso could see them. Of these quipus, there were a
great number in Peru and in the city of Quito.[19]

In the preceding passages, the chronicler informs us of several
things. He tells us that a different type of quipu, distinct from the
mnemonic type described by Garcilaso, was used by the Inca historians "for the tradition and knowledge of the Peruvian kings" and that
the information in these quipus "was contained in themselves." The
text also states that Garcilaso was ignorant about the special quipus
used by the *amauta* for recording history. These quipus could be sent
to someone and read without the assistance of their creators; in other
words, these special quipus were self-contained bodies of knowledge,

---

18. "Mas porque dello no tuvo noticia Garcilaso Ynga, ni de los Quipos, que los
Amautas, o Historiadores Yndios usaban, y su diferencia para la tradición, y noticia de los
Reyes Peruanos, pues para ello fue necesario remitirle algunos, cuya inteligenica se quedó
en ellos mismos; formó la falsa relación . . . destos Quipos, que usaron en lugar de letras . . .
hubo gran número en el Perú, y con especialidad en Quito" (Yale [ca. 1645] ca. 1860, book
1, chap. 4).

19. ". . . y porque desto no tubo noticia Garcilaso dice el autor del manuscrito en el discurso 2, cap. 1 tratando de los Amautas e istoriadores indios y de la diferencia de los quipos
de que usaban para tradicion de los sucesos y hechos de los reis Peruanos . . . ; que saue se
an inbiado a esse año muchos de aquellos quipos para que los viese Garcilaso. Destos
quipos ai de gran número en el Piru, y en la ciudad de Quito" (USevilla 1644, book 1, chap.
4).

rather than mere memory aids. Montesinos is suggesting that the Incas possessed a writing system in the form of these special quipus, in contradiction to Garcilaso's statement that quipus "can give only numbers and not words."

The preceding passages from Montesinos also explain that these special historical quipus were linked to Quito and to the history contained in Montesinos's text. These distinctive quipus were used "for the tradition and knowledge of the Peruvian kings"; by the phrase "Peruvian kings," Montesinos is referring to the line of ninety-three pre-Inca kings, beginning with Pirua, that formed part of this historical tradition shared with Valera. In the passage prior to the one just cited, Montesinos describes how his history of Peruvian kings was derived from the historians of Atahuallpa's time; he then clarifies that Garcilaso only could have known about this line of Peruvian kings if he had access to the quipus used for recording this history. The peculiar history recorded by both Montesinos and Valera was linked to these distinctive quipus "whose information was contained in themselves."

Montesinos's anonymous source, an author who may have been a Jesuit or may have had ties to them, further states that Garcilaso himself was sent many of these special quipus and that he lied about them in his *Comentarios reales*. This accusation echoes claims made in the recently discovered "Naples documents" (see chaps. 9–10). Among the extraordinary assertions made in these documents is the claim that Blas Valera taught his followers that the Incas had a secret phonetic writing system used by the historians of the empire. Moreover, these texts claim that numerous examples of these special phonetic quipus were sent to Garcilaso, who, however, lied about them in the *Comentarios reales* (Laurencich Minelli, Miccinelli, and Animato 1995). A sample of one of these special quipus—representing a portion of the poem "Sumac ñusta," cited by Valera—accompanies these documents.

The quipu writing system that the Naples documents claim was taught by Valera matches the quipus found in an eighteenth-century work by Raimondo di Sangro, prince of Sansevero. In this work, the *Lettera apologética* (1750), Sansevero reflected on the history of writing and, in particular, on the relationship between the mark of Cain described in the Bible (Genesis 4:50 NAB) and early textile-based writing methods. Among the more unusual passages in the book is the description of a secret writing system once used, Sansevero claimed, by the ancient Peruvian bards *("amauta")* in the Inca Empire. According to the prince, this writing system was depicted in a seventeenth-century manuscript that he had purchased from a Jesuit priest, Father Pedro de Illanes (Sansevero 1750, 241–45). In fact, a record of this purchase, dated to 1744, still exists in the Naples city archives (Domenici and Domenici 1996, 54). Unlike the common Inca quipus, Sansevero's "royal" quipus consisted of woven images representing the syllables of Quechua. Therefore, the "royal" quipus formed a writing system capable of denoting any utterance in spoken Quechua. According to the text, the entire system was based on a Quechua syllabary represented by forty symbols. The prince emphasized that the existence of these "royal" quipus had been a closely guarded secret of the *amauta,* the most learned historians of the Inca Empire. Furthermore, in his description of the manuscript purchased from Father Illanes, the prince associated the knowledge of this system with Valera.

In Sansevero's work, the poem "Sumac ñusta," cited by Valera, is depicted by means of this "royal" quipu writing system. As discussed in chapter 4, this poem is a theological statement about the Andean belief in the true God as the source of all natural phenomena. The symbols of the "royal" quipu writing system, as we shall see, likewise reflect Valera's theology about the Andean understanding of the Creator. For Valera, demonstrating that Quechua could have an indigenous writing system would be an important statement about the moral superiority of the Quechua language.

The evidence from Sansevero and Montesinos suggests that the Naples documents were correct in linking this phonetic quipu writing system to Valera. The claims that samples of these special historical quipus were sent to Garcilaso and that he lied about them are repeated in Montesinos's text. The historical quipus "whose information was contained in themselves"—described by Montesinos's source—fit the description of the phonetic quipus; moreover, the specific pre-Inca history linked with these historical quipus is the same unusual history expressed by Valera. Sansevero himself acknowledged that his secret quipu writing system came from an early Jesuit document. Not only do the "royal" quipus found in Sansevero conform to Valera's very high view of Quechua, but the symbols of the system itself reflect Valera's theories about Andean Christianity. In Sansevero's work, the theological poem "Sumac ñusta," cited by Valera, is even the exemplar of the system. It seems clear from Sansevero and Montesinos that Valera and his followers among the Jesuits in Peru were involved in developing a phonetic quipu writing system for Quechua. Yet it is highly unlikely that this represented a secret system used throughout the empire; rather, it seems to have been a writing system developed to express particular Christian ideas. But was this system based on earlier, indigenous quipu variants, or did Valera and the Jesuits develop it in its entirety?

According to the seventeenth-century chronicler Martín de Murúa, there existed a great deal of variation throughout the Andes in the manner of using quipus.

> There was another marvel: that as each province had its own native language, it also had a new type of quipu and a new way [to use] it.[20]

As a Mercedarian friar, Murúa would have been well informed about quipu usages in the Andes. The Mercedarians had employed quipus extensively in Christian evangelization in Peru since the 1580s (see Porres [ca. 1585] 1953). The primary Mercedarian missionary manual, written by Friar Diego de Porres in Peru in the middle to late 1580s, required Mercedarian priests to make considerable use of quipus in evangelization. Porres instructed the friars to encode on the knotted strings detailed information about Christian living. The missionary advised priests to explain to the natives what was required of them by the Third Lima Council of Bishops and then to present the native leaders with this information encoded on a quipu. Friars were also encouraged to oblige the native people to make quipus recording in Quechua the Pater Noster, the Ave Maria, the Gloria Patri, and the Salve Regina, which they would "pray by pauses and syllables."[21] These quipus, Porres continued, should be carried by the local people

---

20. "Había otra maravilla, que cada provincia como tenía propio lenguaje nativo, también tenía nuevo modo de Quipu y nueva razon dello" (Murúa [1613] 1987, 374).

21. ". . . por pausas y silabas" (Porres [ca. 1585] 1953, 176).

at all times, and a quipu with the Ten Commandments should be affixed to the church wall. Additionally, Mercedarian missionaries were to give to local leaders quipus containing thirty-four lengthy points on Christian behavior, such as how to conduct funerals. These quipus included instructions on how other quipus should be used by the villagers. For instance, this quipu ordered natives to make a quipu with an account of the entire Christian year, marking all the feast days; the calendrical quipu was to be kept in the local church. As another example, when anyone in the village died, native Christians were told to make quipus with an inventory of all of the deceased's goods, which they would present to the priest. The priest would then show the quipu to the relatives of the dead man and ensure that the proper heirs had received their inheritance.

Friars following Porres's instructions would have possessed an intimate knowledge of how to create and use quipus. The complex semantic material stored on these quipus could apparently be read by local leaders and other individuals besides their creators. During the sixteenth century, the Mercedarians were the only religious order in Peru actively to pursue accepting mestizos fluent in Quechua into their order; this was in line with the Mercedarians' distinctive missionary philosophy (see Hyland 1994, 242–66). Perhaps Porres had learned the art of quipu making from a fellow Mercedarian who was a mestizo or from an Indian catechist.

The exact nature of these Mercedarian quipus, which were able to record such detailed and complex information, remains a mystery. There is, however, at least one other example of quipus from Peru that do not conform to the standard Inca quipus but, instead, represent a local variation. In the mid–nineteenth century, the explorer Charles Wiener discovered two quipus in Paramonga quite distinct from the known Inca quipus (see fig. 9). These quipus make use of symbols of bunched cloth or fiber in addition to a variety of knots. Unfortunately, Wiener does not provide us with any information about the circumstances in which he found these quipus or how they may be used (Weiner 1880, 71–87, 776).[22]

---

22. I am grateful to Dr. Brian Bauer (personal communication, 2001) for bringing these quipus to my attention.

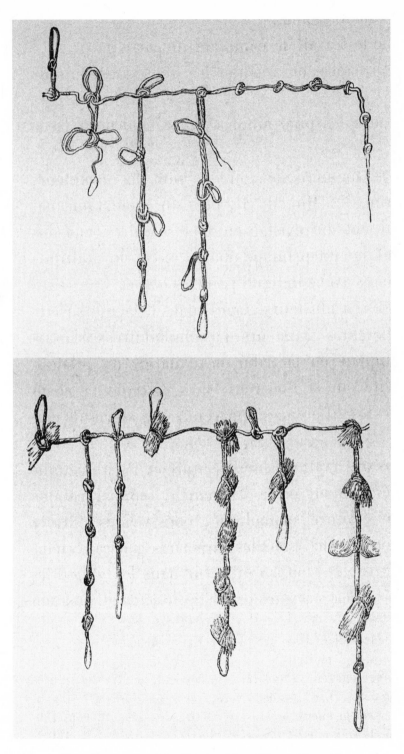

Fig. 9. Paramonga quipus. (Reprinted from Wiener 1880, 776.)

Additionally, we know that the native peoples of the Quito region apparently had developed at least one other type of "quipu," described by the Jesuit Juan de Velasco in the eighteenth century.

> They used a type of writing more imperfect than the Peruvian quipus. They reduced [writing] to certain archives, or deposits, made of wood, of stone, or of clay, with diverse separations, in which they arranged little stones of different sizes, colors, and angular figures worked to perfection, because they were excellent lapidaries. With the different combinations of these, which can be called characters, they perpetuated their deeds, kept an exact note of each one of the provinces, and formed their counts of all.[23]

It is possible, perhaps, that Valera based his quipu writing system on a local quipu variation, altering it to fit his theological requirements. Augustinian friars in the early colonial Philippines, for example, modified the indigenous Tagalog syllabary *(baybayin)* to include distinctions among vowel sounds (Rafael 1993, 39–54). This was part of a missionary attempt to develop a Christian *baybayin* literature on the islands. The extent to which this "royal" quipu system may have been used in Jesuit catechesis—if ever—is of course unclear. However, an analysis of the system itself can help to clarify the manner in which the "royal" quipus reflected the theological understandings of Valera and other Jesuits in the Andes.

The Decipherment of the "Royal" Quipus

Woven forms of communication are known to have been widespread in the Andes at the time of the Spanish conquest. Native Peruvian clothing and blankets frequently contained abstract geometrical symbols called *tocapu,* which were discretely located within a rectangular or square border. On clothing, each *tocapu* could be placed either in a linear pattern across the waist or in a grid pattern covering the

---

23. "Usaban de una especie de escritura, más imperfecta que la de los Quipos peruanos. Se reducía a ciertos archivos, o depositos, hechos de madera, de piedra, o de barro, con diversas separaciones, en las cuales colocaban piedrecillas de distintos tamaños, colores, y figuras angulares labradas a perfección, porque eran excelentes lapidarios. Con las diversas combinaciones de aquellos que pueden llamarse caracteres, perpetuaban sus hechos, tenían la exacta nota de cada una de las provincias, y formaban su cuenta de todo" (Velasco [1789] 1977, 91).

whole surface. It is believed that these geometrical designs denoted ethnic, political, or religious status. Cummins (1994) has analyzed one *tocapu* that represents Tambotoco, the cave from which originated Manco Capac and his wife, the mythical founders of the Inca lineage.

The "royal" quipus described by Sansevero show an affinity to the *tocapus* used on Andean textiles. However, the "royal" quipus represent the sounds of speech, rather than general ideas. Three elements were necessary for the creation of a "royal" quipu. First, one needed a horizontal string onto which the pendant symbols were attached. Second, one used a group of woven pendant symbols; the standardized designs in these pendants symbolized different words. According to Sansevero, there were a total of forty different symbols, each of which represented a distinct word. Finally, each of the pendant symbols had a string hanging down from it. The knots on this string indicated which syllable of the represented word was to be spoken. Sansevero, incidently, does not fully explain how to read the quipus illustrated in his work; only the Naples documents provide a complete explanation of the system.

To create one of the "royal" quipus, an *amauta* first gathered a certain number of the individual woven pendants, each of which carried a woven, multicolored symbol that indicated a word; for example, the symbol for Pachacamac indicated the word *Pachacamac*. The *amauta* then would select a symbol indicating a word containing a syllable that she or he wished to represent. For example, if the *amauta* wanted to use the syllable "cha," she or he would select the Pachacamac pendant and would place two knots on the string hanging down from it; these two knots indicated that "cha," the second syllable of the word *Pachacamac*, was to be enunciated. The *amauta* would then attach the pendant symbol to a horizontal string and would proceed to the next syllable she or he wished to represent. If someone desired to represent the entire word *Pachacamac*, she or he would place no knots on the string hanging down from the Pachacamac pendant. The entire quipu was read from left to right. We do not know the conventions governing the division of words into syllables. Given the redundancy of the syllabary (many syllables are repeated several times), there must have been an agreement that certain syllables could represent lone vowel or consonant sounds. With this proviso, these special "royal" quipus can represent any utterance in Quechua; they represent a complete phonetic writing system.

In his text, Sansevero included a colored drawing of a "royal" quipu representing the Quechua poem "Sumac ñusta" (Beautiful princess), cited by Valera. The syllables of these eloquent stanzas about an Andean rain goddess are pictured through this ingenious system of colored designs and knots. A careful study of the prince's painting reveals the method just described for creating and decoding the "royal" quipus.

The most important section of Sansevero's work is the basic syllabary of forty "master words" on which the system depends.[24] The basic syllabary consists of forty words representing the full range of syllables in spoken Quechua (fig. 10). The "master words" are subdivided into four groups: (1) celestial objects or events; (2) human figures *(figura Umana)*; (3) quadrupeds *(quadrupedi)*; and (4) miscellaneous items, such as royal vestments. The latter group also includes the two symbols depicting the gods Pachacamac and Viracocha. According to the text, the major division is between the nonhuman signs and those symbols—consisting of a top knot followed by three knots and a "skirt"—that represent human figures. In addition, Sansevero provides us with a rough notation for a song to aid in memorizing the list of forty words (Sansevero 1750, plate 2). Ethnolinguists have discovered that syllabic writing systems typically use songs for teaching the basic syllabary (e.g., Conklin 1991); such a song would be expected to exist for a system that reflected an authentic Andean syllabic tradition.

An examination of the individual symbols of Sansevero's syllabary, however, reveals them to echo Western concepts of religion, rather than purely Andean beliefs. The text gives careful explanations for the colors and designs used in the symbols (Sansevero 1750, 246–61); these explanations clearly reflect Valera's attempts to portray Inca religion in a manner acceptable to a Spanish ecclesiastical audience.

The first icon of the syllabary—representing Pachacamac—betrays

---

24. This forty-word syllabary was reproduced by Léon de Rosny (1870), who, however, failed to provide any explanation of how the system worked.

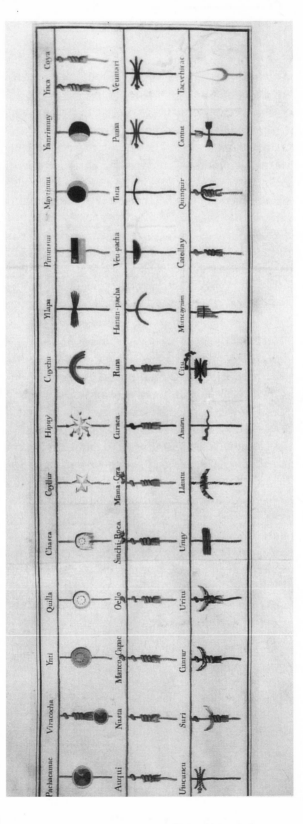

Fig. 10. "Royal" quipu symbols from Sansevero's *Lettera apologética* (1750).

a definite European bias. Pachacamac was a local pre-Inca deity whose cult centered around an oracle and ritual complex on the coast northwest of Cuzco. The Incas and the priests of Pachacamac had formed a powerful alliance during Inca rule; the Incas helped to spread the Pachacamac cult, and in turn, the Pachacamac oracle lent its support to Inca expansion. Some colonial Spanish accounts describe Pachacamac as "he who gives being to the earth" as a creator; other chronicles mention Pachacamac's children and document the offering of sacrifices to him (MacCormack 1991, 352). In Sansevero's text, which ultimately was informed by Valera, Pachacamac is described as "God, the Creator of the Universe."[25] According to Garcilaso, Andean Christians in Cuzco frequently used Pachacamac's name to refer to the Christian God (see MacCormack 1991, 366). We know that Valera certainly considered Pachacamac, also called Illa Tecce, as the true God, equivalent to the supreme deity worshiped by the Hebrews and Christians (e.g., Blas Valera [1594] 1968, 153). Pachacamac's icon, Sansevero explains further, is divided into four equal parts colored to represent the four essential elements of the universe—red for fire, blue for air, brown for earth, and sea green for water. Most Spanish thinkers of the sixteenth century, following classical Greek theories, believed that these four elements comprised the universe. Native Andean cosmography did not share that belief. The depiction of these elements in an allegedly Inca symbol clearly stems from the Spanish colonial period.

Likewise, Sansevero's description of the second symbol—for Viracocha—echoes distinctive European models. Viracocha was a native Andean culture hero whose exact nature has been the matter of some dispute among scholars. A wide variety of native myths exist concerning this figure. In some legends, Viracocha is a creator god; in others, he wanders about the Andes dressed in rags. In some instances, he is doubled with a brother. For example, in the male puberty rituals in Cochacaya, recorded in a Jesuit manuscript dating to 1614, Viracocha and his brother, Yacaylla Viracocha, "to whom they attribute the creation of the earth," were invoked to give the young men "strength, industriousness, ability, and good fortune."[26]

---

25. ". . . Dio Creatore dell' Universo" (Sansevero 1750, 246).

26. "En llegando los uarones a los años de la puberdad les ponian el *huara* que era una faxa de lana de la tierra de largo de media uara . . . y le ponian la *huara* estando en pie en

At times, Viracocha acts for the good of humankind; in other moments, he is a lascivious destroyer and trickster. However, Sansevero's text defines Viracocha in no uncertain terms as a Christlike being who represents the incarnation of God as man. Viracocha is described as "God [i.e., Pachacamac] in human figure" (Sansevero 1750, 247). The fact of the incarnation of the true God is emphasized in the iconography of the symbol for Viracocha. As one can observe in the illustration (fig. 10), the symbol consists of the sign for Pachacamac hanging down from a "flesh-colored" string with knots. The text explains that the flesh color and the knots symbolize the human form of God incarnate. The same pinkish brown skin color and three knots occur in the symbols classified as human—the *figura Umana*. Valera is not merely providing a Christian gloss for a non-Christian symbol; the European bias is intrinsic to the iconography of the Viracocha icon, combining, as it does, the symbols for a human and for the true God.

In the colonial period in Peru, there was a widespread belief that Viracocha may have been one of the apostles. Alonso Ramos Gavilán, an Augustinian writer in Copacabana, described the legend that Virachocha was actually the apostle St. Thomas (see Salles-Reese 1997). In the *Comentarios reales,* Garcilaso informs us that an exclusive fellowship of mestizos in Cuzco believed that Viracocha was the Christian apostle St. Bartholomew, said to have preached the gospel to the pagans. These mestizos, he wrote, "spent a great deal on their celebrations, and took the blessed apostle as their patron, declaring that as he was said to have preached in Peru, whether truly or falsely, they would have him as their advocate, though some malicious Spaniards, seeing the adornments they put on for the occasion, asserted that this was done for the Inca Viracocha, not for the apostle" (Garcilaso de la Vega [1609] 1987, 291–92).[27]

---

medio de la casa con una *chunta* ques una lança en la mano derecha afirmando en ella ynuocandosse assi *uiracocha yacaylla viracocha* su hermano a quienes atribuyan la creación de la tierra pidiendoles que diesen al que ponian la *huara* fuerça, yndustria, abilidad y uentura" (Duviols 1974–76). In Guaman Poma's *Nueva corónica,* an early Andean people named the Wari Wiracocharuna worshiped two forms of Viracocha—Ticci Viracocha and Caylla Viracocha (see Urton 1999, 41). See also Duviols 1977 and Pease 1973.

27. ". . . la cual solenizan con grandes gastos, tomaron por abogado a este bienaventurado apóstol, diziendo que, ya que con ficción o sin ella se havía dicho que havía predicado en el Perú, lo querían por su patrón, aunque algunos españoles maldizientes, viendo

However, in the explanation of this syllabary, Valera goes one step further than the mestizos in Cuzco. For Valera, Viracocha was not St. Bartholomew but Christ himself. In Christian theology, the incarnation of God as man occurred only once, in the person of Jesus Christ. Valera's assertion that Viracocha was God incarnate is therefore equivalent to stating that Viracocha was Christ. In Sansevero's text, it is explained that the true God, Pachacamac, appeared in human form to a young Inca prince, the son of the emperor Yahuar Huacac. This apparition of God in human form—in other words, of Christ—told the prince a message that enabled the young man to lead the Incas to victory against one of their most important rival tribes. As emperor, this prince took the name *Viracocha* in honor of Christ's appearance to him. In fact, most other Spanish accounts claim that it was either the sun god or Viracocha who appeared to emperor Viracocha's son, Prince Yupanqui (who later would become emperor Pachacuti), to urge him to victory against the Chancas.[28] Valera is telling us that this god was Christ and that the Incas, therefore, were very close to being Christians.

In another text by Valera, he writes that the word *Viracocha* should be translated by the Latin word *numen,* meaning "the will and power of God," an appropriate title for Christ (Garcilaso de la Vega [1609] 1987, 288). The Jesuit scholar also stated that *Viracocha* was a name used by modern Andeans to signify "the immense god of Pirua" (Blas Valera [1594] 1968, 153). Garcilaso ([1609] 1987, 128) also notes that Valera referred to Viracocha as a "modern" god worshiped by the Peruvians. According to Valera, *Pirua* was an honorific title for the first inhabitant and king of the Andes in ancient South American prehistory. Valera believed that Pirua's god was the true God, the same as the deity worshiped in the Old Testament. It is fitting that *Viracocha* would have been a relatively more modern name for God, in Valera's theology, because this name could only have been applied by the Andeans to God after the resurrection of Christ. Until that time, of course, there could have been no apparitions of Christ to the Andean people, because God had not yet become incarnate.

---

los arreos y galas que aquel día sacan, han dicho que no lo hazen por el apóstol, sino por el Inca Viracocha" (Garcilaso [1609] 1944a, 272).

    28. See, for example, Sarmiento de Gamboa ([1572] 1972, 90), who claims the sun god appeared to Pachacuti.

One can also see a reflection of Valera's teachings about Andean religion and Christianity in the first line of icons in the syllabary. If one arranges the forty icons, in order, in four groups of ten, according to the importance placed by the Incas on the number four, the first group reads:

Creator *(Pachacamac)*, Christ *(Viracocha)*, Sun *(Ynti)*, Moon *(Quilla)*, Morning Star *(Chaska)*, Star *(Coyllur)*, Comet *(Hipuy)*, Rainbow *(Cuychu)*, Thunder *(Yllapa)*, and Equinox *(Pinunsun)*.

This can be seen as a visual representation of the idea—expressed in the poem "Sumac ñusta" as well as in the *Relación de las costumbres antiguas*—that the Andeans believed the true God to have created all celestial objects and events. As Jeffrey Klaiber described the ideas expressed in the *Relación*, "in the beginning . . . all things, stars, moon and sun, were but servants of the one God, who assigned different tasks to each one" (Klaiber 1976). Likewise, in the first line of the syllabary, Pachacamac and Viracocha come first, followed by the heavenly objects created by God and, according to Valera, adored by the Andeans as secondary objects infused with life and power by the Creator.

Valera's discussion of Pachacamac and Viracocha portrays an image of native Andean beliefs that, in European terms, placed Peruvian religion on a high level. By arguing that the Andeans worshiped the true invisible God, along with God incarnate, Christ, he was implying that Inca religion and customs could serve as a solid basis for Christianity. In his estimation of native religion, Valera was opposed by most of the church leadership in Peru at the time. For example, José de Acosta, Valera's Jesuit superior, believed that Andeans held only a "sparse and attenuated" knowledge of the true God. Furthermore, Acosta argued that native worship of Viracocha, Pachacamac, and other gods was so profoundly compromised by blasphemous idolatries that such native cults must be rooted out in their entirety (Acosta [1590] 1987, 314–16). Any aspect of Andean faith or ritual that seemed similar to Christianity was, Acosta contended, merely an act of demonic imitation. To Acosta and to those who shared similar views, Valera's definitions of Pachacamac as the invisible, true God and of Viracocha as Christ, God incarnate, would have seemed idolatrous and dangerous to the spread of Christianity.

The preceding analysis reveals that two of the primary symbols of the "royal" quipu syllabary—Pachacamac and Viracocha—pertain to the colonial Spanish period rather than to the Inca past. Pachacamac is pictured in accordance with European ideas about the four elements of the universe—earth, air, fire, and water; Viracocha is depicted as God incarnate, a combination of the symbol for Pachacamac and of the knots and flesh-colored symbol for a human. The definitions provided for these two icons correspond closely to Valera's views on the Inca church. Moreover, argumentation through lexicography, that is, through providing Spanish definitions for Quechua words, was a central aspect of Valera's thought. In his *Vocabulario* and other writings, he bases important points on the proper definition of Andean terms. In his works, he begins by stating that Quechua religious phrases, such as *tocricoc* (prelate), *supay* (demon), and *huancaquilli* (hermit), have equivalents in Spanish and Latin. This alone, of course, was a significant and controversial assertion. His view on translating Quechua religious terms was opposed by those in charge of the Quechua catechism of the Third Lima Council of Bishops, although the Spanish author Domingo de Santo Tomás supported Valera's point of view (Santo Tomás [1560] 1891, 9). Yet Valera makes many of his most substantial arguments strictly within the limits of his lexicon. For example, in the *Vocabulario*, he informs us in his definition of Atahuallpa, that the last Inca emperor was a Christian saint who is now in heaven (Anello Oliva [1631] 1998, 107–8); this "fact" had important implications for Valera's view of the natives' role in Andean Christianity (see chap. 7). In another example, he used lexicography to deny that the Incas had ever practiced human sacrifice. Such authors as Polo de Ondegardo believed that the Incas had sacrificed humans, but Valera argued that these Spaniards did not understand the Incas' common use of the words *huahuas* and *yuyac* to describe sacrificial victims. *Huahuas* normally referred to human children and *yuyac* to adults, thus giving rise to the belief that the Incas sacrificed humans. However, Valera writes,

> these *huahuas* are not understood to be children, sons [and daughters] of men, but baby llamas, which were also called children in that language; and in the same way, *yuyac* are understood to be animals that are already grown adults, which were sacrificed in place of men.[29]

---

29. ". . . mas estos *huahuas* no se entienden niños hijos de hombres, sino corderitos, que también se llaman niños en aquella lengua; y al mismo modo, *yuyac,* se entienden

We see in this example another instance of Valera's use of word definition to make essential arguments in defense of native religion. The use of lexicon in Sansevero's syllabary to show the compatibility between Andean beliefs and Christianity is perfectly in accord with Valera's work; the definitions provided in Sansevero's syllabary demonstrate Valera's personal influence in the "royal" quipu "script."

Valera's Quipu Tradition

For Valera, the greatness of the Quechua language was a reflection of the superiority of the Inca civilization. In Valera's writings, Quechua takes on the character of a sacred language, equal to Latin and superior to vernacular tongues. A writing system was considered a marker of a language's—and a civilization's—moral worth; it is not surprising that Valera would be associated with a phonetic form of Quechua "writing."

The analysis of two of the primary symbols used in the "royal" quipus reveals that the system was, at the very least, greatly modified in the early colonial period. It is most likely that Valera, similar to the Cherokee intellectual Sequoya, invented the "royal" quipu writing system on his own. This in itself would have been a tremendous accomplishment. Sequoya's efforts at establishing literacy in the native Cherokee script led to a flowering of Cherokee literature and civic discourse. Valera's dissemination of the "royal" quipus may well have inspired a similar outpouring of colonial Indian literature among his closely knit disciples in the Nombre de Jesús confraternity. Valera refers to several accounts of Inca legends encoded on quipus by the Cuzco noblemen Juan Huallpa Inca and Don Francisco Yutu Inca (Blas Valera [1594] 1968, 153); these quipus may have been knotted in the manner of the "royal" quipus. This is not to say that a quipu system that recorded speech was intrinsically superior to any other system of quipus. Rather, the "royal" quipus, if they represent a purely sixteenth-century invention, form a vital strand of native colonial discourse.

---

animales ya crecidos adultos, que en lugar de hombres se sacrificaban" (Blas Valera [1594] 1968, 157).

The possibility remains, however, that the "royal" quipus may have been based on a regional quipu variant. Typically, Valera based his discussions of Inca culture on some facet of Inca life that actually had existed, then he modified this aspect until it conformed to European norms. It is possible that he might have done the same with the "royal" quipus; however, it must be noted that no quipu exhibiting the characteristics of the "royal" quipus has ever been found. More research remains to be done on the question of Andean quipu variation, as well as on the use of quipus by missionaries. The iconography of the "royal" quipu syllabary was created to express some of Valera's heterodox beliefs concerning Inca religion; these religious ideologies are examined in greater depth in chapter 7.

CHAPTER SEVEN

"... the laws of religious ceremonies and of the priesthoods ..."

The previous chapters have presented Valera's ideas concerning Inca religion and Andean Christianity. In this chapter, Valera's writings about religion are examined in greater detail. The Jesuit thinker based his descriptions of the Inca faith on a typology of religion developed by the classical Roman writer Marcus Terentius Varro (116–27 B.C.). The following pages will demonstrate how Valera defended native Peruvian religion using Varro's analyses of Roman paganism. The views of other chroniclers of Inca religion, particularly those of José de Acosta, Valera's Jesuit superior, will also be discussed. Acosta was renowned during his lifetime for his insights into Inca religion; this chapter will reveal how Valera was in dialogue with his superior's conclusions regarding Andean ritual practices and beliefs. Finally, this chapter will address how Valera and Acosta stood in relation to other members of the Society of Jesus on matters of native evangelization. An examination of Acosta's censored writings shows him to have been a considerably more moderate figure than is often portrayed; unfortunately, his Peruvian provincialate

---

Citing St. Augustine.

would be followed by the leadership of those Jesuits hostile to native religiosity in general and to Valera in particular.

Varro, Augustine, and the God of Pirua

Because we have only partial access to Valera's body of works, his thoughts on Andean religion must be reconstructed from what survives of his texts. A key to his understanding of religion can be found in one of Garcilaso's citations from the *Historia Occidentalis*. In chapter 6, book 2, Garcilaso ([1609] 1987, 81–83) quotes at length from Valera's descriptions of native Mexican and North American deities. Valera contrasts the "demonic" and "filthy" gods "of all the natives of Mexico, Chiapas, Guatemala, Vera Paz and other places" with the "natural gods" of "great Florida [North America] and all the islands."[1] He writes that the natural deities of the latter conform to Marcus Terentius Varro's description of "natural gods—the elements, the sea, lakes, rivers, springs, hills, wild animals, snakes, crops, and similar things." Furthermore, Valera adds, this practice of natural religion originated with the Chaldeans and then "spread to many various nations." According to Garcilaso (ibid., 82–83), Valera argued that the Incas "worshipped only the sun and planets"—the highest form of Varro's natural gods—and that the Incas, like the natives of North America, imitated the Chaldeans in this. Valera is careful to note, however, that the Incas paid primary homage to the Creator, who made the sun and planets.

Garcilaso's quotation from the *Historia Occidentalis* suggests Varro's importance to Valera's thought. This supposition is reinforced by the study of Valera's other writings on native religion, in which he clearly uses Varro's categories of Roman paganism to describe Inca belief. Throughout the *Relación de las costumbres antiguas,* the *Vocabulario,* and the remnants of the *Historia Occidentalis,* the author repeatedly compares the Incas to the ancient Romans, although always to the Peruvians' advantage.

It is not surprising that Valera would have been familiar with Varro's writings. The discussion of Varro's work forms a central

---

1. Valera's sources on Mexican religion include Francisco López de Gomara, Peter Martyr d'Anghiera, and Jerónimo Román y Zamora.

theme in one of the most widely read books of the medieval and early modern periods, St. Augustine of Hippo's *De civitate Dei* (The city of God). Varro was considered to be one of the greatest Roman scholars. St. Augustine referred to Varro as

> a man of pre-eminent, of unparalleled erudition, succinctly and neatly described in one line of Terentian,
>
> "Varro, that man of universal science";
>
> a man who read so much that we marvel that he had any time for writing; who wrote so much that we find it hard to believe that anyone could read it all. (Augustine 1984, 230)

In the course of his life, Varro composed some seventy-four works, only two of which survive, *Rerum rusticarum libri III* (The three books of rural life) and *De lingua Latina* (On the Latin language) (in part). His most significant work, the *Antiquitatum rerum humanarum et divinarum* (On human and divine antiquities) is known primarily through Augustine's critique of it in *De civitate Dei*. The first twenty-five books of the *Antiquitatum* treat human matters, while the last sixteen books deal with divine things. In these final books, he writes about Roman priests, temples, and shrines; theater and mythology; public and private worship; and the gods. Augustine explains Varro's religious thought in detail; however, his purpose is not to laud the ancient Roman but to criticize Roman paganism as part of his defense of Christianity. Augustine concedes that there existed admirable aspects of the Roman Empire that were important in preparing the ground for the gospel of Christ. Nonetheless, he finds little truth in the Roman religion and attacks it vehemently. Valera claimed that Inca religion shared many of Rome's finest qualities and even surpassed the classical religions. He answers Augustine's criticisms of this type of paganism by asserting that the Incas possessed the qualities of "true religion," which Augustine believed ancient Roman religion lacked.

Varro divides Roman religion, or "theology," into three categories: mythical, civil, and natural. His category of mythical theology consists of the aspects of religion expressed by poets. It includes the fables and myths of the gods and is best exemplified by the Roman theater. Augustine held this form of religion in contempt; he intimated that Varro believed it to be the basest kind of theology, necessary only because "people in general are more inclined to listen to poets than to scientists [i.e., philosophers]" (Augustine 1984, 176). Augustine quotes the following passage from Varro concerning mythical theology.

> [This] contains a great deal of fiction which is in conflict with the dignity and nature of the immortals. It is in this category that we find one god born from the head, another from the thigh, a third from drops of blood; we find stories about thefts and adulteries committed by gods, and gods enslaved to human beings. In fact, we find attributed to gods not only the accidents that happen to humanity in general, but even those which can befall the most contemptible of mankind. (ibid., 234)

Augustine considered mythical theology, "with all its lies and filth," to be a completely unworthy form of religious expression. Likewise, he was critical of Varro's second category of Roman paganism, civil theology, which consists of the religious practices of the citizens of the city. According to Varro, this form of religion

> is that which the citizens in the towns, and especially the priests, ought to know and put into practice. It contains information about the gods which should be worshipped officially and the rites and sacrifices which should be offered to each of them. (Augustine 1984, 236)

Varro holds civil theology in higher esteem than mythical theology. He contends that inasmuch as the highest form of theology, natural theology, is too difficult for most people to grasp and the lowest, mythical theology, is too debased to serve as the religion of the city, civil theology forms an appropriate meeting ground for the two. Augustine writes:

> For [Varro] distinctly states that what the poets write is inadequate to serve as a model for the people to follow, while the writings of the philosophers are too demanding for the common people to find profit from their study. "These two theologies," says Varro, "are incompatible; and yet quite a number of ingredients have been taken from them to help form the principles of 'civil' theology." (ibid., 238)

While Varro accepts civil theology as a positive good for the citizens of the town, Augustine criticizes it severely. The author of *De civitate Dei* questions whether the "disgusting" rites of civil religion in the towns differ much from the "degradation and obscenity" of the "theology of the theater." Augustine mocks the Roman temple rituals, calling them "degraded," "disgusting and dishonorable" (Augustine 1984, 241). Particular disdain is reserved for the Galli, the young priests castrated in rites to the mother of the Gods. Of these, Augustine writes, "the effeminates consecrated to the Great Mother . . . violate every canon of decency in men and women" (286).

In natural theology, Varro—and to some extent Augustine—finds the highest form of paganism. Natural theology is not simply the worship of nature, as one might suppose. Rather, it is the religion of the philosophers. Varro states:

> [This] type which I have pointed out, is one on which the philosophers have left a number of works, in which they discuss who the gods are, where they are, of what kind and of what character they are. (Augustine 1984, 234)

The "true gods," Varro writes, consist of the Soul of the World and its diverse manifestations: "God is the Soul of the World, or as the Greeks say, the *cosmos,* and this world itself is God" (Augustine 1984, 262). All the gods are manifestations of different aspects of this abiding World Soul. Images of the gods were first invented by humans, Varro explains, to help those initiated into the divine mysteries "fix their eyes on [the mysteries], and apprehend with their minds the true gods, namely the Soul of the World and its manifestations" (ibid., 261). Idolatry, therefore, arose as the philosophers created images to assist humanity in understanding the many different aspects of the World Soul. So, for example, Varro explains that the god Jupiter, who represents the fulfillment of all things, also represents the fecundity of the world, as well as wealth and possessions. Jupiter is merely, however, a manifestation of these particular functions of the World Soul, and his images were created by philosophers to help the people to comprehend the variety and diversity of this World Soul. In his discussion of the World Soul, Varro is following the Platonic tradition, in which the World Soul is a bridge between the realm of Ideas and the transitory appearances of daily consciousness.

Augustine thoroughly criticizes Varro's notion of natural theology, arguing that despite its appearance of profundity, it is a disguise for the "wretched" superstitions of Rome's mythical and civil religion. He ridicules the multiplicity of Roman gods who watched over minutia, and he wonders how the religion of the philosophers can be reconciled with the "squalid" rites of the Roman temples and theater (Augustine 1984, 261–86).[2] For Augustine, idolatry arose from men who wished to be worshiped as gods, rather than from metaphysical speculation on the nature of the World Soul. Yet his most important criticism of natural theology is directed against the notion of the World Soul. He condemns natural theology because it supports worship of something created—the World Soul—rather than of the Creator himself. As he states, "it is blasphemy to worship anything, whether material or spiritual, in place of the true God, who alone can bring happiness to the soul in which he dwells." If the Romans, he continues, believed that through their "monstrous" ceremonies, they were "worshipping the one true God, the creator of every soul and material being," their "sin would consist not in worshipping an unworthy object, but in worshipping the proper object of worship by improper means." Likewise, he argues, if any "created spirit" is worshiped with the temples, priests, and sacrifices pertaining to the Creator, the worshipers sin because these rites "should be employed only in the worship of him to whom such worship and service are due" (288). For Augustine, the Romans' natural theology was false because, even at its most sublime, it advocated the worship of a created being in place of the true God, the Creator.

Although Valera undoubtedly had access to *De civitate Dei,* he would not have been entirely dependent on this text for an understanding of Varro's theology or of Augustine's criticisms of it. Most Catholic theology books of the sixteenth century bore some influence of Augustine's thought. For example, Jerónimo Román's work on comparative religion, which Valera cites, was influenced by Augustine; in fact, Román was probably Valera's source for the idea that the Chaldeans spread natural theology throughout the world.

The influence of Varro's category of mythical theology can be seen

---

2. Augustine's view of idolatry was influenced by the Book of Wisdom.

in Valera's description of native Mexican religion. Unlike Las Casas,[3] who praised native Mexican and Peruvian religion alike, Valera believed that religions of the Aztecs and Mayans were vastly inferior to that of the Andeans. One hears echoes of Augustine's criticisms of mythical theology and the Roman gods in Valera's description of the deities of the ancient Mexicans.

> The Mexicans had gods and goddesses they worshipped including some very filthy ones who were looked on as gods of the vices. They included Tlazolteutl, the god of lust; Ometochtli, god of drunkenness; and Vitcilopuchtli, god of strife and murder. Icona is the father of all the gods whom he begot on various wives and concubines; he was the god of fathers of families. Bacab was the god of sons of families; Estruac god of the air; Chiripia mother of the gods and the earth; Ischen, stepmother of the gods; and Tlaloc god of the waters. . . . They had innumerable idols and effigies of gods invented for various purposes. Many of them were very base. Some gods were in common; others were special. They were annual, and every year everyone changed and varied them at will. (Garcilaso [1609] 1987, 82)[4]

As cited in the beginning of this section, Valera contrasts the "filthy" gods of the Mexicans with the "natural" deities of the Incas, as defined by Varro. The theme of Incaic religion as a form of natural

---

3. Although Valera criticized the native Mexicans, whom Las Casas so admired, both authors agreed that the Incas had knowledge of the Creator. Las Casas's name for the Andean creator god, *Condici Viracocha,* varied slightly from the *Illa Tecce Viracocha* used by Valera. A major difference between Las Casas and Valera is that Las Casas believed that the Incas were responsible for introducing worship of the Creator into the Andes, whereas Valera argued that Illa Tecce had been adored continuously in Peru since the time of Pirua. For a discussion of Las Casas's writings on Peruvian religion, see MacCormack 1991, 205–40.

4. ". . . porque los mexicanos tuvieron dioses y diosas que adoraron, entre los cuales huvo algunos muy sucios, los cuales entendían aquellos indios que eran dioses de los vicios, como fue Tlazolteutl, dios de la luxeria, Ometochtli, dios de la embriaguez, Uitcilopuchtli, dios de la milicia o del homocidio. Icona era el padre de todos sus dioses: dezían que los engendró en diversas mujeres y concubinas; teníanle por dios de los padres de familias. Bacab era dios de los hijos de familia. Estruac, dios del aire. Chiripa era madre de los dioses, y tierra misma. Ischen era madrastra de sus dioses. Tlaloc, dios de las aguas. . . . Tuvieron innumerables imágines y figuras de dioses inventados para diversos oficios y diversas cosas. Muchos dellos eran muy suzios. Unos dioses tuvieron en común, otros en particular. Eran anales, que cada año y cada uno los mudava y trocava conforme a su antojo" (Garcilaso [1609] 1944a, 78).

theology is further developed by Valera in the *Relación de las costumbres antiguas.* In this text, Valera writes that the ancient Peruvians lived for many years without idols, worshiping only "the luminaries of the sky and the stars."[5] As he explains, the Peruvians primarily honored Illa Tecce, whom they believed created "the world, heavens and earth, sun and moon."[6] The name *Illa Tecce,* meaning "Light Eternal" *(Luz Eterna),* referred to the same God, the Creator, as do *El* in Hebrew, *Theos* in Greek, and *Deus* in Latin, according to Valera. Additionally, *Tecce* denotes "the first thing without beginning" *(principium rerum sine principio),* a traditional Christian formulation for the Creator. In more recent times, Valera continues, the honorific title *Viracocha,* which signifies the god of Pirua, was added to the name *Illa Tecce.*[7] However, he adds, the Peruvians believed that

> this immense and true God had communicated his divinity and potency to diverse created beings, so that each one functioned according to the office or virtue that it had; and that these were companion and councilor gods to the great God and principally were in the heavens, such as the sun, moon and stars, and planets.[8]

Valera concedes that the Peruvians erred in thinking that the Creator had divided his powers this way. Yet the author firmly maintains that the ancient Peruvians understood the Creator to be the force behind all of the secondary gods. Eventually, Valera states, the ancient Andeans began to make statues of these celestial gods to keep in mind the ideas and virtues represented by each.

> The great god Illa Tecce had certain ideas of everything present and to come and, for the good government of the world, distributed [these ideas] to each [stellar god]. . . . in each one of these gods or

---

5. ". . . las luminarias del cielo y las estrellas" (Blas Valera [1594] 1968, 153). This assertion accords with Garcilaso's statement that Valera "dize [Blas Valera] que los Incas no adoravan sino al sol y a los planetas" (Garcilaso [1609] 1944a, 79).

6. ". . . el mundo, cielo y tierra, y sol y luna" (Blas Valera [1594] 1968, 153).

7. See chapter 3 for a discussion of Valera's historiography, according to which Pirua was the first king of Peru.

8. ". . . que este Dios inmenso y verdadero tenía comunicada su divinidad y potencia a diversas criaturas, para que cada una obrase según el oficio o virtud que tenía. Y que estos eran dioses compañeros y consejeros del gran Dios, y principalmente estaban en los cielos, como son el sol, luna y estrellas y planetas" (Blas Valera [1594] 1968, 153).

stars were the ideas or models of those things they had in their care and office; and thus they said that such and such a star had the shape of a sheep [llama], because it was its task to guard and watch over the sheep; another star [had] the shape of a lion [puma]; another star the shape of a serpent. And [the natives] agreed that here on earth they would make statues or images of those ideas or things, according to the office that each [god] had. And in this way began the idols of stone, of wood, of gold, [of] silver, etc. that they said represented the gods that were in the sky; although later they said that those [images] also represented the same ideas.[9]

As one can see, Valera's description of the ancient Peruvian religion mirrors Varro's natural theology, from the explanation of the rise of idolatry to the understanding of celestial gods as manifestations of the one great God. The only distinction, in Valera's view, between the Inca and Roman religions, is, however, absolutely crucial: whereas the Roman philosophers understood the minor gods to be expressions of the World Soul, the Inca wise men knew that the secondary gods were all reflections of the Creator. In this, Valera is responding to Augustine's primary objection to pagan natural theology. It is not surprising, therefore, that in every text we have of Valera, there is mention of the Peruvians' knowledge of the true God. For example, in Garcilaso's *Comentarios reales* ([1609] 1987, 288), we read that Valera translated the name *Viracocha* by the Latin term *numen*—"the will and power of God"—to indicate "the divinity attributed by the Indians to this phantom." This is consonant, of course, with the idea that Viracocha is Christ, the Word of God made flesh. Anello Oliva ([1631] 1895, 126), following Valera, defines the Andean creator god as "eternity, without beginning or end" [Eterno sin principio ni fin]. Likewise, according to Montesinos's history ([1644] 1930, 7, 32), which Valera shared, the first Peruvian king,

---

9. ". . . el gran dios *Illa Tecce* había ciertas ideas de todas las cosas presentes y venideras, y que para el buen gobierno del mundo repartió a cada uno de estos dioses o estrellas cosas que tenía por cuidado y oficio; a así decían que tal estrella tenía figura de cordero, porque era su oficio guardar y conservar las ovejas; tal estrella figura de león; tal estrella figura de serpiente. Y que convenía que acá en la tierra se hiciesen estatuas o imágenes de aquellas ideas o cosas, según el oficio que tenía cada uno. Y por esta vía comenzaron los ídolos de piedra, de madera, de oro, plata, etc. que decían ellos representar a los dioses que estaban en el cielo; aunque despues dijeron que también aquellos eran las mismas ideas" (ibid., 154).

Pirua, and his successors worshiped Illa Ticci Huiracocha as "the supreme creator." Moreover, as I showed in chapter 6, Valera also taught that the Incas maintained a distinction between the first two persons of the Trinity—the creator of the universe (Pachacamac) and his incarnation on earth (Viracocha), who was also fully the creator.

In agreement with Varro's definition of natural theology as the religion of the philosophers, Valera extolled the virtues of the ancient Peruvian *amauta,* or wise men. For example, about the emperor Capac Raymi Amauta, the thirty-ninth Peruvian king, Valera writes:

> [he] was a very wise philosopher. He governed forty years during the fourth sun before the birth of the Lord; he discovered the solstices and called them Raymi in his name.[10]

Valera also claimed that at least two of the Inca kings, Inca Roca and Topa Inca Yupanqui, were philosophers who speculated on theological matters. To the latter, for instance, Valera attributes the reflection that the sun is not alive because "it does not grow tired from its continuous burning; for if it were a living thing it would tire as we do" (Garcilaso [1609] 1987, 497).[11]

Valera furthers his analogy between Inca beliefs and Roman religion by claiming a similarity between Andean celestial gods and those of the classical pantheon. Contrary to any other commentator on Inca religion, he writes that the ancient Peruvians worshiped Mars *(Aucayoc)* as a god of war, Mercury *(Catuilla)* as a god of messengers and merchants, Saturn *(Huacha)* as a god of pestilence and misfortune, and Jupiter *(Pirua)* as a god of empire and of harvests and plenty. Interestingly, he avoids suggesting an equivalence between the Andean earth goddess, Pachamama, and the Roman great earth mother, Tellus, perhaps because Augustine was particularly scathing in his criticisms of the worship of the earth mother. While many of Valera's contemporaries would use Augustine's criticisms of paganism to justify violent campaigns against alleged idolaters in the high-

---

10. ". . . fue muy sabio philosopho: este governó quarenta años en tiempo del quarto Sol antes del naçimiento del Señor: halló los solstiçios y llamolos Raymi de su nombre" (Anello Oliva [1631] 1998, 95); this is a direct quote from Valera's *Vocabulario.* Montesinos's description of Capac Raymi Amauta is in identical words: "fue muy sabio filossofo. Este gouerno quarenta años en tiempo del quarto sol antes del nacimiento del Señor, hallo los Solsticios y llamolos Raymi de su nombre" (Montesinos [1644] 1930, 57).

11. ". . . si fuera cosa viva se cansara como nosotros" (Garcilaso [1609] 1944b, 175).

lands (see MacCormack 1985b), Valera answered Augustine's complaints about paganism by defending Inca belief. In *De civitate Dei,* Augustine writes that divine providence led Christianity to be founded in the Roman Empire, because, despite its faults, Rome provided a solid moral and ethical base for new faith (Augustine 1984, xxvi). It is the same with the Inca religion, in Valera's view; the natural theology of the Inca prepared the way for the coming of Christ's gospel to the diverse peoples of the Andes.

Hermits, *Aclla,* and Vestal Virgins

Inca priests and priestesses, hermits and saints, also formed an integral part of Valera's vision of the Andean past. The Inca priesthood, in particular, was described by Valera in a manner combining classical and Christian features against a native Peruvian backdrop. According to the Jesuit author, the Inca religious hierarchy was headed by a pontiff called the *vilahoma (villac-umu).* The *vilahoma,* Valera taught, lived a life of holy simplicity. He eschewed sexual contact, abstained from meat, wore simple garments, and lived in the countryside, the better to meditate on the stars. His primary responsibility, apart from prayer, was directing the activities of his ten *hatun vilca,* "prelates who were like bishops."[12] Valera claims that there was one *hatun vilca* for each of the following regions: Collao, Collasuyos, Condesuyos, Chincha, Huaylas, Cajamarca, Ayahuaca, Quito, Trujillo (whose temple was located in the great pyramid called Chimo), and, finally, Canas and Canchis, near Cuzco. The *hatun vilca,* like the *vilahoma,* were celibate. Valera is unusual in claiming such austerity for the Peruvian pontiff and his bishops. Clearly, Valera wished to claim Christian virtues for the native Andean prelates, whom he compared to the hierarchs of the Catholic Church (Blas Valera [1594] 1968, 161–66).

The clergy under the rule of the *vilahoma,* Valera continues, were charged with presiding over the public religious ceremonies of the empire. They taught the people about the gods, the idols, and the laws of religion. The lowest level of this Inca priesthood were the *yanavillca* (black priests). They were equivalent to parish priests, although they

---

12. "... los prelados eran como obispos" (Blas Valera [1594] 1968, 163).

lived together in communities dedicated to Illa Tecce Viracocha (Blas Valera [1594] 1968, 164, 168–69). The *yanavillca* did not always maintain the high moral standards of their superiors, Valera writes. At times, he claims, they demonstrated a "pharisaical" pride when preaching to the people. Some of the priests were persuaded by the Devil—who "appeared to them in diverse shapes of men and animals" (Blas Valera [1594] 1968, 169)—to castrate themselves, to bleed themselves, or even to throw themselves off of cliffs. Those who castrated themselves in honor of the gods were known as *corasca;* Valera is the only chronicler of Peru to mention their existence. The *corasca* are reminiscent of the "effeminates" belonging to the ecstatic Roman earth cults derided by Augustine (1984, 286). In fact, their very name, *corasca,* denotes those who consume the hallucinogenic herb *cizaña (cora),*[13] suggesting that these Andean priests participated in ecstatic rituals similar, at least superficially, to the rites of Demeter. Although the exact role of hallucinogens in Inca state rituals is unclear, there is little doubt that Andean shamans used psychotropic herbs to induce trance states (Sharon 1978, 23–33). In describing the *corasca,* Valera apparently is referring to an actual Andean practice of using *cizaña,* but he is casting it according to the classical model of the Galli, who were castrated as well as ecstatic.

The Jesuit chronicler readily admits that the Devil influenced the *corasca,* by appearing to them as animals and people. Likewise, he concedes that another class of religious practitioners, the *huatuc* (diviners), were routinely deceived by Satan. The *huatuc* served the major oracles of the empire: Mullipampa (Quito), Pacasmayo (Trujillo), Rimac (Lima), Pachacamac, and Inticaca (Lake Titicaca). According to Valera, the *huatuc* maintained a pact with the Devil, who spoke to them through the oracles.

> [When] the time [came] to hear the oracle, the minister was taken with a diabolical furor that they called *utirayay,* and afterward he declared to the people what the oracle had told him.[14]

---

13. *Cizaña,* the Spanish word for darnel *(Lolium temulentum),* was generally used in the sixteenth century to refer to hallucinogenic herbs. Although darnel itself has no hallucinogenic properties, it is highly susceptible to ergot infestation and thus gained a reputation as a dangerous plant.

14. "Al tiempo de oír el oráculo, se tomaba el tal ministro de un furor diabólico que ellos decían *utirayay,* y despues declaraba al pueblo lo que el oráculo le había dicho" (Blas Valera [1594] 1968, 164).

The frenzy—*utirayay*—of the *huatuc* certainly sounds similar to some of the hallucinogen-induced trances used by shamans in the Andes today to contact the spirit world. Valera tells us that the other types of diviner, who include the *hamurpa,* who prognosticate by reading omens and animal entrails, and the *ichuri,* confessors, had no dealings with the Devil. Neither, he asserts, did most of the other native Andean religious practitioners, such as the officers of animal sacrifices or the *aclla,* the celibate priestesses.

In fact, the only other native priests who had occasional contact with diabolic forces, he writes, were the native hermits. He explains that certain *yanavillca* chose to live in holy seclusion on lonely mountain peaks. These hermits were known as *huancaquilli,* which means "those who were disinherited and bereft of all riches and exiled."[15] According to Valera, they were led by an "abbot," the *tocricoc.* Valera was unique in defining the term *tocricoc*—literally, "he who sees all"—as "abbot"; *tocricoc* was more usually applied to an Inca provincial governor. With the permission of the *tocricoc,* the hermits were allowed to live in "solitude and austere penance" amid remote cliffs in the wilderness, where they occupied themselves with contemplation, worship, discipline, and assisting the common people.

> There they contemplated the sun, the moon, and the stars, and they adored them almost without ceasing; they did not lack for their idols; the mountains, the narrow river valleys, the rocky plains, served them as temples, oratories, and sanctuaries. Who doubts but that the Devil appeared to them there? . . .
>
> They slept on the ground; they ate roots; they drank cold water; they whipped themselves with well-knotted cords; and, just as the ancient anchorites were, in ancient times, much visited by the faithful, so also were these visited by the heathen.[16]

To emphasize the regard in which the hermits were held, Valera enumerates the types of assistance that the people would seek from the *huancaquilli:* to find lost objects, to discover the fate of a husband

---

15. ". . . desheredados y desechados de todas las riquezas, y desterrados" (ibid., 169).

16. "Allí contemplaban al sol, la luna y las estrellas, y las adoraban casi sin cesar; no carecían de sus idolillos; los montes, las cuencas de los rios, las peñas, les servían de templos, de oratorios y sanctuarios. Quién duda sino que allí se les aparecía el Demonio? . . .

who went to war, to pray to the moon for assistance in giving birth, and to receive aid in all their necessities. In return, the hermits were provided for by the local villagers. When one of the hermits died, he was buried by other *huancaquilli,* who came down from their lonely solitude to attend to his funeral.

In many ways, Valera depicts the native hermits in a very positive light. The *huancaquilli* lived in holy solitude and penance comparable to that of the early Christian desert fathers with whom Valera compares them. The lives of the first Christian anchorites, who dwelt in Egypt in the third and fourth centuries A.D., were one of the primary models of the Christian religious life in the sixteenth century. Such hermits as St. Anthony the Great (d. 355) served as a continuing inspiration to the creators of new religious orders, from St. Benedict of Nursia, author of the Benedictine rule in the sixth century, to St. Ignatius Loyola, founder of the Jesuits in 1540. As a Jesuit, Valera would have been very familiar with the sainted lives of the early desert hermits. In the passage just cited, he is clearly showing that the pagan Andean hermits shared in many of the same penitential virtues exhibited by the desert fathers, whose example is one of the bases of Christian spirituality. Thus, he implies, the Andean peoples were well prepared to accept these virtues under Christian instruction.

The Jesuit author acknowledges that no other writer has mentioned the existence of these pagan Andean hermits. However, he attributes this oversight to the early conquistadors' passion for gold and wealth.

> The excessive concern for seeking gold and silver with which the Spaniards entered Peru was part of the reason why neither the first [conquistadors] nor [those] in the later years were able to learn much about the false religion of the Peruvians; this was helped by the civil wars that the Spanish fought among themselves for more than thirty years, instigated by this concern and greed; if they [i.e., the conquistadors] did find out something, it was not because they wanted to learn but because [while] seeking treasures, burials, and

---

Dormían en el suelo, comían raíces, bebían agua fría, disciplinábanse con cordeles bien añudados, y así como los antiguos anachoretas fueron antiguamente muy visitados de los fieles, así también lo fueron estos de los infieles" (ibid.).

tombs, where there was gold and silver, . . . they asked by whom and how [the treasures] were placed there.[17]

In other words, the European knowledge of native religion was motivated primarily by the search for treasure. Therefore, Valera concludes, the religious lives of those priests and hermits who lived in poverty, in remote areas, escaped notice. Valera accuses the influential Spanish chronicler Polo de Ondegardo of being particularly remiss in his understanding of Inca religiosity. Polo, he wrote, was only concerned to find hidden loot, and that is why he bothered to discover the graves of the kings and lords of Cuzco. He was not, Valera emphasized, interested in Andean religion for its own sake (Blas Valera [1594] 1968, 168).

Valera's belief that there were non-Christian Andean ascetics living in isolated mountain peaks should not be dismissed out of hand as merely romanticism of the Inca past. The Augustinian friars in sixteenth-century Huamachuco, in northern Peru, described encountering a non-Christian Andean hermit who lived in the wilderness as penance for his sins (*Relación de idolatrías* [1560] 1918, 43). According to Acosta ([1590] 1987, 366), native confessors *(ichuri)* in the region of Juli would assign penances of living in the remote mountain wilderness for a period of a year or more for extremely serious sins. These lonely penitents possibly served as Valera's model for the *huancaquilli*. Valera may be describing actual pre-Hispanic native practices, in a manner that conforms to Christian ideals. His assertion that the Devil frequently appeared to these men should not be taken as a condemnation of the *huancaquilli*. The Christian desert fathers suffered likewise from demonic visitations and temptations, according to legends about them.

The *aclla*—the beautiful "chosen" women of the Inca—comprised the final category of religious discussed by Valera. Consecrated attendants in Cuzco and in Inca temples throughout the empire, the *aclla*

---

17. "La demasiada solicitud de buscar oro y plata con que entraron los españoles en el Piru fue parte para que ni aún los principios ni en los años venideros se pudiesen saber muchas cosas antiguas de la religión falsa de los piruanos; ayudaron mucho a esto las guerras civiles que por más de treinta años tuvieron los españoles entre sí unos con otros, instigados desa solicitud y codicia; y si supieron algo, no fue porque lo quisieron saber, sino porque buscando tesoros, entierros, sepulcros, donde hubiese oro y plata, y teniendo noticia de algunos, preguntaron quién y cómo los puso allí" (ibid., 168).

were responsible for serving the shrine of the moon and for carrying the moon's silver image. The Inca *coya*, or queen, had charge over the women dedicated to the moon cult. But a large number of *aclla* were also consecrated to serving in the sun temples. According to the chronicler Bernabe Cobo, the *aclla* were responsible for worship in the sun temple in Cuzco as well as in the provinces. They also, he continued, spun very fine cloth for use in sacrifice, in clothing the images of the gods, and as gifts to the Inca. Preparing food and corn beer for the gods and the other attendants in the temple was another important aspect of their duties. Finally, Cobo emphasizes that in Cuzco the women cared for a sacred fire that burned in front of the sacred image of the sun. He compares these sacred women to cloistered Christian nuns, who, like the *aclla*, were considered to be the spouses of God. Moreover, the virginity of the *aclla* was of the utmost importance and was fiercely guarded. Any chosen woman caught in an illicit relationship with a man was immediately sentenced to death (Cobo [1653] 1990, 172–73).

In his *Relación de las costumbres antiguas*, Valera claims that the first *aclla* were chosen by the emperor Pachacuti VII, the lord of Pacari Tampu, who restored the empire after a foreign invasion and a series of devastating epidemics (Blas Valera [1594] 1968, 169; Montesinos [1644] 1930, 66–69). This emperor, we are told, first built the temples of the sun and of the moon in Cuzco. To ensure the perpetual worship of these deities in the temples, he ordained female ministers,

> who were chosen virgins, beautiful and of noble blood, called *acllas*, that is, elect and consecrated to the sun: and thus they were called *intip chinan* or *punchao chinan*, that is, caretakers of the sun, servants of the light of day, but never *intip huarmin* or *punchaopa huarmin*, wives of the sun.[18]

Valera describes in some detail the girls' three-year novitiate, after which, he states, they took solemn vows. He disagrees vehemently

---

18. ". . . que fuesen virgines escogidas, hermosas y de sangre noble, llamadas *acllas*, esto es, electas y consagradas al Sol; y así se llamaban ellas *intip chinan*, o *punchao chinan*, esto es criadas del Sol, siervas de la luz del día, pero nunca *intip huarmin*, o *punchaopa huarmin*, mujeres del Sol" (Blas Valera [1594] 1968, 170). Valera claims that most of the women chosen for their beauty came from Chachapoyas, Cuzco, and the region of Huánuco; never once was an *aclla* selected from the province of Collas in the south. In this statement, one sees the author's bias in favor of Chachapoyas.

with Polo de Ondegardo's contention that most *aclla* were forced into this life; Valera insists that entering the *acllahuasi* (house of the chosen women) was a voluntary choice and even a desired honor for young Peruvian girls. His list of the *acllas*' duties agrees with that of other sources. They were responsible for weaving fine *cumbi* cloth, making corn beer, cooking sacrificial foods, cleaning and adorning the various shrines, and performing ritual ceremonies. Valera also emphasizes that the *acllas*' primary duty was to care for the eternal flame, the *nina villca,* that burned in the sun temple known as Coricancha (fig. 11). This echoes the accounts of the vestal virgins of ancient Rome, who tended to the eternal flame in that city. However, Valera goes on to declare that the *aclla* were superior to any other non-Christian priestesses for the rigor with which they guarded their virginity for life: "It is not known of any gentiles that they made vows of perpetual virginity and that they kept [their vows], except for only the Peruvians, with their virgin *aclla.*[19] Moreover, the women kept their vows solemnly. "It is not known in any history or quipu," he writes, "that any of these virgin *acllas* have ever fallen into the weaknesses of the flesh" (Blas Valera [1594] 1968, 172).[20] The Peruvian priestesses were similar to the vestal virgins, therefore, in their care for an eternal flame. Yet they were superior to their classical counterparts, both in the seriousness with which they kept their vows of chastity and in the fact that their vows were perpetual, not temporary. In fact, Valera compares the sacred women of the Inca to Christian nuns, informing us that the *acllahuasi* was the same as a monastery and that the head priestess, the *mama aclla,* "was like an abbess."[21]

Valera concedes that the *aclla* helped to spread superstition and "lies" as agents of a pagan religion. Nonetheless, his portrayal of their annual ceremony to renew their vows emphasized their worship of God, the Creator. Valera, who is the only writer to describe this rite, states that this ritual was performed after the harvest, presumably as part of the harvest moon festival (Aymoray Quilla) in May

---

19. "No se sabe de gentilidad ninguna que haya prometido virginidad perpétua y que la haya guardado, sino sólo la piruana en sus vírgines *acllas*" (Blas Valera [1594] 1968, 172).

20. "No se sabe ni tal historia ni quipo hay que tal diga, de que alguna destas *acllas* vírgines hayan caído en flaqueza de carne" (ibid.).

21. ". . . era como abadesa, la cual . . . se decía *mama aclla*" (ibid.).

Fig. 11. Remains of Coricancha, surmounted by the Church of Santo Domingo. (Photo courtesy of Brian S. Bauer.)

(for a different view of this feast, see Cristobal de Molina [1575] 1989, 118–20). During this ritual, the emperor and his queen, along with the most important nobles, would seat themselves with great pomp in one of the central plazas in Cuzco. In front of the royals, the *aclla* would erect lavishly decorated altars bearing the idols to whom the women would renew their vows. Preeminent among these shrines was that dedicated to Illa Tecce Viracocha—the Creator. In the ceremony, the chosen women would present to the notables a variety of gifts, including embroidered cloth, elaborate sandals, brooches, jewels, belts, and garlands. In return, the *aclla* would receive from the emperor and his court gifts of livestock, land, gold, silver, wool, and food. As part of their reconsecration, the women also would walk among the guests and serve corn beer and a sacred bread called *illai tanta*. To eat this bread was an act of reverence, Valera states, and the sacred bread itself was carefully guarded "as if it were a relic."[22] The parallels with the Eucharist are obvious and reinforce Valera's view of the natural holiness of the Inca *aclla*, whom he depicts as pre-Christian precursors of Catholic nuns.

What was the fate of the *aclla* once the Spanish soldiers entered Tahuantinsuyu? Certainly, many were raped; Valera tells us that the Spanish initially believed them to be witches (Blas Valera [1594] 1968, 172). However, he continues, a great many of these holy women accepted baptism.

> Many of these [*aclla* in Cajamarca and Huaylas], receiving sacred baptism, remained virgins, offering themselves newly as *acllas* of Jesus Christ our Lord, and others fled to the hills. The nuns in Cuzco did the same; more than two thousand of them converted to the Lord, and most remained virgins until death, and others married recently baptized Indian men, and others fled to diverse parts; however, all or most came to be Christians, and those [native women] who most flowered in devotion and chastity were these [former *aclla*].[23]

---

22. "Tenían este pan por gran regalo y guardábanlo como si fuese reliquia y llamábanle *illai tanta*, pan divino, pan sagrado" (Blas Valera [1594] 1968, 173).

23. ". . . muchas dellas, recibiendo el baptismo sagrado, se quedaron virgines, ofreciéndose nuevamente por acllas de Jhesu Cristo Nuestro Señor, y otras huyeron al monte. Las monjas del Cusco hicieron lo mismo, que se convirtieron al Señor más de dos mill dellas, y las más permanecieron vírgines hasta la muerte, y otras casaron con indios recién

During his time in Cuzco, when he was a spiritual leader of many Christian Inca elites, Valera may have known some former *aclla* living under Christian vows of chastity. Their saintly lives after conversion to Christianity underscores, for Valera, the holiness inherent in the Inca way of life. This is the same holiness apparent in Valera's story of Atahuallpa's conversion, in which the pagan emperor is able to become a Christian saint whose soul ascended directly to heaven. Valera clearly believed—based in part on his experiences with the Nombre de Jesús, the confraternity of Inca nobles in Cuzco—that the Inca faith was uniquely able to guide people to a Christian life.

Acosta and Valera

Valera was not the only Jesuit chronicler of Peruvian antiquities writing in Peru in the 1570s and 1580s. His direct superior, José de Acosta, wrote two highly influential works—*De Procuranda Indorum Salute* (On procuring the salvation of the Indians) and *Historia natural y moral de las Indias* (The natural and moral history of the Indies)—based, in part, on his experiences in Peru. No discussion of Valera's work, therefore, would be complete without a comparison with the writings of Acosta. The two men often disagreed with each other, and Valera frequently criticized opinions expressed in Acosta's work. Examining the relationship between the two men can provide new insights into Acosta's thought, despite the extent to which his writings have already been studied (see MacCormack 1991, 261–80; Lopétegui 1942; Pina 1990; Lisi 1990). Acosta, who steadfastly praised Valera, even after the latter's mysterious imprisonment, is a difficult figure to assess. Although he criticized Andean culture freely and believed the Incas to have been barbarians, many of his fellow Jesuits in Peru considered Acosta to be too lenient in matters regarding the native Peruvians. In fact, Acosta saw his own work rigorously censored by the Society; he was forced to remove entire passages critical of Spanish abuse of the Indians from *De Procuranda*. Toward the end of Valera's life, Acosta, who had witnessed the riots that shook Cuzco on Valera's behalf in 1577, intervened for Valera to end his imprison-

---

baptizados y otras se huyeron a diversas partes; aunque todas o las más vinieron a ser cristianas, y las que más florecieron en devoción y honestidad fueron éstas" (ibid., 172).

ment. The association between the two men was complex and must be analyzed to understand how the work of each writer was constrained by the internal Jesuit politics in Peru—politics that would eventually lead to Valera's imprisonment and to Acosta's departure from Peru amid a severe personal crisis.

José de Acosta was born in Medina del Campo, Spain, in September or October 1540. When he entered the Society of Jesus in 1554 at the age of fourteen, his older brothers were already Jesuits (Lopétegui 1942, 8–36). As a young Jesuit, Acosta petitioned repeatedly to be sent to the Indies. According to a manuscript by Anello Oliva, Acosta said that he was inspired in this desire by the appearance to him of an angel carrying a burning ax (Anello Oliva [1631] 1998, 307). Upon his arrival in Lima in 1572, Acosta's intelligence and leadership abilities were quickly rewarded: in 1572, he was made novice master; in 1575, he was chosen to be rector in the Jesuit school in Lima, where he taught theology; and in 1576, he was named provincial for the Jesuit province of Peru, thereby assuming the leadership over the Jesuits in virtually all of Spanish South America.

While he was provincial, Acosta finished *De Procuranda,* his monumental treatise on Peruvian missions, begun when he was a theology professor in Lima. Through his writings and leadership role in the Society, he gained a considerable reputation in the colony. In 1581, when his term of office ended, it was already known that he was to play a major role in one of the most important events in Peruvian church history—the Third Lima Council of Bishops. This council, held by Archbishop Toribio Mogrovejo, laid the foundations for the Catholic Church in Peru, especially in matters regarding the care and conversion of the native peoples. Acosta was the leading theological advisor to the council and had a profound impact on its legislation. He was also put in charge of the production of the council's trilingual catechism in Spanish, Quechua, and Aymara. According to Lopé-tegui, Acosta composed the Spanish text of the catechism, along with the accompanying confessional and sermons. Throughout Acosta's work, one can see the influence of the Spanish lawyer Polo de Ondegardo. Polo de Ondegardo had penned a tract on native Andean religion, based on his own research among native informants in Cuzco, which was published by the council in 1585.[24] His influence was profound, not only on Acosta's work on the catechism, but also on Acosta's ethnographic writings. As Sabine MacCormack has written (1991, 269), "Acosta's guide in all matters of Andean religion was Polo de Ondegardo, whom he often quoted verbatim." Valera, who was one of the translators for the catechism of the Third Lima Council, took great exception to Polo de Ondegardo's understanding of native beliefs and attacked him vigorously in his writings. Although Valera never mentions Acosta by name, one can sense his frustrations over his superior's dependence on Polo de Ondegardo for knowledge of Peru.

Several areas of disagreement between Acosta and Valera have already been discussed in chapters 3 and 6. One major source of conflict was over the translation of the catechism. While Valera, following Domingo de Santo Tomás, advocated the use of Quechua words for Christian concepts, Acosta insisted on the imposition of Spanish neologisms within the Quechua text. The Jesuit provincial did not share his subordinate's faith in the ability of Inca culture to prepare the native peoples for Christianity; rather, he argued that the Andeans possessed only a "sparse and attenuated" knowledge of the true God and that their customs were too corrupt for the natives to accept Christ into their hearts. Similarities between Christianity and Andean religions, Acosta contended, were due simply to demonic imitation of the "true faith."

Moreover, Acosta disagreed with Valera over the sources of the Andeans' idolatry. For Acosta, the Peruvians' idol worship did not stem from the desire to make images of the sun, moon, and stars to explain the manifestations of God. Instead, in *De Procuranda*, Acosta followed Augustine's criticism of Roman religion by stating that the Inca gods were derived from heroes who were later adored as gods (Augustine 1984, 276). Yet he deepens his criticism of Inca religious worship by arguing that it most resembled the idolatry of the ancient Egyptians.[25] In this, he was employing the religious categories of St. John of Damascus

---

24. Polo de Ondegardo's tract is entitled *Tratado y averiguación sobre los errores y supersticiones de los Indios.* It was published by the council as part of a confessional manual, *Confesionario para curas de Indios* (1585).

25. An outstanding discussion of Acosta's views on idolatry can be found in MacCormack 1991, 261–80. MacCormack focuses specifically on Acosta's later analysis of Andean idolatry in the *Historia natural y moral,* rather than on his discussion in *De Procuranda.*

(ca. 675–ca. 749), who divided idolatry into three types. According to John of Damascus, the highest form of idolatry consisted of the worship of the stars and natural phenomena, the second category was that of the ancient Greeks and Romans, and the final and most pernicious type was that of ancient Egypt. In *De Procuranda*, Acosta writes:

> the idolatry of the Egyptians, in which, not only are the stars and men taken as gods, but also the sordid and vile animals and the very stones and senseless pieces of wood are granted divine honors. . . . That which touches on the superstitions of the Egyptians has such a hold on the Indians that the types of sacrilege and idol cannot be counted: mountains, hills, prominent rocks, water fountains, rivers that flow swiftly, high peaks in rocky cliffs, great dunes of sand, the opening of a dark hole, an ancient and gigantic tree, a vein of metal, a rare and elegant form of any little stone. . . . This evil pestilence of idolatry fills the mountains, fills the valleys, the towns, the houses, the roads, and there is not a portion of land in Peru that is free of this superstition.[26]

Acosta's negative assessment of Inca religion, in which it is not even accorded the honors of Greek and Roman idolatry, must have been a disappointment to Valera. In his writings, Valera attacks Acosta's source of information, Polo de Ondegardo, for spreading ignorance about the Inca gods and Inca rituals. "When Polo says that there were Incas who wished to be adored as gods and who ordered that this be done," Valera writes, "it is a certain thing that this was a conjecture of his." Valera explains that the *amauta* Amaro Toco held a disputation in Cuzco in the time of the Incas, in which he proved "that no man born of woman can be a god."[27]

---

26. ". . . la idolatría de los egipcios, en que no sólo los astros o los hombres son tenidos por dioses, sino también a los animales sórdidos y viles y a las mismas piedras y leños sin sentido se tributan honores divinos. . . . Pues lo que toca a la superstición de los egipcios está tan en vigor entre los indios, que no se pueden contar los géneros de sacrilegios y guacas: montes, cuestas, rocas prominentes, aguas manantiales útiles, ríos que corren precipitados, cumbres altas de las peñas, montones grandes de arena, abertura de un hoyo tenebroso, un árbol gigantesco y añoso, una vena de metal, la forma rara y elegante de cualquier piedrecita. . . . De este peste perniciosa de la idolatria están .llenos los montes, llenos los valles, los pueblos, las casas, los caminos y no hay porción de tierra en el Perú que esté libre de esta superstición" (Acosta [1577] 1954, 559, 560–61).

27. "En lo que dice Polo que hubo ingas que quisieron ser adorados como dioses, y que lo mandaron así guardar, es cosa clara que fue por conietura suya"; ". . . que ningun hombre nacido de hombre y de mujer puede ser dios" (Blas Valera [1594] 1968, 160).

Therefore, he concludes, the Incas knew that no mere mortal could ever be worshiped.

Another matter on which Acosta and Valera differed was the question of whether the Incas practiced human sacrifice. In *De Procuranda,* Acosta wrote:

> The victims, the libations, the order of the ceremonies followed by the leading Incas in all their cults, would be infinite to recount; whoever reads the history carefully written about this by licentiate Polo, a serious and prudent man, will see that within the boundaries of the city of Cuzco alone there were more than 370 idols counted, to all of whom were given divine honors; to some they offered the fruit of the land; to others, precious metals and gold and silver; and in honor of others, much blood from innocent children was shed in sacrifice.[28]

Although most chroniclers in the sixteenth century accepted that the Incas practiced human sacrifice, Valera protested vociferously against this notion. "But the worst error or false testimony that Polo said about the Peruvians was that they practiced the sacrifice of adults and children," he wrote. Valera argues that there were three primary reasons why Polo mistakenly believed that the Incas had offered human sacrifices. For one thing, he explained, when Polo researched Inca antiquities in Cuzco, "all of the old men and Indian historians had fled to the mountains ... because of the war of Francisco Hernandez Girón."[29] Therefore, there were no reliable sources to inform Polo about the truth of the Inca faith. The second cause of Polo's misapprehensions, Valera states, was that he did not know the native lan-

---

28. "Pues las víctimas, las libaciones, el orden de las ceremonias con que seguían todos estos cultos los principales de los Ingas, sería infinito contarlo; lea quien quiera la historia que cuidadosamente escribió de esto el licenciado Polo, varón grave y prudente; verá que sólo dentro del Cuzco había más de trescientas sesenta guacas contadas, a todas las cuales se daban honores divinos; a unas ofrecían frutos de la tierra; a otras, vellones preciosos y oro y plata; y en honor de otras se derramaba en sacrificio mucha sangre de niños inocentes" (Acosta [1577] 1954, 561).

29. "Pero el mayor borrón o falso testimonio que Polo dijo de los piruanos, fue, que ellos usaron sacrificar hombre adultos y niños"; "Hizo Polo esta averiguación ... cuando todos los viejos y historiadores indios se habían ido al monte, por cause de la guerra de Francisco Hernandez Girón" (Blas Valera [1594] 1968, 155). Hernandez Girón rebelled against the Spanish Crown in 1553; Alonso de Alvarado, from Chachapoyas, was placed in charge of the royal forces against him.

guages and had no reliable interpreters. Thus, most of his conclusions were pure fabrication; "one can hardly read in his papers anything that is not full of his conjectures," Valera tells us. Because of his inability to understand Quechua, Valera claims, Polo reversed many things that were told to him by the Indians: "He could not help but write many things that were the reverse of what had happened and of how the Indians had understood it." Moreover, Valera added, Polo had arrived in Peru too late to appreciate how the land had prospered under the Incas. "He arrived very late to the kingdom [of Peru]," Valera continues.[30] Therefore, by the time he reached Peru, many things had changed, and Polo attributed to the Inca elites many things that pertained only to the Andean peasantry.

In the matter of human sacrifice, Valera explained, Polo failed to comprehend the metaphorical nature of Quechua and so misunderstood what he was told. When the ancients spoke of sacrificing "babies" *(huahuas)* and "men" *(runa)*, they were simply referring to animals in human terms, Valera writes. The Inca informants were not, the chronicler insisted, speaking about actual human sacrifice. Likewise, Valera tells us that *aclla* were never sacrificed in the time of the Inca.

> I do not know where Polo could have divined such an interpretation, unless he heard it said that they sacrificed *pasñas* [young maidens] and *ñustas* [princesses] and *acllas* and *huahuas;* but he did not understand the language of the Indians, that the lambs and sheep that were sacrificed in the name of these or other young women were called *pasña, chusña,* and *ñusta* and that those [animals who were sacrificed] in the name of the same *acllas* were also called *acllas....* And he who does not observe the tropes and representations that this language has will always say one thing for another and lead into error everyone who follows him.[31]

---

30. ". . . que apenas se puede leer en sus papeles cosa que no vaya llena destas coniecturas . . . . no pudo dejar de escribir muchas cosas al revés de lo que ello pasaba y de como los indios lo entendían . . . . Nota que Polo lo revolvió todo; que lo que era de los Andes lo aplicó a los ingas, y al revés; porque entonces no tuvo más luz de las antiguedades del Pirú sino las que se le dijeron en confuso; que él no vió nada de esto, pues vino ya muy tarde al reino" (Blas Valera [1594] 1968, 156).

31. "Ni sé a donde pudo Polo adivinar tal interpretación, si no es que oyó decir que se sacrificaban *pasña,* y *ñustas,* y *acllas,* y *huahuas;* mas no entendió el lenguaje de los indios, que a las corderas y ovejas que se sacrificaban en nombre destas o de otras doncellas, se

Garcilaso tells us that Valera expressed the same opinion in his *Historia Occidentalis.*

> Padre Blas Valera, speaking of the antiquities of Peru and of the sacrifices the Incas made to the Sun, recognizing it as their father, says the following words, which I copy literally: "In whose veneration their successors made great sacrifices to the Sun of sheep and other animals, but never of men, as Polo and those who follow him falsely assert." (Garcilaso [1609] 1987, 92)[32]

Whereas Las Casas had tried to justify the Aztecs' and Incas' practice of human sacrifice, Valera argued that the Incas had never sacrificed a human being. In fact, Valera seems to be making an implicit comparison between the Inca idea of sacrifice, in which llamas are given in the place of men, and the Old Testament sacrifice of Abraham, in which a ram is substituted for his son Isaac.[33] Nonetheless, in Valera's view, Polo bore the responsibility for leading other scholars into this serious error concerning the Incas.

Valera clearly objected to Polo's influence over Acosta. It must have been deeply galling to the mestizo scholar that his superior put more faith in the works of a non-Jesuit lawyer than in the advice of one of his own men. Moreover, Acosta's use of Polo's writings extended beyond the scope of Andean religion. Based on Polo's observations, Acosta, in the *Historia natural y moral,* developed a hierarchy of pagan civilizations that placed the Incas near the bottom, lower than the ancient Mexicans, Chinese, Romans, and Greeks. This, of course, would have been anathema to Valera, who boasted of the Incas' superiority, not only to the ancient Mexicans, but to the classical Greeks and Romans as well.

---

llamaban *pasña, chusña,* y *ñusta,* y las que en nombre de las mismas *acllas,* se decían *acllas.* . . . Y quien no repara en los tropos y figuras que tiene esa lengua, dirá siempre una cosa por otra, y hará errar a todos los que le siguieren" (ibid., 173–74).

32. "El Padre Blas Valera, hablando de las antigüedades del Perú y de los sacrificios que los Inca hazían al Sol reconociéndole por padre, dize estas palabras, que son sacadas a la letra: 'En cuya reverencia hazían los successores grandes sacrificios al Sol, de ovejas y de otros animales, y nunca de hombres, como falsamente afirmaron Polo y los que le siguieron'" (Garcilaso [1609] 1944a, 88).

33. I am indebted to Sabine MacCormack (personal communication, 2001) for suggesting the comparison between Valera's description of Inca sacrifice and Abraham's sacrifice of the ram (Genesis 22:1–19).

Given the areas of disagreement between Valera and Acosta, one must ask why Valera never criticized Acosta directly; he places the blame for Acosta's misunderstandings entirely on Polo de Ondegardo. In part, this reticence must have been due to prudence. It probably would not have been wise for Valera to disparage his powerful superior in writing. Yet it is also possible that there was a degree of sympathy between the two men. These two priests, who knew each other personally, shared certain attitudes toward the native Peruvians, and both disagreed with the harsher policies of their Jesuit colleagues in Peru.

Despite Acosta's criticisms of Andean religion, he partook of Valera's deep sense of outrage over the abuses of the native Americans by the Spaniards. In *De Procuranda,* Acosta wrote movingly about the miseries and sufferings endured by the Peruvian Indians at the hands of their European conquerors. According to his text, one of the three primary reasons for the Peruvians' difficulty in accepting Christianity was the violence that accompanied evangelization, and he provides disturbing examples of this.[34] However, his discussion of Spanish atrocities was removed from his text by the order of the Jesuit general Aquaviva and has never been published. Apparently, the general felt that such criticisms of Spanish actions might threaten the reputation of the Society and incur the wrath of the Spanish Crown. In a letter to the provincial of Toledo dated November 8, 1582, Aquaviva instructs the provincial to remove from *De Procuranda* "the chapter that discusses the conquistadors' cruelty and the manner they had."[35] Acosta's distress over the fate of the native peoples was similarly expressed in a letter he wrote to King Philip II of Spain. In this letter, dated March 7, 1577, Acosta describes at length the hardships suffered by the Indians because of new taxes levied against them. He concludes by requesting that the Crown send a special visitor to "undo the abuses" endured by the indigenous communities.[36] However, the general of the Society at the time, Everardo Mercurian, reacted very negatively to Acosta's efforts to ameliorate the sufferings

---

34. For Acosta's original manuscript of *De Procuranda Indorum Salute,* see Lopétegui (1942).

35. ". . . el capítulo se dize de la crueldad y por el modo que tuvieron los conquistadors." The original text of this letter is published in Egaña 1961, 195–96.

36. A copy of this letter can be found in Egaña 1958, 299–302.

of the natives. In a strongly worded letter, Mercurian ordered the Jesuits in Peru to refrain from any criticism whatsoever of Spanish colonial policy in the Indies and to avoid giving the Spanish Crown any reason for becoming angered with the Society.[37] Concern over the hardships of the native people would have been a potential point of sympathy between Acosta and Valera.

Likewise, Acosta shared Valera's anger over missionaries who were more concerned with making a profit in the *doctrinas* than with saving souls. Acosta strongly condemns those missionaries who, by their corruption, impede the spread of the gospel. In an unpublished memorial from 1583, Acosta discusses at length how the abuses of the Catholic priests in native *doctrinas* impede evangelization. In this text, one of his primary complaints is directed against *doctrina* priests who use Indian labor in their fields: "the Indians receive a notable scandal and bad example because they determine that the law of Christ is nothing more than greed and that the priests are in the *doctrinas* for no other reason than to become rich from the labor and lands of the Indians."[38] In the original text of *De Procuranda,* he argues that the exploitation of the native people by Christian missionaries is one of the most important causes of the Indians' rejection of Christianity (Lopétequi 1942). The natives cannot be brought to the faith, he wrote, by those priests who were misusing them. In particular, he criticizes the *encomienda* system, in which, he argues, priests virtually become employees of the wealthy *encomenderos*. In such a system, he wrote, the priest is unable to protect the native people from abusive and unscrupulous *encomenderos,* and evangelization suffers. However, his analysis of the impact of corrupt missionaries was also expunged from the printed version of *De Procuranda,* again by order of Aquaviva. Only his most general comments on the need for morally upright evangelists were allowed to remain in the work.

The general's censorship of *De Procuranda* resulted in a transformation, or shifting in emphasis, of Acosta's arguments about why the Andean peoples have been hesitant to embrace Christianity. In his original text, Acosta posits three reasons for the natives' indifference

---

37. General Mercurian's letter to Provincial Acosta is published in Egaña 1958, 477–78.

38. ". . . los indios resciben notable escandalo y mal exemplo porque juzgan que la ley de Cristo no es mas de cobdicia, y que los sacerdotes por ninguna otra cosa doctrinan sino por hazerse ricos con trabajos y hazienda de indios" (Pius XII Library 1583, 759).

to the gospel: (1) the violence of the Spanish conquistadors, with whom the Indians associate Christianity; (2) the immorality of many Spanish missionaries; and (3) the tenacity of the Andeans' "corrupt" customs. By eliminating many of the passages that blamed the European soldiers and priests for the native unwillingness to accept Christianity, the censored version of *De Procuranda* places undue emphasis on the role of Andean culture in hindering the faith. Acosta's original analysis of impediments to Christianity in the Andes were much more in harmony with Valera's beliefs than has been apparent. Because of censorship, Acosta's strident denunciations of Spanish activities in Peru were never printed and, except for a very brief mention by Lopétegui (1942, 219–20), have been little known.

Likewise, Acosta's leadership during the Third Lima Council of Bishops suggests a difference of opinion over native matters with his fellow Jesuits in Peru. As Archbishop Mogrovejo's primary theological advisor, Acosta was intimately linked to the policies of the council (Lopétegui 1942, 489–512).[39] Kenneth Mills has skillfully demonstrated that the policies followed by Mogrovejo in this council were not universally agreed on by members of the Peruvian church. According to Mills (1997, 20–24), there existed in Peru since the time of Pizarro two competing modes of converting the Indians: a "patient and gradualist tradition" and a more systematically coercive approach. Mogrovejo represented the slower and more persuasive tradition. In his extensive travels throughout the most remote regions of Peru, Mogrovejo responded optimistically to the Andeans as potential Christians. He was pleased with what he saw of Andean Christianity, and he felt that the natives needed only better instruction with adequate clergy to receive the fullness of the faith. The policies of the Third Lima Council, which Acosta helped to draft, reflected his positive, gradualist approach.

However, as Mills indicates (1997, 20), Mogrovejo was only holding back "the more aggressive undercurrents favored by some churchmen in their relations with non-Christians." St. Toribio's episcopate

---

39. Mogrovego acknowledged Acosta's assistance and friendship during the council in a letter to Aquaviva, in which he wrote: ". . . Padre José de Acosta, persona de muchas letras y christianidad y de gran reputación en estas partes, con cuia doctrina y sermones están todos mui edificados y le tienen en lugar de padre. Yo en particular le tengo mucha afición. . . ." A transcription of this letter can be found in Egaña 1961, 416–17.

was followed by a series of harsh episcopal campaigns to extirpate idolatry from Peru. Among the most vocal supporters of the extirpation campaigns were some of Acosta's former subordinates, now raised to positions of dominance within the Society in Peru. Such Jesuits as Juan de Atienza, Juan Sebastián, Luís de Teruel, and Diego Alvarez de Paz, who had held powerful, if subordinate, positions during Acosta's provincialate, became leaders in the struggle to eradicate idolatry from the highlands. Imprisonment, fines, and public floggings against suspected Indian idolaters were commonplace in the campaigns against idolatry (see Griffiths 1996). Such campaigns were counter to the spirit of Mogrovejo's councils; in fact, the Jesuit José de Arriaga, a leading extirpator, delicately criticized the archbishop for not perceiving the secret idolatry that filled the hearts of the baptized natives (Arriaga [1621] 1968, 73–74; Mills 1997, 24). It is known that Atienza, who was Acosta's assistant during the Third Lima Council, chafed under his superior's supervision. In a letter to Aquaviva, Atienza criticized Acosta for being overly domineering and not in agreement with the other Jesuit leaders in Peru.[40] A comparison of the conciliar policies endorsed by Mogrovejo, to whom Acosta was a principal advisor, with the extirpation campaigns promoted by the later Jesuit leadership suggests a difference of opinion between Acosta and the other Jesuits over relations with the native Andeans.

This suggestion of an ideological division between Acosta and his confreres is furthered by an examination of Acosta's role in the controversy over mestizo priests. The question of whether mestizos should be ordained as Catholic priests was a highly contentious issue in Peru (Hyland 1998a, 1994). On December 14, 1582, the Jesuit fathers in Peru voted unanimously—"nemine discrepante"—to forbid all mestizos from entering the Society. According to their decision, they agreed to "close the door to mestizos . . . because experience has shown at length that this class of people does not prove worthy."[41] Acosta took part in this vote against mestizos. As I discussed in chapter 2, Acosta explained the concern over mestizo priests in *De Procuranda*. According to Acosta, the Jesuits in Peru had become increas-

---

40. This letter is published in Egaña 1961, 255–56.

41. ". . . cerrar la puerta a mestizos . . . porque la experiencia ha mostrado a la larga no probar bien este género de gente." The legislation of this provincial council was published in Egaña 1961, 205–6.

ingly apprehensive over the religious orthodoxy of mestizo priests. It was believed that the mestizos were too enmeshed in the "immorality" and "idolatry" of their Indian mothers to be trusted as Christian priests. Acosta, writing after a 1576 Jesuit decision greatly restricting the entrance of mestizos into the Society, cites Scripture along with actual experience to argue against the ordination of mestizos. As he wrote, "Experience has shown that most of these [mestizos] impede [evangelization] more with their corrupt customs than [they] aid it with their skilled tongues."[42]

Yet while Acosta voted with his fellow Jesuits in 1582 to exclude mestizos from the Society, he was simultaneously working to persuade both the archbishop and the viceroy to create a mestizo secular clergy to serve in native *doctrinas*. On August 5, 1583, Acosta provided four pages of testimony in a petition to Mogrovejo, arguing that mestizos must be granted the sacrament of ordination (Acosta 1953). The Crown had recently prohibited the ordination of mestizos, and the archbishop was going to determine the Peruvian church's policy on this issue at the Third Lima Council. In Acosta's prepared testimony, he stated that he personally knew many mestizo priests— including Blas Valera, whom he mentioned by name—who were exemplary Christians and missionaries. He emphasized the mestizos' crucial role in evangelization; because of the mestizos' linguistic skills and their familiarity with native culture, he wrote, they were ideal missionaries to the native Peruvians. Acosta also described his efforts to persuade Viceroy Don Martín Enríquez de Almansa and other notables of the necessity of granting holy orders to mestizos.

The arguments of Acosta and the others involved in this issue bore fruit. During the Third Lima Council, the archbishop convened a committee of sympathetic bishops who found in favor of mestizo ordination. Despite royal decrees barring mestizos from the priesthood, the actions of this council permitted mestizos to be ordained in Peru, but only to serve in *doctrinas*. The ordination of mestizos then became a common custom throughout the Andes, one that would continue to be controversial, however. Acosta was opposed in the Third Lima Council by one of his fellow Jesuits, the theologian Esteban de Avila, who campaigned ardently against the policy of ordain-

---

42. "La experiencia ha mostrado que la mayor parte de éstos impiden más con sus corrompidas costumbres que no aprovechan con su buena palabra" (Acosta [1577] 1954, 518).

ing mestizos. In his efforts, Avila apparently was supported by his friend Atienza, who would later show great resistance against accepting into the Society anyone born in Peru.[43] However, Avila and Atienza were not able to prevail against Acosta and the archbishop in this matter. It is worth noting that the colonial Mexican church never developed the custom of ordaining mestizos as the Peruvian church did. Lacking a powerful spokesman like Acosta, mestizos in colonial Mexico were consistently denied the priesthood.[44]

Acosta's actions in the controversy over mestizo ordination reveal a degree of ambivalence in his activities. While he refused to vote against his confreres on the question of mestizos in the Society, he worked against their policies in the Third Lima Council. This seeming contradiction deepens as one examines his petition to the archbishop on mestizo ordination. In August 1583, when Acosta presented his petition, Valera had been imprisoned in Lima for several months, accused of a secret crime so heinous that the Jesuits said it could not be described in writing; the details of Valera's delict had to be communicated only verbally to the general. Yet in his petition, Acosta singles out Valera for praise.

> In the general catechism that was made for the Indians, by order of the provincial council, . . . some of the aforesaid mestizo priests have helped a great deal; and with their diligence and work, they have made very good translations in the languages of Cuzco and Aymara; and of these were two from the Society of Jesus, Father Blas Valera and Bartolomé de Santiago.[45]

---

43. The friendship between the two men is evident in a letter of April 23, 1584, from Esteban de Avila to Aquaviva, in which Avila has the most fulsome praise for Atienza and his reforms of the Society in Peru; this letter is printed in Egaña 1961, 410. Atienza's hostility toward creoles and mestizos is apparent in many of his letters to the general. See, for example, Atienza's letters to Aquaviva of April 8 and 22, 1584, in which Atienza complains about the corrupt nature of those born in Peru (ibid., 385–99, 405–8).

44. In addition to benefiting from Acosta's powerful advocacy, the mestizos in Peru enjoyed the support of the Mercedarian order, which accepted many men of Indian descent. The Peruvian Mercedarians played a key role in establishing the Peruvian custom of ordaining mestizos to serve in Indian *doctrinas*. See Hyland 1998a.

45. "... en el catecismo general que por mandado del Concilio provincial ... se a fecho para los indios, algunos de los dichos mestizos sacerdotes an ayudado muy bien e con su diligencia y trabajo se an hecho muy buenas traduciones en las lenguas del Cuzco e aimara, y dellos son dos de la Compañía de Jesús, que son el Padre Blas Balera y Bartolomé de Santiago" (testimony on mestizo ordination, 1583, published in Barriga 1953, 279–80).

Several years later, in Italy, Acosta would attempt to ameliorate Valera's difficult situation in Peru by recommending his removal to Spain. Apparently, Acosta thought well of Valera at a time when the mestizo priest was suffering imprisonment and censorship at the hands of his fellow Jesuits.

Acosta was a complex and difficult thinker, subject to bouts of depression and anger. The relationship between Acosta and Valera is not simple to ascertain. The two men disagreed vehemently on many issues yet were in perfect accord on others. Both priests were subjected to the censorship of their ideas by their superiors within the Society. Examining the role of Acosta in Peru helps to demonstrate the divisions among the Jesuits there. Acosta seems to have been a relatively moderate figure, balancing such radicals as Valera against individuals—such as Atienza and Sebastián—who were hostile to mestizos and in favor of aggressive actions to eradicate idolatry. Eventually, Acosta, plagued by a profound melancholy, asked to leave Peru. He sailed from the port of Callao in 1586, arriving in Spain in 1587. Many of his later years would be devoted to fighting a losing battle against General Aquaviva and "foreign" (i.e., non-Spanish) control of the Society. In these struggles within the Society, he would again reveal two faces. During the Fifth General Congregation of the Jesuits in 1594, he submitted obediently to the will of his brothers yet wrote passionate and angry letters expressing the ideas of the rebellious anti-Spanish Jesuit writer Juan de Mariana (Mateos 1954, xxviii).

Acosta was also one of the few Jesuits familiar with the entire history of Valera's "crime" and imprisonment. The story of Valera's fall from grace, the subsequent Jesuit attempts to conceal his misdeeds, and the rumors that would surround Valera for many decades after his death are explored in chapter 8.

CHAPTER EIGHT

A Danger to Peru

When the Jesuits in Peru voted on December 14, 1582, to refrain from accepting more mestizos, Valera was still officially in good standing. The provincial catalog compiled in early January 1583 makes no criticism of Father Valera.

> Father Blas Valera—from Chachapoyas in Peru—thirty-two years old—good health—fifteen years in the Society—Latin and Humanities—preacher to and confessor of Indians—professed of three vows.[1]

Valera apparently had returned to Potosí by January, where he had been appointed to a professorship of grammar over the objections of the Jesuit college rector, Father Juan Sebastián. On February 12, Atienza wrote to Aquaviva, complaining bitterly against Valera's selection for this post, specifying that he had been selected without

---

1. "El Padre Blas Valera—de Chachapoyas en el Pirú—de treinta y dos años—buenas fuercas—quinze años de Compañía—latinidad y Artes—predicador y confessor de indios—professo de tres votos" (Egaña 1961, 225). Among the Jesuits, it is a great honor to be asked to take a fourth vow of obedience to the Holy See. Only those who have taken a fourth vow cannot be forcibly removed from the Society.

consulting the Jesuit leadership in the province.[2] It is not clear what events occurred in Potosí during the following month; however, it is certain that by April, Valera was incarcerated in an underground prison cell located in the Jesuit house in Lima, charged with a mysterious crime of a highly serious nature. When the Jesuit procurator for the Peruvian province, Father Andrés López, left for Europe on April 11, 1583, part of his mission was to explain to General Aquaviva in Rome the nature of Valera's crime and whether the chronicler ought to be dismissed from the Society. This information had to be communicated personally, it was stated, because the Valera affair was considered too sensitive to commit to paper.[3] Juan Sebastián later wrote to Aquaviva that the case of "Blas Valera, mestizo, that is, son of a Spaniard and an Indian" had been a cause of "notable pain" in the Potosí college. The rector added that Valera's crime (which he never specifies) demonstrated that "[i]t is important for our Society in these parts to receive very few creoles and to have the door completely closed to accepting any mestizos ever."[4] It is worth noting, however, that none of the other mestizos in the Society in Peru at this time were charged with any crimes.[5]

---

2. The letter of February 12, 1583, from Atienza to Aquaviva is reproduced in Egaña 1961, 252–55.

3. The letter from Father Juan de Atienza to General Aquaviva describing López's commission to discuss Valera is reproduced in Egaña 1961, 675. It was common for institutions and individuals in the Spanish colonial world to be concerned over the possibility of their written words falling into the wrong hands. Many of the Spanish state papers, for example, were written in code so that foreign governments could not have easy access to these documents. The Jesuits occasionally used ciphers in their communications between Peru and Rome. However, as this instance reveals, the Jesuits also relied on personal communication to limit the possibility that their enemies might acquire sensitive information about the Society. Maurizio Gnerre (2001, 199) has suggested that documents about Valera in the Archivum Romanum Societatis Iesu (ARSI) may have been destroyed in 1617, when General Vitelleschi personally searched the archives and destroyed any documents deemed unedifying.

4. "Al presente no se offresce más de que el estado deste collegio a sido . . . sin aver avido cosa en él que aya dado notable pena, sacados dos, de las quales la una que fue de un Padre professo de tres votos, llamado Blas Valera, mestico, ques hijo despañol y india. . . . Impórtale a nuestra Compañía en estas partes en recebir criolla ser muy limitada, y tener la puerta del todo cerrado para no recebir jamás mestico ninguno" (letter from Juan Sebastián to Aquaviva, February 6, 1585, printed in Egaña 1961, 547–50).

5. See Hyland 1994, 88–119. The other seven mestizos accepted by the Jesuits in Peru in the sixteenth century were (in the order of joining the Society) Gonzalo Ruiz, Juan Rodriguez, Juan de Añasco, Pedro de Añasco, Alonso Camacho, Bartolomé de Santiago,

The concern over secrecy about Valera's crime reflects the insecurity experienced by the Jesuits during a period in the order's early history when the Spanish Crown and the Spanish Inquisition came close to destroying the fledgling order. Throughout the latter part of the sixteenth century, Philip II of Spain worked fervently to bring the Spanish Jesuits under his personal supervision for the stated goal of enforcing religious and political orthodoxy.[6] Although Philip was ultimately unable to assert his authority over the Society, the Jesuit generals Everardo Mercurian and Claudio Aquaviva were forced to use extreme care not to give the Spanish Crown an excuse for subsuming the Jesuits under Spanish control. Likewise, the Spanish Inquisition resented the newly founded Society and periodically tried to suppress it. For example, in the 1580s, the inquisitors in Valladolid imprisoned the leading Jesuit theologian Father Marcenius on trumped-up charges of heresy and attempted to use these charges as an excuse for driving the Jesuits out of Spain (Caurson 1879, 159–60). The inquisitors' efforts failed, but they illustrate the pressures faced by the Jesuits in Peru. The members of the Society were strongly discouraged from any theological or political discussions that suggested heresy or criticism of the Spanish Crown. General Mercurian's repeated orders that the Peruvian Jesuits refrain from any activities—such as criticisms of colonial policies—that would provide the Crown with a reason to remove the Jesuits from its South American missions demonstrate the Society's sense of vulnerability to outside pressures.[7]

Although the crimes of other Peruvian Jesuits of this period—such as Father Miguel de Fuentes and Father Luis López, both of whom were convicted by the Inquisition of fornication—were discussed in

---

and Domingo de Vermeo. All were accepted during the tenure of the first provincial in Peru, Jerónimo de Ruiz de Portillo. Two of these mestizo Jesuits left the Society while novices (Juan Rodriguez and Juan de Añasco), two remained as lay brothers (Ruiz and Vermeo), one died before taking holy orders (Camacho), and two became renowned missionaries (Santiago and Pedro de Añasco).

6. Philip II was initially suspicious of the Jesuits, in part because of the prominence of Italians within the Society. Influenced by English Jesuits who had taken refuge at the Spanish court, he eventually looked more kindly on the Society; nonetheless, he attempted to have the Society placed under direct Spanish governmental supervision. See Lopétegui 1942 and Schneider 1967.

7. Mercurian's instructions to this effect can be seen in his letter of October 1, 1578, to Provincial Acosta, reproduced in Egaña 1958, 477–78. Similar instructions are found in Mercurian's next letter to Acosta, dated November 15, 1578 (ibid., 565).

Jesuit letters to Rome, Valera's delict is never openly described in writing. General Aquaviva eventually would instruct the Peruvian Jesuits,

> if it is judged appropriate to dismiss Father Blas Valera, take as the reason that which he did with the woman and dismiss him; and if not, then keep him [in prison], etc.[8]

The unusual wording of this order suggests that Valera's alleged activities with a woman were not the real reason for his incarceration yet were to be given as the ostensible cause for his punishment. Valera himself claimed that he was completely innocent of any wrongdoing. Father Hernando Morillo, whom Valera met in Quito in 1594 when he was on his voyage to Spain, reported that Valera "denies everything."[9]

Rubén Vargas Ugarte, modern historian of the Jesuits in Peru, has stated unequivocally that Valera was a victim of the Inquisition, imprisoned for fornication with a woman (Vargas Ugarte 1963–65, 1:251). However, one of the "Naples documents," the seventeenth-century manuscript allegedly written by the Jesuits Joan Antonio Cumis and Giovanni Anello Oliva, tells a different story of Valera's crime. Cumis and Oliva both assert that Valera had been imprisoned by the Jesuits for his writings on Inca religion—not by the Inquisition for fornication, as the Jesuits had falsely claimed (Laurencich Minelli, Miccinelli, and Animato 1995). Their allegations are supported by documents from the archives of the Spanish Inquisition in the Archivo Histórico Nacional in Madrid. According to manuscript sources in the archive, Valera was convicted not by the Inquisition but by his own religious order, for his potentially heretical teachings. Moreover, direct testimony in the Inquisition archives indicates that the Jesuit superiors lied about their role in his conviction, stating untruthfully that his harsh punishment was by order of the Holy Office.[10]

---

8. ". . . si se juzga que conviene despedir al Padre Blas Valera, tome por ocasión lo que hizo con la muger y le despida; y si no, que le tenga etc." (letter from Aquaviva to Father Juan de Atienza, June 1584, published in Egaña 1961, 251). Aquaviva wrote similar instructions several years later, in a letter to Atienza dated March 23, 1587 (Egaña 1966a, 188–89).

9. ". . . traté este Padre [Valera] en Quito y niega todo" (letter from Father Hernando Morillo to General Aquaviva, December 31, 1594, published in Egaña 1970, 646).

10. See appendix B, "Testimony of Father Lucio Garcete, S.J., to the Inquisitors of Panama City, August 11, 1591," and the references cited throughout this chapter. For an excellent study of the Peruvian Inquisition, see Hampe Martínez 1998.

According to unpublished Inquisition documents, the Jesuit house in Lima rented out prison cells to the Inquisition during the late 1500s. This custom first arose when the Peruvian inquisitors asked the Lima Jesuits to house some captured English pirates—Joan Oxnem, Joan Butler, Enrique Butler, and Thomas Xeroel—who were to be tried by the Inquisition for heresy before being handed over to the secular courts on charges of piracy. The inquisitors requested this arrangement out of the belief that among the Peruvian Jesuits, there would be some who spoke English and could translate for the pirates.[11] Over time, the use of Jesuit facilities by the Inquisition seems to have become customary due to a shortage of cells in the Inquisition prison. Thus, the Jesuit superiors would have been able to maintain plausibly that any prisoner in their house, such as Valera, was a charge of the Holy Office; only the inquisitors and the Jesuit superiors would have known the true reasons for any prisoner's incarceration.

A comparison of Valera's case with that of two Jesuits who were convicted of fornication by the Inquisition reveals striking differences, both in the manner in which the cases were handled and in the severity of the punishments. In the early 1580s, both Miguel de Fuentes and Luis López ran afoul of the Lima inquisitors on charges of seducing young women. According to case reports in the Inquisition archives, Fuentes was found guilty of seducing most of the younger nuns of the Convent of La Concepción in Lima, along with a group of young laywomen. The women who testified against him reported that he told them that if they practiced certain austerities, such as shaving their head, they would commit no sin by allowing him to kiss them, to fondle their breasts, or to have sex with them. For his crimes, the Holy Office in Lima sentenced him to be reprimanded in front of his superiors in the Jesuit house in Lima and to not hear confessions from women for ten years (AHN n.d.b; 1580–81b; 1581–82a). However, Fuentes was able to continue to serve as a priest (except for hearing women's confessions) within the Society in Peru and served in the Jesuit house in Juli after his conviction.

Luis López was convicted of the rape of several young women in Lima, including a brutal assault on Doña María Pizarro. In the case

---

11. See AHN 1580a. In 1595, the Jesuits obliged the Inquisition by housing the captured English pirate Richard Hawkins and his crew. See AHN 1595.

of the latter, he had been asked by Doña María's parents to investigate some visions that the teenage girl claimed to have experienced. During his conversation with her in her bedroom, he savagely raped her, causing severe bleeding and a variety of injuries. This violent act seems to have precipitated her descent into madness. After López had been brought before the Inquisition on rape charges, the inquisitors searched López's room, where they found papers containing criticisms of Viceroy Toledo. However, in all of López's writings, the only statement judged objectionable by the inquisitors was the following: "God wanted our first pontiff St. Peter to be first tempted and to fall into temptation."[12] The inquisitors judged this proposition, perhaps intended as a self-justification for López's own lapses, as "heretical blasphemy." For his crimes of rape and his one expression of heresy, the Lima tribunal sentenced López to a slightly harsher punishment than that received by Fuentes. He was ordered to return immediately to Spain, where he was to endure two years of house arrest in a Jesuit house and could never again confess women.[13] Neither he nor Fuentes were removed from the Society, and both were able to continue as priests, with the stipulation that they could not confess women. Nothing was added to their sentences by the Society; the Jesuit superiors clearly believed that the priests' relatively mild sentences were appropriate for their crimes.

The cases against Fuentes and López lasted for several years and appear repeatedly in the Inquisition archives. Valera, by contrast, is never once mentioned as a suspect in the detailed reports prepared by the Peruvian inquisitors; there is no evidence whatsoever to lend credence to the supposition that he was convicted by the Inquisition. Furthermore, in the spring of 1583, when Valera was first imprisoned, a flotilla arrived from Spain bearing authorization from the Roman Curia for the Jesuits in Peru to deal with cases of heresy without recourse to the Inquisition (Yale 1508–1634, fol. 3b). Prior to receiving

---

12. "Quiso Dios que nro primer póntifice san pedro fuesse primero tentado y caydo en la tentación. En la propiedad de las palabras, es blasfemia heretical."

13. AHN; 1580–81a; 1581–82a. While López was being tried for his crimes by the Inquisition tribunal, he shared a prison cell in the Jesuit house with the pirate Enrique Butler, a young boy who was mentally retarded. The Inquisition absolved Enrique of any culpability for his piracy or his heresy, but despite the inquisitors' protests, he was sentenced by the secular courts to life on a galley ship.

this privilege, the Jesuits legally had to turn over to the Holy Office anyone, priest or layperson, whom they suspected of heresy. This privilege applied only to instances of suspected heresy, not to cases of fornication or adultery. It is a significant coincidence that Valera was imprisoned just when the Jesuits received the privilege to handle cases of heresy on their own.

Valera's punishment, which was decided on by General Aquaviva and the Peruvian provincial, not by the inquisitors, was very severe for his alleged crime of fornication, in contrast to the sentences of Fuentes and López.[14] Sentenced to spend four years in a prison cell in the Jesuit house in Lima, he was forced to fast, pray, and practice weekly "mortifications," which consisted of floggings under the supervision of the provincial. Valera's health appears to have broken down during his difficult incarceration: prior to his imprisonment, the Jesuit reports about him stress his hardiness and good health; while in prison and for the rest of his life, however, he was constantly plagued by illness. After the first four years of incarceration in an underground cell, Valera was offered the opportunity to leave the Jesuits and join another religious order. Maintaining his innocence, he refused to leave the Society and, according to the terms of his initial sentence, was put under house arrest in Lima for six years, from 1587 to 1593. During this time, he was not allowed to perform any of the sacramental functions of a priest, talk to outsiders, or leave the house for any reason. He was also required to perform only "low offices" in the house, such as cleaning and tending to the sick and elderly priests. He was, however, permitted to attend mass and take communion in the house chapel.

While Valera was in prison, we know that he wrote at least two letters to General Aquaviva, dated April 20, 1585, and May 3, 1586, requesting to be transferred to Rome for health reasons. Although Valera's letters have been not been found, Aquaviva refers to them in a letter of March 3, 1587, to Provincial Atienza. In this communication, Aquaviva imparts that Valera has written asking to be moved to Rome because the climate in Lima has proven damaging to his health. The general adds that Acosta, who was currently in Rome, had told

---

14. The letter by Aquaviva outlining Valera's punishment is printed in Egaña 1966a, 302–3.

him that Valera had not only performed his penance well but had practiced additional mortifications of his own free will.[15] Even after he was released from prison, during his period of house arrest, Valera continued to practice weekly fasts and other disciplines and to recite daily the seven penitential psalms. Later that same month, on March 23, Aquaviva wrote a brief letter to Valera.

> I have received [the letter] of Your Reverence of May 3 of 86, and earlier another of those of April 20 of the year 85, and because for such a long journey as that to Rome from Peru . . . it is appropriate that there is a cause or a need so urgent, and because Your Reverence does not write this, nor do I know [a reason so urgent], it seems to me that you can with total confidence communicate your [desires] of making such a journey, or of the transfer that you ask from that province, with the father provincial, to whom I will write to listen to you and to console [you] in that which he judges to be suitable for the service of God and the good of your soul.[16]

At this point, therefore, it had not been decided whether Valera would actually be transferred to Europe as he wished. However, Acosta continued to press the general in Rome to allow Valera to move to Europe, and by the following year, Aquaviva granted his permission. In a letter to Provincial Atienza dated October 31, 1588, the general wrote,

> From Father Joseph de Acosta we have understood that Father Blas Valera will not be well in that province because of the danger of doing harm to others and of receiving harm himself and for other considerations.[17]

---

15. Letter from Aquaviva to Atienza, March 3, 1587, printed in Egaña 1966a, 188–89.

16. "He recevido la de V. R. de 3 de Mayo del 86, y antes otra de los de 20 de Abril del año 85, y porque para tan larga jornada como es la de Roma desde el Perú, y en que tanto se suele mirar que venga desde tan lejos, conviene que aya causa o precisa tan urgente, y porque ésta ni V. R. la escrivía ni yo la sé, me parece que podría con toda seguridad comunicar la que tuviere de hazer tal jornada, o de la mudanza que pide de esa Provincia, con el Padre Provincial, al que le escrivo que le oiga y consuele en lo que juzgare convenir al servicio divino y bien de su alma" (Egaña 1966a, 189).

17. "Del Padre Joseph de Acosta hemos entendido que el Padre Blas Valera no estaría bien en esa Provincia por el peligro que ay de hazer daño a otros y de recibirlo en sí mismo y por otros respetos" (ibid., 432–23).

Note the unusual wording, that Valera might do harm to others and likewise be harmed himself; none of the Jesuits convicted of fornication were spoken of in this manner. Aquaviva continued his letter by stating that it would be best if Valera would simply leave the Jesuits to join a mendicant order in Peru. Nonetheless, the general had decided to follow Acosta's advice and ordered that Valera should be sent to Andalusia with a "good and safe companion" when his sentence was complete.

In 1593, Valera was transferred to Quito with the intention that he would sail to Spain the following year.[18] However, in Quito, he fell very ill, and his journey was delayed until 1595. In May 1596, Valera finally arrived in Spain, where he was sent to Cádiz and placed under the care of Father Cristóbal Méndez, the provincial of Andalusia, who was ordered to keep him locked up until further notice. However, on June 3, 1596, Méndez wrote to Aquaviva that Valera had made a good impression on the Jesuits in Cádiz.[19] The Andalusian provincial had permitted Valera to teach in the Jesuit grade school of that city, and he requested of the general that Valera be allowed to resume his duties as a priest. Aquaviva's reply was adamantly negative, emphasizing that although Valera could teach other subjects, by no means was he ever to be allowed to teach grammar. By "grammar," Aquaviva was referring to teaching Quechua; Valera was providing free Quechua classes to the public at the time of his incarceration (see chap. 3). Since Fathers Fuentes and López had been restricted from confessing women, one may gain insight into the nature of Valera's crime from the nature of his punishment.

The suggestion that Valera was imprisoned not by the Inquisition for fornication but by the Jesuits themselves for his teachings on grammar and religion is supported by the testimony of Father Lucio Garcete, an Italian Jesuit living in the Indies. On August 11, 1591, Garcete testified about Valera's case before the Inquisition tribunal in Panama City. In his deposition before the Holy Office, Garcete stated that he had taught theology for five years in the Jesuit house in Lima and had recently been made superior of the Jesuit house in Panama

---

18. Valera's departure is mentioned in a letter of December 1594 from Father Hernando Morillo to Aquaviva, printed in Egaña 1970, 646.

19. The letter from Méndez to Aquaviva is printed in Egaña 1974, 168–69.

City. During his time in Peru, he wrote, he had become concerned about the actions of the Peruvian superiors, citing what he called "the very harsh and long imprisonment" [estrechissima y larga prission] of Blas Valera as an example of the Peruvian Jesuits' questionable activities. Garcete emphasized his superiors' fears of the Spanish Inquisition, mentioning Atienza and Cabello by name, and stated that these fears increased during the Inquisition's imprisonment of Father Marcenius in Valladolid and the subsequent attempt to drive the Jesuits out of Spain. One can certainly imagine the Jesuits' concern over this; had the inquisitors been successful in using Marcenius's alleged heresy to remove the Jesuits from Spain, the Jesuits would have had to abandon their Peruvian missions as well. In discussing his superiors' abuse of the privilege to deal with cases of heresy without consulting the Inquisition, Garcete mentioned that the Jesuits claimed that Valera was a prisoner of the Holy Office. This, he believed, was simply not true. Moreover, he implied that Valera's incarceration was carried out according to this privilege, which was relevant only for cases of heresy, not for cases of fornication (AHN 1591).[20]

Garcete's testimony against Atienza and Cabello before the Holy Office in Panama City was never investigated further by the tribunal, which suffered from a serious shortage of manpower.[21] Soon after giving his deposition in Panama, Garcete was recalled to Italy. According to a letter sent from Padre Juan Ordoñez in Seville to Aquaviva, Garcete had threatened to go to the Inquisition tribunal with reports of Jesuit misdoings in Peru. Therefore, Ordoñez wrote, it was judged safer to send him as soon as possible to Italy, where his threats could do little damage. In 1593, he arrived in Cádiz, from where he booked a passage to Italy (Egaña 1966a, 30–32). In Italy, he was sent to the Jesuit house in Naples, where he would have met Gio-

---

20. According to Garcete, Valera served only three years of his four-year prison term before beginning his sentence of house arrest. The full text of Garcete's testimony is presented in appendix B.

21. Many of the accusations received by the Inquisition tribunals in the Americas were never investigated. See, for example, the inquisitor's statement in AHN 1571–73 that many of the cases reported to the tribunal in those years were not investigated due to limitations of time and resources. The situation had not improved by 1590, according to a letter written in Lima by Don Antonio de Arpide y Ulloa (AHN 1590), which states that the Holy Office's caseload was severely backed up and that cases were being improperly dismissed, because of the lack of assistants to aid the inquisitors.

vanni Anello Oliva, who was a novice there at the time. It is quite likely that Garcete told Anello Oliva about Valera's troubles with the Peruvian Jesuits over his writings about Inca religion; when Anello Oliva left for Peru in 1597, he apparently took with him the tale of Valera's disgrace and imprisonment.

It is interesting that Garcete singles out Atienza, who was the provincial, and Cabello, his principal advisor, for notice in this matter. Atienza, a supporter of those Jesuits—such as Juan Sebastián—who advocated harsh measure to stamp out idolatry in the highlands, had written repeated complaints to Aquaviva about the "laxity" and corruption of both creoles and mestizos born in Peru. Given his views on mestizos and on native religion, it would not be surprising for him to have objected strongly to Valera's writings; he certainly had expressed anger over Valera's appointment to the professorship in grammar at Potosí (Egaña 1961, 252–55). Father Esteban Cabello was Atienza's confessor, secretary, and trusted advisor. In his letters to Aquaviva, Cabello wrote that he had felt great "repugnance" at the laxity and freedom he first found among the Jesuits in Peru; with the provincialate of Atienza, however, he believed that discipline and rigor were returning to Jesuit life in Peru, especially because Atienza had forced many "unworthy" members to leave the Society.[22] Not only were Valera's ideas on native religion and evangelization contrary to the policies of his superiors, including Atienza and his successor as provincial, Juan Sebastián, but Valera's teachings about Viracocha as Christ were heretical. Given the climate of fear described by Garcete among certain Peruvian Jesuits in the 1580s, one would expect Valera to have been perceived as a threat, as he indeed was.

For Valera, however, the question of being allowed to teach grammar in Cádiz soon became moot. During the latter half of 1596, the English pirate Robert Devereux, earl of Essex, sacked the city of Cádiz, and his men roamed the city, savagely beating any priests they found.[23] Valera, whose health was already weak, was badly injured in

---

22. See Cabello's letter of January 15, 1585, to Aquaviva (printed in Egaña 1961, 504–5) and Aquaviva's letter of February 24, 1587, to Cabello (printed in Egaña 1966a, 170).

23. Two of the men most responsible for Valera's death, Robert Devereux, who led the assault on Cádiz, and Sir Walter Raleigh, who was active in the attack, would themselves be executed by the English Crown years after Valera's demise.

the brutal attack and was removed to Málaga, where he died on April 2 of the following year. The modern scholar José Durand found Valera listed among those who died in the College of Málaga in 1597, according to handwritten necrology in the archives of the Jesuit province of Toledo. Valera was fifty-three years old at the time of his death, an exile far from the homeland to which he had devoted his tumultuous and difficult life.[24]

---

24. Valera's last days are described in Durand 1987. According to Durand, "En un necrologio manuscrito . . . existente en el Archivo de la provincia jesuita de Toledo, aparece Blas Valera, del colegio de Málaga, entre los muertos en ese año [1597]" (410).

CHAPTER NINE

The "Naples Documents"

Valera's story should have ended with his tragic death in Spain in 1597. A great scholar and a passionate advocate for the rights of native peoples, Valera was killed by English buccaneers after years of ignominious imprisonment. Claiming falsely that he was jailed by the Inquisition for fornication, then exiling him to Spain, his superiors clearly were trying to suppress his unorthodox religious ideas, beliefs that he shared with his Indian followers, such as the members of the Nombre de Jesús confraternity, who marched through the streets of Cuzco on his behalf in 1576. Yet Valera's story is of the kind that lingers on in religious communities. Father Lucio Garcete reported on Valera's case to the Inquisition in Panama (see app. B) and probably recounted it again when he returned to the Jesuit house in Naples, where a young Giovanni Anello Oliva was preparing to go to Peru. Valera's friends—such as Onofre Esteban, who wrote to General Aquaviva asking for any news of Valera—would have retained the memory of his extraordinary and tragic life.

Now, four centuries after his death, Valera has taken center stage in the world of Andean studies, with the discovery of two documents, the *Historia et Rudimenta* and *Exsul Immeritus,* from the private family collection of Clara Miccinelli. These manuscripts not only recount some of the events surrounding Valera's imprisonment and exile, which were unknown at the time of their first publication, but also make astonishing claims about Valera's life and work. They allege, for example, that Valera's death in 1597 was faked by the Jesuits who wanted to remove him from the Society; after 1597, the documents continue, he returned to Peru, where he secretly wrote the *Nueva corónica y buen gobierno,* a massive chronicle of Andean life, attributed to Felipe Guaman Poma de Ayala. These allegations, if true, would have profound implications for our knowledge of the Incas as well as early colonial times in Peru, and they have therefore led to heated controversies.

This chapter describes the two manuscripts found in Naples, each of which contains several texts, allegedly pertaining to Valera. One of the difficulties that has existed in assessing these texts is that they were released to the scholarly world in a piecemeal fashion. Therefore, this chapter concludes with a brief history of the collection and a chronology of the two documents. At the time of this writing, Miccinelli has agreed to allow any interested scholar to examine the documents at her home in Naples; until recently, scholars have been deeply frustrated over their lack of access to the original manuscripts.

The *Historia et Rudimenta*

The first of the "Naples documents" that was presented to the public is the complex text known as the *Historia et Rudimenta* (Laurencich Minelli, Miccinelli, and Animato 1995). This manuscript consists of nine folios with Spanish, Latin, and ciphered Italian texts, bound in a tan-colored cover bearing the title *Historia et Rudimenta Linguae Piruanorum* (History and rudiments of the language of the Peruvians). The document contains four basic texts: (1) a Latin text signed "JAC," which Laurencich Minelli believes to represent the name of Joan Antonio Cumis; (2) a ciphered Italian text dating to 1637 and signed "JAO," which is attributed to Giovanni ("Juan") Anello Oliva; (3) another ciphered Italian text signed "JAO" but dating to 1638; and (4) a brief note in Spanish written in 1737 and signed by the Jesuit Pedro de Illanes. Accompanying this manuscript are three half-pages of drawings depicting the "royal" quipu writing system—the same system found in Sansevero's *Lettera apologética* (discussed in chap. 6)—with Blas Valera's signature on the third page. Finally, an envelope enclosing a woven woolen quipu fragment representing a line from the poem "Sumac ñusta," cited by Valera (Garcilaso de la Vega [1609] 1987, 128), was found with the *Historia et Rudimenta*. JAO claimed to have found this quipu fragment in the Acatanga *huaca*; the location of this *huaca* is unknown.

The first text, written in Latin by JAC, purports to recount the story told to Joan Antonio Cumis (1537–1618) by the elderly *curaca* Mayachac Azuay. Mayachac Azuay came to JAC in Cuzco with information about Blas Valera, whom Azuay had known personally. Azuay claimed that Valera had been a defender of native rights and a spiritual guide for the Andean peoples. In particular, the *curaca* continued, Valera defended the Christian beliefs of the native Andeans, arguing that the Indians were not idolatrous, because their native practices were completely in harmony with the Christian faith. However, he explained, Valera was persecuted for his religious beliefs and for his work with the religious sodalities in Cuzco. According to Azuay, Provincial Juan de Atienza wished to expel Valera for the latter's pro-Indian beliefs; however, as an excuse to try to remove him from the Society, the provincial used the false pretext that Valera had fornicated with a woman. Failing Valera's expulsion, the mestizo author was robbed of most of his writings by his enemies within the Society. Fortunately, Azuay continued, he was able to deliver some pages of his work to one of his native disciples in Cuzco.

JAC then describes Valera's teachings about native Peruvian writing, as recounted by Azuay. There was allegedly a sacred and secret form of Quechua writing, known only to the Inca priests, the *aclla*, the *amauta*, and the poets of the empire. Unlike the common form of quipu, which used knots, this "holy language" used woven textiles along with images in jewels and small objects. Not only could Valera read these sacred quipus easily, but he taught his disciples how to make and read them. Because the Spaniards destroyed many of these holy quipus, the Inca leaders collected the most important ones and placed them in "arks" [arcis] of "unripe gold" [auro immaturo]. These arks were then sunk in Lake Titicaca and hidden in the Orcos valley to keep them out of the hands of Catholic priests. According to Valera, JAC writes, the Incas honored the special ark containing the laws given by the Creator to Manco Capac; this is a clear reference to the Old Testament and the idea of the Incas as a chosen people. The manner in which the sacred quipus functioned, identical to those described in Sansevero's *Lettera apologética,* is explained in the text.

JAC also adds a brief outline of Quechua grammar, which is followed by two prayers in Quechua.[1] The astonishing first verse seems to imply that the sacred quipus allegedly were used by a religious group with millenarian overtones.

> Ruru curipac Ynti Quilla Coyllircuna Pachacamac rimacunaman chucumanta Viracochapac allapacamasca runaruryan unumanta Viracochapa Yancaripi cancuna chacuenacuna Pachacamacripa Illatecceripa Apo Manco Capac hiacollaripi qupucunacanqui apuychimanca manaricana caylla llapi Viracocha yanusca quipac causcarina.

> [Golden Egg, Sun, Moon, and Stars, the Creator of the World is speaking in the heart of Viracocha; the living earth is made man by the waters of Viracocha. In the ark [?] are the laws of Pachacamac Illa Tecce; Lord Manco Capac, with your square mantle, knot the prayer in a quipu. At the song, Viracocha will come back to life.]

The next prayer, JAC states, is in honor of emperor Huayna Capac.

> Ah! Huahina Capac ninahuan yacuyachinacanqui huascata curipa chapunacanqui runacunata huascapi curipa hananpachata allapata huascapi curipa puchauta tutata huascapi curipa; Huahina Capac atinacanqui Zupayta Apichiquipa Pichunsipa; Huahina Capac ricunacanqui Yntita.

> [Ah! Huahina Capac, with fire you forged the golden rope; you united the people in the golden rope, heaven and earth, day and night, in the golden rope; Huahina Capac, you defeated the demons of Apichiqui and Pichunsi; Huahina Capac, you fastened the sun.]

According to Garcilaso ([1609] 1987, 543–44), Huayna Capac celebrated the birth of his son Huascar by creating a great cable of gold to be used in the dances honoring the young prince. The chronicler further explains that the prince's name *Huascar* was derived from the word *huasca,* "rope," in remembrance of his father's gift. While the

---

1. The Quechua grammar exhibited in these hymns incorporates many aspects of Spanish syntax and is not that of a native Quechua speaker.

prayer recorded by JAC certainly seems to recall this golden rope, this oration gives the golden rope an entirely different meaning, one focused on a curious mysticism, with no mention of the young prince. Montesinos writes a curious note about Huascar, based on his anonymous source from Quito: "The proper name of this prince was Inticuse Hualpa; they gave him the other [name (i.e., *Huascar*)] for the nursemaid who gave him milk. The rest that Garcilaso and some others say about the name of this prince and the great chain of gold are fictions of theirs."[2]

A Quechua/Spanish vocabulary list follows JAC's discussion of the Quechua prayers and the "royal" quipu writing system. This list of "fundamental" Quechua words contains fifty-six words arranged in alphabetical order. All of the words from Sansevero's "royal" quipu master syllabary are represented on this list except for *Ynca* (king), *curaca* (feudal lord), *veu-pacha* (hell), and *veumari* (bear). The word given for "bear" on JAC's list is *ucumari* rather than *veumari*. *Uku* signifies "inner"; if *veu* and *uku* are equivalents, then *veu-pacha* means "inner world," which could certainly be a gloss for the Christian concept of hell.

Bruce Mannheim, an expert in Quechua linguistics, has concluded that the vocabulary list and other examples of Quechua in the Naples documents reveal an origin in the northern Andes: "the vocabulary lists in the Naples manuscript are of a type appended to several colonial writings, most notable the *Doctrina Cristiana y Catecismo para Instrucción de los Indios* . . . [Christian doctrine and catechism for the instruction of the Indians . . .], an ecclesiastical document dating to 1584. From its sound, scribal practice, and grammatical forms, however, the Quechua itself is likely of northern, probably Ecuadorian, origin and resembles that used by the Jesuits in the mid- to late seventeenth century—no earlier" (Domenici and Domenici 1996, 55). Significantly, Mannheim rejects the idea that this document could date to 1618 (the year of Cumis's death), arguing that its language, while similar to that used by the Jesuits, is from the latter half of the seventeenth century.

---

2. "El nombre proprio deste príncipe era Inticuse Hualpa, diéronle el otro por la ama que le dio leche. Lo demás que dice Garcilaso y algunos otros del nombre deste príncipe y de la cadena grande de oro son ficciones suias" (Yale [ca. 1645] ca. 1860, book 2, chap. 28).

The author concludes this text by explaining why Mayachac Azuay chose to reveal these secrets to him. As the elderly *curaca* was facing death, JAC writes, Azuay wished, by imparting these secrets, to take revenge against the conquistadors and Catholic priests who had destroyed his lineage. Feeling "honored" by his confidence, the Jesuit brother has written down his story in two days in the month of April (for JAC, see Laurencich Minelli, Miccinelli, and Animato 1995, 382–87).

The next two texts in the document are both by JAO, presumably Giovanni Anello Oliva (1574–1642)—also known as Juan Anello Oliva—and are in ciphered Italian (Laurencich Minelli, Miccinelli, and Animato 1995, 388–413). The first text, JAO I, is dated July 30, 1637, and was written in Lima. The author begins by stating that Blas Valera was not the only one who suffered because of his desire to tell the truth about the native Peruvians. Anello Oliva also, the document claims, has been coerced by his superiors and had his work censored because of his desire to tell the truth about Peru. In fact, the author writes, he does not know if even now he will be able to write the truth, for fear of censorship.

JAO then expounds his theory that all religions have similar foundations and venerate the different aspects of the one God by worship of many gods. The Incas, he claimed, knew that the different gods were merely aspects of the Creator, venerating "the invisible god" Pachacamac and the "incarnate god" Viracocha, along with the forces of nature and the king, the child of the sun. It is difficult to gain the confidence of the Peruvian people, however, the author states, because it is not easy to learn to speak their language. Once JAO did gain their confidence, however, he was shown "great geometrical buildings" that stored their special quipus. These quipus were unknown to the common people and contained the "true" Inca history. Unlike the common quipus, these "royal" quipus used elaborate symbols woven by the priestesses of the sun. Many of these "royal" quipus, he continued, were burned by the Spaniard; therefore, the Inca leaders hid the remaining quipus in inaccessible places. Blas Valera, who was persecuted by the Jesuits, encoded the history of his people and of the treasures buried in the "lake of ten" in one of these "royal" quipus.[3]

---

3. It is not clear which lake is referred to as the "lake of ten." According to Montesinos, Atahuallpa's treasures were buried in a series of sixteen lakes: "Lo que escondieron

According to JAO, Valera was buried with this quipu in his grave in the Spanish city of Alcalá de Henares.

JAO interrupts his discussion of these "royal" quipus by providing a brief outline of the history contained in one of them, which was showed to him, he claims, by the *quipucamayoc* Chahuarurac. He then recounts a history of the Incas, beginning with the arrival of strangers from Tartaria; these strangers nearly exterminated the inhabitants of Peru, but the two peoples eventually intermarried to produce the Inca population. This history is followed by a section describing the author's discussions with Chahuarurac. The Indian sage commented that Christ's words, written in the Bible, were irrelevant, because writing with pen and paper was useless; quipus, he claimed, were the "true writing, because, containing both spirit and thought, they bind God and man together."[4]

JAO next criticized two Andean customs, cranial deformation and "the barbaric slash of the clitoris on little girls,"[5] both of which Chahuarurac defended. The lengthened skull, Chahuarurac explained, connects humans with the world and was a custom already practiced by the Chinchoros, Chimu, and Uari when they were conquered by the Incas. Concerning the slash of the clitoris on young girls, the *quipucamayoc* argues that the Andeans believe that the clitoris is symbolized by the scorpion's sting and that by this act they venerate the male soul of the woman. Chahuarurac also translated the quipu fragment JAO found in 1627 in the *huaca* of Acatanga, which accompanies the manuscript.

After this discussion, the author accuses Francisco Pizarro and three Dominican friars, Vicente Valverde, Joannes Yepes, and Reginaldus Pedraza, of giving poisoned wine to Atahuallpa, thereby defeating the Inca ruler through treachery. JAO claims that the Dominican Ciprianus de Medina swore to him that on that fateful day in Cajamarca, Pizarro first gave Atahuallpa unadulterated wine but then offered the ruler and his guards poisoned wine. Only by poi-

---

los indios cuando supieron la muerte de Atahuallpa, no se puede hacer número. Tengo por cierto que lo echaron en lagunas, hay 16 en diversas partes" (Yale [ca. 1645] 1860, book 1, chap. 23).

4. ". . . e per lui vera scrittura, in quanto legamento infra Dio e l'Huomo, sono racchiusi lo spirituo e 'l pensiero" (Laurencich Minelli, Miccinelli, and Animato 1995, 389).

5. ". . . il barbaro taglio del clitoris alle bimbe" (ibid.).

soning Atahuallpa and his bodyguards was Pizarro able to win the kingdom of Peru.

Finally, the author has included a list of "Inca hieroglyphics" that he claims to have learned from the native writer Uaman Poma. This list is composed of eighteen symbols, each of which bears a short explanation. For example, the first symbol, ~, is said to represent the waning and waxing moon; the second symbol, *, purports to portray the human and animal worlds in the sky; and so forth. On the back of the page containing the list of "hieroglyphics" is a schematic representation of the poem "Sumac ñusta" (cited by Valera), along with the following shortened version of the poem.

Sumac Ñusta	Beautiful Princess,
Torallay Quin	Your Brother
Puy nuy quita	Your Jar
Paquir cayan	Now breaks.
Unuyquita	Your water
Pachacamac	Pachacamac
Viracocha	Viracocha,
Paramunqui.	You rain.

The third major text of the *Historia et Rudimenta,* JAO II, is dated May 7, 1638. In this text, JAO states that as a son of St. Ignatius, he must tell the whole truth about Valera, despite the censorship of his previous published works. The mestizo priest, JAO wrote, was a master at using the "royal" quipus and had illustrated one of the "royal" quipus so that others would know how to read it. Valera himself told his story to JAO, "giving his confidence in a moan of suffering."[6]

According to JAO II, Valera's mother was a native woman named Allpa Urpi (the name means "turtledove"), who was raped by Captain Alonso Valera, a soldier in Pizarro's suit. During the rape, Allpa Urpi was infected with scabies, earning her the nickname *Piri* (meaning "sore"). Alonso decided to marry Allpa Urpi, after having baptized her with the name *Francisca Perez; Perez* was chosen as a slightly altered version of *Piri.* As a boy, Valera learned Quechua along with Spanish and Latin. He also preserved an account of the Spanish conquest written by Francisco de Chaves and given to Luis

---

6. ". . . che in me ripose la sua fiducia, altro se non un gemito di sofferenza" (ibid., 396).

Valera, Blas's uncle. As a Jesuit, Valera distinguished himself, eventually writing an account of the conquest of Peru, detailing Pizarro's use of poisoned wine. This narrative was sent to General Aquaviva, who, however, wished to dismiss Valera from the Society. Valera asked for permission to travel to Rome to explain himself to Aquaviva personally, but he was prevented from doing so by his superior Juan de Atienza. Instead, he was exiled to Spain, "so that he could not do any harm with the truth."[7] José de Acosta, "defender of the Indians," knew the truth in his "restless soul" and admits this in the twenty-third sermon in the *Doctrina cristiana y catecismo*.[8] But, the text continues, Acosta accuses the Indians of idolatry, which is not true.

After describing Valera's youth and early career, JAO explains how he met Valera. In 1611, in Santa Cruz de la Sierra, when Valera was officially dead, JAO met a white-haired mestizo in the courtyard of the Jesuit mission. This individual greeted JAO with the Jesuit motto *Ad maiorem Dei gloriam* [For the greater glory of God] and proceeded to confide in the younger priest. Valera was inspired to do so, JAO added, because he had been informed by the natives that JAO was trustworthy and sympathetic to the native cause. The elderly Valera recounted how Aquaviva, because of Valera's heretical and anti-Spanish beliefs, had made Valera choose between leaving the Jesuits or faking his own death. Valera chose the latter course and, during his period of hiding in Spain, gave his writings to Garcilaso de la Vega, who promised to copy them faithfully. Yet Garcilaso "contorted and censored" Valera's work and "particularly sullied the things that Valera had written profusely about the royal quipus"; he also omitted what Valera had written about the sacred geometry of the Incas, including the quipus and the *ceque (sique)* lines "that knotted the *huacas* to the heart of the Inca."[9]

After the sack of Cádiz in 1596 and his faked death in Málaga in 1597, continues JAO, Valera finally left Spain for Peru in June 1598, traveling incognito. Landing in Cartagena, he journeyed overland and by river to Quito and from there to Cuzco. In Cuzco, he was received

---

7. ". . . acche non potesse nuocere con la verita" (ibid., 397).

8. ". . . avvocato degl' indios"; ". . . anima l'inquieta" (ibid.).

9. ". . . stravolse il contenuto censurandolo"; "In especie, deturpo quanto il P. Valera havea scritto a profusione su' quipos regali"; ". . . ch'annodavano le huacas al core dell' Inca" (ibid., 398).

by his fellow mestizo Gonzalo Ruiz, who hid him among the Indians of Cuzco, among whom were the members of the Nombre de Jesús sodality. In Cuzco, Valera wrote his most ambitious work yet, the *Nueva corónica y buen gobierno* (New chronicle and good government). However, because Valera was already sixty-six years old in 1611, Gonzalo Ruiz copied out the manuscript and created the drawings accompanying the text. The Indian Guaman Poma, "for his faults of arrogance and vainglory,"[10] was chosen to serve as the alleged author of the document, since Valera, who was supposed to be dead, could not acknowledge his own work. Finally, Valera returned to Spain in 1618, where he died the following year.

The remainder of JAO II describes specific examples from the *Nueva corónica* that supposedly reveal Valera's authorship of the chronicle. For example, in the section on the Spanish conquest, where the message of Atahuallpa is reported, Valera uses a sentence with a double meaning: "Y anci vino adelante" could mean "and thus he came before" or "and thus the wine before." This sentence, JAO argues, is a secret reference to the wine that was used to poison Atahuallpa's guards. Another instance demonstrating that JAO and Valera were involved in composing the *Nueva corónica*, JAO continues, can be found in the song "Panipani Chunaychuna," which includes two words—*cavalluch* and *mulach* from the Neapolitan dialect—translated into Aymara. Incidently, all of the examples from the *Nueva corónica* provided in this text pertain to a fairly small portion of this monumental work.

After JAO's coded texts are three half-pages depicting a colored "royal" quipu of the poem "Sumac ñusta" signed by Blas Valera. This abbreviated version of the poem matches that found in Anello Oliva's first text in the *Historia et Rudimenta*. On the back of the third page, JAO has written in code, "In the woven quipu, the number of knots in the body of the keyword is not important, but the number of syllabic knots is important."[11] On the paper used as an envelope to enclose the quipu fragment, JAO has added in ciphered

---

10. ". . . d'esser prescelto per la soperbia e la vaingloria" (ibid., 399).

11. "Nel quipu intessuto non importa il n. dei nodi nel corpo della parola chiave, si come invece quello dei nodi sillabici" (ibid., 401).

Italian, "Quipu that I discovered in Acatanga's *huaca* and here enclosed as a relic." This quipu represents the fourth and part of the fifth line of "Sumac ñusta," "pa-quir ca-yan / unuy."

The final major text of the *Historia et Rudimenta* is the note written in Spanish by Father Pedro de Illanes in 1737. In this brief message, the Jesuit missionary writes:

> The Indian Juan Taquic Menendez de Sodar gave me this manuscript on his deathbed in the sacristy of the Church of Saint Francis Xavier, S.J., in Concepción, Chile. Juan Taquic, after having piously confessed all of his sins, handed me a bag containing a small image of the Holy Rosary, some quipu fragments, and this manuscript. The more I read it, the Latin language and the style that is used make me certainly suppose that the author was a priest; the initials "Jac" make me think that the name was *Jacinto* or *Jacob*. Whomever it may be, he has written a truly dramatic page of history; it is a minor part, without doubt, of that which remains from the ancient "Jerusalem" over which the mighty and ravaging conquistadors passed.[12]

Pedro de Illanes sold the manuscript and enclosed quipu to Sansevero seven years later. A record of this transaction still remains in the Naples city archives (Domenici and Domenici 1996, 54).

A complex document containing multiple texts, the *Historia et Rudimenta* raised a number of extremely controversial issues that the other Naples document, *Exsul Immeritus*, has done nothing to quell.

Exsul Immeritus

After the discovery and publication of the *Historia et Rudimenta*, Italian researchers encountered another manuscript in the Miccinelli

---

12. "El indio Juan Taquic Menendez de Sodar me hizo entrega en el momento de su muerte de este manuscrito, en la Sacristia Ecclesia S. Fran. Xaverij S. Jesu de Conceptione de Chille. Juan Taquic despues de haberse piadosamente confesado, me confio una bolsa que contenia una pequeña imagen del S.S. Rosario, algunos fragmentos de quipu y este manuscrito. Cuanto mas lo leo, la lengua latina y el estilo que empleo me hacen ciertamente suponer que el autor era un Clerigo; las iniciales Jac. hacen pensar que el nombre sea Jacinto o Jacob. Quienquiera que sea, ha escrito una pagina de historia verdaderamente dramatica: es poco, sin duda, lo que queda de la antigua "Jerusalem" sobre la cual pasaron poderosos y devastadores Conquistadores" (ibid., 402).

archive, *Exsul Immeritus Blas Valera Populo Suo*.[13] *Exsul Immeritus* consists of twenty-two folios bound together with parchment. Nineteen folios were written and signed (allegedly) by Blas Valera; the remaining folios comprise the supposedly original account by Valera's relative Francisco de Chaves of Pizarro's treacherous defeat of Atahuallpa. Also included in the document are two sealed envelopes. The first envelope contains thirteen woven or metallic ideograms of Quechua keywords, a tiny parchment book with paintings, and a silver disc earring. The second envelope encloses a variety of objects: two pages painted by Blas Valera, one of the Inca succession and one a calendrical quipu; and four wax items, including two wax medallions, an oval reliquary with a cross on the front and containing a tiny book in which Valera described his false death, and a sealed square wax item with a mosaic of the mythical land of Paytiti on its cover. This final wax item was opened by Laurencich Minelli in front of witnesses. Although it was partially destroyed upon opening, it was revealed to hold two documents: (1) a fragment of a letter from Christopher Columbus, on the front of which Valera had written a song and on the back of which he had noted that this letter was given to him by the Jesuit theologian Juan de Mariana (see Fernandez de la Mora 1993); and (2) one page recording the contract whereby Guaman Lazaro Poma agreed to allow the Jesuits to use his name on the *Nueva corónica* in return for the gift of a cart and a horse.

The oldest document within *Exsul Immeritus* is a letter from Chaves to the emperor Charles V, dated August 5, 1533, and written in Cajamarca (Laurencich Minelli, Miccinelli, and Animato 1998). This is, presumably, the *relación* described in the *Relación de las costumbres antiguas*.

> Francisco de Chaves, Jerezano, who was a great friend of Tito Atauchi, brother of King Atahuallpa; [Chaves] not only informed himself of a thousand things but saw with his eyes that which here is told, and [he] wrote a copious account and left it with his friend and relative Don Luis Valera, and he [i.e., Luis] gave it to Diego de Olivares.[14]

---

13. For information about *Exsul Immeritus,* see Laurencich Minelli, Miccinelli, and Animato 1998; Laurencich Minelli 2001a, 2001b; Miccinelli and Animato (1999).

14. ". . . Francisco de Chaves, jerezano, que fue grande amigo de Tito Atauchi, hermano del rey Atahuallpa; el cual no sólo se informó de mill cosas, pero vio con sus ojos esto

In the Chaves account from *Exsul Immeritus,* the author explains how he has been a companion of Pizarro. He left Panama on December 27, 1530, in the company of the conquistador's men. While he was aboard the ship, however, he overheard a secret conference between Francisco Pizarro and three Dominicans, Vicente de Valverde, Juan de Yepes, and Reginaldo de Pedraça. This conference, he believed, was of major significance for determining whether the Inca Empire had been defeated through a just war. Pizarro, Chaves wrote, knew from his previous trips that the native South Americans were fond of wine made from grapes, having none of their own. Therefore, the four men made a pact that they would secretly poison some of the wine intended as a gift for the native emperor. In this manner, they believed, they would be able to defeat the native ruler through poisoning his generals and bodyguards, without the risk of a fair fight. By assuring their success against the natives through the secret use of poison, they would be able to gain new souls for heaven as well as many riches and honors for themselves. The conspirators, Chaves continues, swore in front of an altar prepared for mass to keep their plan a secret.

Chaves then explains how Pizarro and the Dominicans used poison to win a victory over Atahuallpa. First, he writes, they offered unadulterated wine to Atahuallpa and his advisors. Then, he continues, Pizarro, with the greatest affability, presented the poisoned wine. Once this was consumed, the Incas were unable to defend themselves against the Spanish onslaught, and the Spaniards captured Atahuallpa, winning the kingdom for themselves. Chaves expresses his deep unhappiness that the Inca Empire was conquered through deception rather than through an honorable military engagement.

Furthermore, the letter condemns the execution of Atahuallpa by the Spaniards, claiming that this was an act of great injustice against an innocent man. Chaves explains that when Atahuallpa was first imprisoned by the Europeans, the native ruler expressed his desire to travel to Spain to swear fealty in person to Charles V. However, Pizarro did not want Atahuallpa to meet with the emperor, for fear that Atahuallpa might reveal how much gold Pizarro and his men had

---

que aquí se dice, y hizo una relación copiosa y la dejó en poder de su amigo y deudo Don Luis Valera, y éste se la dio a Diego de Olivares" (Blas Valera [1594] 1968, 155).

illegally kept for themselves. Therefore, Chaves writes, it seemed prudent to Pizarro and to his Dominican advisors to execute the native king. The author is careful to place most of the blame for Atahuallpa's tragic death on the Dominicans who were counseling Pizarro. On July 26, a month before this document was written, Chaves concludes, Atahuallpa was shamefully put to death, although he was guiltless of any crime.

The letter from Chaves carries two additional signatures, those of Licenciado Polo de Ondegardo and José de Acosta. In *Exsul Immeritus,* Valera explains that he had given the letter to Acosta to pass on to his superiors but that Acosta did not do this, choosing to keep the *relación* for himself. Presumably, Chaves retained this letter for at least a year before passing it on to his relative Luis Valera, who did not arrive in Peru until late in the year 1534. It is uncertain why Valera, in both the *Relación de las costumbres antiguas* and the *Vocabulario* cited by Anello Oliva, identified Chaves as a native of Jerez, when in this letter, Chaves clearly refers to himself as a native of Trujillo (Laurencich Minelli, Miccinelli, and Animato 1998, 71–73, 80). It is also unclear how Valera acquired this document that Luis had given to Diego de Olivares.

Most of *Exsul Immeritus,* however, does not concern Chaves and his letter but, rather, is Valera's autobiographical account of his life, exile, and faked death. According to the text, dated May 10, 1618, Valera wrote this work in Alcala de Henares, a village outside of Madrid. As Laurencich Minelli has observed (2001a), the text can be divided into four parts: (1) an account of Valera's life; (2) information on Andean language, "writing," and cosmology; (3) a description of the "Babel" in Peru created by the Spanish invasion and destruction of native culture; and (4) a pictographic synthesis of the ideal evangelization of Peru.

The story of Valera's life in *Exsul Immeritus* is very similar to that found in the *Historia et Rudimenta* but incorporates additional details. In *Exsul Immeritus,* Valera writes that he was born in Levanto, Chachapoyas, on the feast of St. Blaise (February 3). His father was Alonso Valera, the brother of Luis Valera. However, Blas considered Luis to be his father, because of Alonso's brutality: when Blas was only thirteen years old, Alonso murdered Blas's mother in front of him. Blas's mother was named Urpay and was the daughter of the native healer Illavanqa. Alonso initially raped Urpay and infected her with scabies, earning her the nickname *Piri,* after the Quechua word *quiri* (sore). As a child, Blas became acquainted with the *relación* of the Spanish conquest written by Francisco de Chaves, which his uncle Luis gave to him. Eventually, Blas decided to become a Jesuit in order to help his people, although he already had a son by a native woman. Valera then describes how General Aquaviva wished to expel him from the Society for the sins of disobedience, using fornication as a mere excuse. He also criticizes Acosta for his inertia in protecting him and praises General Vitelleschi, who succeeded Aquaviva, for his assistance. The author next mentions his false death and secret flight to Peru, adding a list of other Jesuits who have secretly aided him, including Anello Oliva, Alonso de Barzana, and Jerónimo de Montesinos, a Jesuit Latin professor.

In this first section of the work, Valera also discusses all of his writings. In addition to *Exsul Immeritus,* he claims credit for the catechism printed by Antonio Ricardo in 1584 and states that he collaborated with other Jesuits on the Quechua vocabulary printed by Ricardo in 1586. Another work of his, he writes, was *De Tahuantinsuyus Prischis Gentibus* (Concerning the ancient peoples of Tahuantinsuyu), which he gave to Acosta in 1586; Laurencich Minelli (2001b, 264–65) believes that *De Tahuantinsuyus* served as the basis for the *Relación de las costumbres antiguas.* Valera also mentions, but does not name, his work that he gave to Garcilaso to publish; it is unclear whether *De Tahuantinsuyus* was this manuscript. Unfortunately, he writes, Garcilaso, in the *Comentarios reales,* censored and fictionalized much of what Valera had written, especially concerning the quipus. To answer the lies in Garcilaso's work, Valera claims, he wrote the *Nueva corónica y buen gobierno,* with the assistance of Gonzalo Ruiz ("GR") and Anello Oliva ("AO"). Ruiz, the author tells us, was responsible for drawing the almost four hundred illustrations in the *Nueva corónica;* Ruiz also created other illustrations, which he sold to Guaman Poma, who in turn gave them to the Mercedarian chronicler Martín de Murúa. Valera mentions that he did not include the story of Pizarro's use of poison in the *Nueva corónica* because he did not wish to lead the Indians to resent all Spaniards, including the missionaries.

The second section of the work, on Andean "writing," language, and beliefs, forms the longest portion of *Exsul Immeritus*. In these pages, Valera describes his work to save the Quechua language from the conquistadors' onslaught. Quechua, he notes, is poorly adapted to the Spanish alphabet but ideally suited to the indigenous writing system of the "royal" quipus. This quipu writing system, he narrates, was invented by Manco Capac, who wished to create a form of writing that would imitate the rays of the sun, the colors of the rainbow, and the knots of the mountains. Paintings of literary quipus, along with lists of keywords and an explanation of how the system worked, are included in the text. According to Laurencich Minelli (2001a), Valera also mentions that the directionality of the knots conveys either addition or subtraction.[15] After further discussion of quipus, the author turns to an examination of *yupana*—checkerboards or tablets containing small colored stones or objects. These were employed, Valera informs us, for counting as well as for communicating ideas. Moreover, he adds, they were used to transform the syllabic quipus into numerical ones.

Finally, the second section concludes with a paragraph entitled "Cequecuna." *Ceques* were the forty-two ritual lines radiating out from the center of Cuzco. Each *ceque* line contained at least several shrines; different groups of nobility in Cuzco were responsible for caring for the shrines along the different *ceque* lines.[16] According to the text, Valera states that the lines were understood as quipu cords radiating out from a central point in the plaza of Coricancha, the temple of the sun in Cuzco. The *ceque* lines in the Chinchaysuyu and Antisuyu quarters were read in a clockwise direction, while those in the Collasuyu and Condesuyu quarters were read counterclockwise. Within the *ceque* lines for each of the four *suyus ("sections"), the lines* were grouped in threes by color, according to whether they were Cayao, Payan, or Collana, except in Condesuyu, which included extra colors for the anomalous *ceques* of Cayao-Collana and

---

15. This statement replicates Gary Urton's recent discoveries about quipus (Urton 1994).

16. For a comprehensive discussion of the Inca *ceque* system, see Bauer 1998. Bauer combines extensive archaeological survey work with archival research on the position of the shrines to offer a comprehensive and empirical understanding of the *ceque* system. One of the more important observations demonstrated in this work is that the *ceque* lines were not always straight, as has been usually assumed. See also Zuidema 1990.

Anahuarque. The actual shrines, he concludes, were indicated by knots along the quipu cords representing each *ceque* (Laurencich Minelli 2001a, 119–20).

In the third section of *Exsul Immeritus,* Valera bewails the destruction of the Andean world by the Spanish conquistadors. He does so primarily through painted images and phrases in Quechua. For example, in this portion of the text, he includes a page showing his mother's murder; a painting of Friar Yepes poisoning the wine that Pizarro will offer to Atahuallpa; and an image of the apocalypse in the Andes, with the words "Yntim tutayanca" [The sun became dark]. He refers repeatedly to the "Babel" of the Spanish conquest and paints thirteen ideograms of keywords in Quechua used in the literary quipus, the only solution to this confusion of languages. There are strong apocalyptic overtones to this and the following sections of the text.

The final portion of Valera's work is quite brief and expresses the utopia that is possible in the Andes with the appropriate Christian evangelization. Here, Valera describes his efforts to defend the native peoples by writing the true history of the conquest by Pizarro. In this section, he includes one of the more dramatic paintings in the work: an image of Christ crucified in the center of the four quarters of Tahuantinsuyu (Miccinelli and Animato 1999, 198). Laurencich Minelli (ibid.) has suggested that this section was written for Valera's followers and disciples, to inspire them to spread a truly Andean form of Christianity.

The History of the Manuscripts

The recent history of the *Historia et Rudimenta* and *Exsul Immeritus* can be traced in large part through materials accompanying the texts. According to notes found with both manuscripts, the documents had been in possession of a member of Italy's royal family, Duke Amadeo di Savoia-Aosta, by the early twentieth century (Laurencich Minelli 2001a). Eventually, the duke presented both works to Riccardo Cera, his companion in the military academy La Nunziatella in Naples. On November 11, 1927, the duke gave the *Historia et Rudimenta* to his boyhood friend, as indicated by a dedication written by Savoia-Aosta on the last page of the text. Several years later, on April 10, 1930,

Exsul Immeritus was given to Cera by the duke. In a letter accompanying the document, Savoia-Aosta explained that this gift was presented in memory of the times that the two men had spent together in their youth and for all that Cera had done to defend the duke's life and honor. The letter continues by explaining that Amadeo I, king of Spain, had acquired the two documents during his short reign (1870–73).

On the cover of *Exsul Immeritus,* written in blue ink, is "Peru 66EspaX." Laurencich Minelli (ibid.) has suggested that this notation indicates that the document was held by a private library in the latter half of the nineteenth century; had the manuscript been owned by a public library, she notes, it would have carried a seal. She speculates, moreover, that the documents may well have been housed in the private library of the Savoia-Aosta family during that period.

In 1951, Carlo Miccinelli, a Jesuit and a relative of Riccardo Cera, was allowed to examine the *Historia et Rudimenta,* along with the quipu fragment. Miccinelli brought the document and quipu to show to Lidio Cipriani, former director of the Anthropological Museum of Florence, and to Paul Rivet at the Museum of Man in Paris. Both Cipriani and Rivet demonstrated interest in obtaining the quipu; however, Riccardo Cera chose not to sell or donate it (Domenici and Domenici 1996, 54).

Upon Cera's death in 1958, the two documents were left to his sister, Anna Cera Miccinelli, with the understanding that she pass them on to her daughter, Clara Miccinelli, when the latter reached adulthood. Clara Miccinelli is currently the sole owner of both texts. Apparently, the manuscripts remained unnoticed in the family archives until 1985, when Miccinelli discovered the *Historia et Rudimenta* (Domenici and Domenici 1996, 54). After several years spent studying the documents with Carlo Animato, Miccinelli, Animato, and a third individual, the noted scholar Paolo Rossi, published their findings in *Quipu: Il nodo parlante dei misteriosi Incas* in 1989. This work included a rough transcription of the first two texts of the *Historia et Rudimenta,* JAC and JAO I. However, the book received virtually no attention until a senior professor from the Università di Bologna, Laura Laurencich Minelli, came across Miccinelli's book and began further inquiries about the curious texts from the Cera family archives.

The first complete and accurate transcription of the *Historia et Rudimenta* was published by Laurencich Minelli, along with Miccinelli and Animato, in 1995. Continued research in the Cera family archives brought *Exsul Immeritus* to light after that. In 1999, Miccinelli and Animato published two illustrations from *Exsul Immeritus* allegedly drawn by Valera (Miccinelli and Animato 1999). Laurencich Minelli has discussed this document in numerous academic presentations and in her article in the volume based on the 1999 Rome symposium on Blas Valera and Guaman Poma (Laurencich Minelli 2001a). However, the publication of the text of this work has been hindered by the bitter controversy over its authenticity, and it is unclear when it will be published.

CHAPTER TEN

The Continuing Controversy
over Blas Valera

The "Naples documents" present quite a challenge to scholars of the ancient Andes. If all of the allegations made in the documents were true, they would require a radical rethinking of our understanding of Inca writing systems, as well as of the authorship and purpose of one of the most important colonial descriptions of the Andean world, the *Nueva corónica y buen gobierno*. They also, of course, would have major implications for our knowledge of Blas Valera's troubled life, informing us about the murder of his mother by his father, Alonso (not Luis), and about his life in hiding after his faked death in 1597.

Yet soon after the publication of the *Historia et Rudimenta,* some scholars rejected the information in the text, claiming instead that this document was a modern forgery, possibly concocted with the complicity of the renowned medieval scholar and novelist Umberto Eco (Estenssoro 1997). Laura Laurencich Minelli, among others, has emphatically denied that the manuscripts are forgeries and has maintained that the claims about Valera as the secret author of the *Nueva corónica* and as the purveyor of an ancient Andean writing system are reasonable and true (Laurencich Minelli 1997, 1998, 1999). Finally, several scholars, including R. T. Zuidema (2001), Juan Ossio, and Father Borja de Medina, the former head of the Institutum Historicum Societatis Iesu in Rome, have argued that these texts are old forgeries, dating to the seventeenth or eighteenth centuries, compiled by Jesuits who knew the tragic story of Valera and were dedicated to what they viewed as his program for evangelization in the Andes.

Accusations of Forgery

The most extensive arguments that the documents are recent forgeries of very poor quality are found in an article by Juan Carlos Estenssoro (1997). Estenssoro had been asked by the Société des Américanistes to determine whether the document was authentic. John Rowe, who likewise examined a copy of the document for the Société, found the *Historia et Rudimenta* to be a genuine work from the seventeenth century (Albó 1998, 322). Estenssoro, however, presents a long list of reasons why he believes that the *Historia et Rudimenta* is undoubtedly a recent fake, and he suggests Laura Laurencich Minelli along with Umberto Eco as the authors of this alleged fraud. Working with a cloudy photocopy of a photocopy of the manuscript, Estenssoro claims to be able to determine that the punctuation of the text is anachronistic and pertains to the late nineteenth or twentieth century, particularly in the frequent use of commas. He also suggests that the fact that the text is written in two columns on each page also proves that it is a modern forgery; never, he asserts, does such a short document contain writing in two columns in the seventeenth century. He also finds the Spanish and Latin vocabulary to be anachronistic; for example, he points out that the word *genocidium,* which he found in Miccinelli's and Animato's transcription of the text, was coined only in the twentieth century. Likewise, he states, the use of the phrase "hombre blanco" ("white man") to describe the Spaniards was unknown in the colonial era; rather, this phrase seems for him to reflect "an indigenous tongue forged in Hollywood."[1]

Estenssoro also criticizes the language of the document. He notes that in the texts allegedly by Cumis and Anello Oliva, both men make

---

1. ". . . una lengua indígena forjada en Hollywood" (Estenssoro 1997, 572).

grammatical errors in their use of Spanish; presumably, he believes that the alleged Italian forgers spoke such poor Spanish that they were unaware of these errors. Additionally, Estenssoro is adamant that the manner of dating the manuscript found in Anello Oliva's text was never used in the seventeenth century but is seen only in more recent centuries. Fault can also be found, he maintains, in the Quechua texts contained in the *Historia et Rudimenta*. Here, Estenssoro refers to Gerald Taylor's work on the manuscript, in which Taylor finds that the Quechua texts were probably not written by a native speaker of Quechua. Taylor, as cited by Estenssoro (1997, 573), claims that many of the so-called Quechua prayers in the document use Quechua words with an essentially Spanish syntax. This, as Estenssoro points out, is not consistent with Blas Valera's well-known command of the Quechua language, which he learned as a child from his mother. Moreover, Estenssoro notes, the document occasionally uses previously unknown Quechua words, which, in his opinion, also proves that the document is a poor-quality forgery.

He continues his discussion by noting that the quipu fragment accompanying the document is poorly made, with inferior weaving, unlike what one would expect from a royal textile. Estenssoro also considers it incredible that the only "royal" quipu discovered would reproduce an already published poem ("Sumac ñusta"). If the "royal" quipus reflected an ancient, secret writing technique of the Incas, he suggests, they presumably would contain some new Inca literature.

Much of the content of the manuscript is patently false, which, Estenssoro states, also reveals the work to be a forgery. For example, Estenssoro draws the reader's attention to the assertion made allegedly by Anello Oliva that all the native Peruvians speak Quechua; this fact, he assures us, is false and therefore demonstrates the problems with the document. Moreover, the "proofs" provided in the document to show that Valera was truly the author of the *Nueva corónica* are extremely poor and unconvincing. The primary evidence of Valera's authorship in the *Nueva corónica,* according to the *Historia et Rudimenta,* is the chronicle's inscription "CORONA REAL," which should read "COROVA REAL"; this phrase can be converted to "VA REAL," an anagram for "VALERA." Estenssoro argues that this supposed "proof," like the other "proofs" offered in the document, is extremely unconvincing; he states, "We can rest tranquilly—

there is no proof that Huaman Poma did not write the *Nueva corónica y buen gobierno.*"[2]

Estenssoro concludes his article by stating again that there is no doubt that the *Historia et Rudimenta* is a recent forgery and by asking whether Laurencich Minelli could be innocent of this fraud. His rather cryptic answer to his own question does not exonerate Laurencich Minelli but, rather, leaves the reader with the suggestion that this senior professor at the Università di Bologna is part of an intentional forgery. He points out that Laurencich Minelli was aware of his criticisms of the manuscript's authenticity but went ahead with publicizing it anyway. He adds: "there is a detail that does not lack a great deal of meaning in this game of words that is the manuscript. And it is that Ms. Laura Laurencich Minelli might have fallen in a trap of her own making. The owner of the manuscript is called Clara Miccinelli, [whose name] is an imperfect anagram of her [Laurencich Minelli's] own name, but not much worse than that which transforms *Corona real* to *Valera.*"[3]

Estenssoro's criticisms of the document as a recent forgery, however impressive they may seem at first glance, are unconvincing on further examination. How is he able to determine with certitude that the punctuation of the text is anachronistic based on examining a photocopy of a photocopy of the manuscript? His observation that it was unknown for short documents from this period to have writing in two columns is likewise puzzling. He admits that longer seventeenth-century manuscripts were written in two columns; how short does a text have to be to make this unacceptable? In the Madrid manuscript of Montesinos's *Memorias historiales,* written prior to 1644, the writing in book 4 begins as one column with marginal notations and then occasionally, for the space of several pages, becomes two columns with additional marginal notations; at times, there are even three columns of writing on a page. Yet according to Estenssoro's observa-

---

2. "Podemos estar tranquilos, no hay ninguna prueba de que Huaman Poma no haya escrito Nueva Coronica y Buen Gobierno" (ibid., 576).

3. ". . . hay un detalle que no deja de tener mucho sentido en este juego de palabras que es el manuscrito. Y es que la Sra. Laura Laurencich Minelli puede haber caido en una trampa hecha a su medida. La dueña del manuscrito se llama: Clara Miccinelli, lo que es un anagrama imperfecto de su propio nombre, pero no mucho peor que el que transforma Corona real en Valera" (ibid., 577).

THE JESUIT AND THE INCAS

tion about the use of columns in the seventeenth century, it would have been impossible for Montesinos to have written short parts of his text with two columns; Estenssoro's claim that the presence of two columns of writing in a short text reveals the *Historia et Rudimenta* to be a modern forgery does not bear scrutiny.

The presence of the word *genocidium* (genocide) in the text would probably indicate a twentieth-century origin for the manuscript—if, in fact, *genocidium* had been used. Laurencich Minelli's transcription of the manuscript indicates that where Estenssoro read *genocidium,* the text actually reads "gen. ocidium," an abbreviated form of the phrase *generis ocidium* (murder of a lineage or family). The abbreviated phrase "gen. ocidium" occurs in a passage in which the author was recounting how Mayachac Azuay bemoaned the destruction of his noble lineage by the Spanish. Given the context of the passage, which focuses on the death of the *curaca*'s family, the phrase *generis ocidium* actually suits the meaning of the text much better than does the modern term *genocidium,* which refers to the destruction of a whole nation.

The Italian phrase *gente bianca,* which Estenssoro takes as meaning "white men" and as referring anachronistically to Europeans, occurs in JAO I. The phrase is used in the context of a narrative read from a "royal" quipu by Chahuarurac to the author (Laurencich Minelli, Miccinelli, and Animato 1995, 388–89). The story begins in A.D. 650, when men from Tartaria invade South America and fight with the Peruvian natives, who had "incarnado bianco" [white skin] and were descendants of giants. According to the text, these giants, described as "gente bianca" [white people], had come to Peru in A.D. 550, one hundred years before the Tartarians. During the combat, the Peruvians were nearly exterminated. Those Peruvians who remained mixed with the newcomers to create a new lineage that eventually gave rise to the Inca. In the aftermath of this war, the sacred "royal" quipus were first introduced to Peru. It is not at all clear from this narrative that the phrase *gente bianca* used to describe the ancestors of the Incas in this account refers to Europeans; rather, the story is quite ambiguous about the identity of these people. Curiously, Montesinos tells a similar version of this legend in which Peru is invaded by foreigners in A.D. 550; however, in his account, the invaders are "of the color black."[4] It is not at all certain that the "gente bianca" mentioned in JAO 1, but who are "de color prieto" in Montesinos, signifies Europeans; Estenssoro's argument that the phrase "white people" in the *Historia et Rudimenta* is a modern anachronism remains undemonstrated.

Estenssoro also claims that the manner of writing the date that occurs in JAO I is totally inappropriate to seventeenth-century Spanish. He has charged that the way in which the date is given in the text, "De Los Reyes 31 de Julio 1637," is never found during this period. Instead, he writes, the date would be preceded by *a*—as in "a 31 de Julio"—in a manuscript that was authentic and not a recent forgery. However, dates could be and were written in the sixteenth and seventeenth centuries without *a* preceding the day. For example, if one looks at Anello Oliva's own *Las vidas de los varones insignes,* one sees that Father Alonso Messía dated his approval for the publication of Anello Oliva's work "de Lima 10 de marzo de 1631." Likewise, the date on Provincial Nicolás Duran's approbation of Anello Oliva's text reads, "Lima diez de marzo," without *a* before the day (Anello Oliva [1631] 1998, 17, 19). Yet again, Estenssoro's arguments about alleged anachronisms in the *Historia et Rudimenta* prove incorrect.

Another aspect of Estenssoro's critique of the *Historia et Rudimenta* concerns the grammatical mistakes made by both Cumis and Anello Oliva in their writings in Spanish. According to Estenssoro, these mistakes provide another confirmation that the document was not written by these men but penned by recent Italian forgers. However, both Cumis and Anello Oliva were native Italian speakers for whom Spanish was a second language. It would not have been impossible for them to have made errors in their written Spanish. Rolena Adorno has maintained that while Cumis might have committed mistakes in his Spanish grammar, such an event would be unlikely for Anello Oliva (Adorno 1998). Pointing out that Anello Oliva's written Spanish in his *Las vidas de los varones insignes* is exemplary, she questions whether he is really the author of JAO I and JAO II. However, one does see grammatical errors in Anello Oliva's original manuscript of *Las vidas,* which he corrected. It would not be unthinkable

---

4. "... de color prieto" (USevilla 1644, book 2, chap. 14).

for him to have made and not noticed several errors in his Spanish while writing in a numerical code. After all, there are only two grammatical mistakes in the Spanish attributed to Anello Oliva in the *Historia et Rudimenta*. The existence of these two mistakes, made while writing in code, hardly seems sufficient to label the document a modern forgery.

All of Estenssoro's remaining arguments focus on disputing the content of the document rather than addressing the age of the manuscript. He makes a cogent argument that the Quechua texts were not dictated by a native speaker of the language, that the "royal" quipu is not of the quality associated with the Inca royalty, that the "proofs" of Valera as the author of the *Nueva corónica* are unconvincing, and that the document contains false statements concerning the native peoples. Yet none of these assertions, however correct they may be, prove that the document is not an authentic seventeenth-century manuscript.

Rolena Adorno (1998) has presented additional evidence, she states, of an anachronism in the text that proves that it could not have been written in the early seventeenth century. Adorno notes that the first documented use of the Greek word *clitoris* in Latin occurs in 1615. Its use, therefore, in a text dating to 1637 is surprisingly early, she argues, and not humanly possible for someone who was a missionary in Peru. However, the Jesuit college of Lima, the capital city of the viceroyalty of Peru, was hardly a backwater in the seventeenth century. Rather, Anello Oliva, as rector of the college, was at the heart of one of the great centers of baroque culture and learning of the time. It does not seem particularly surprising that he would have been capable of employing a Greek word that had already been in use in Latin for at least twenty years, if not longer. According to Adorno, the word *clitoris* in the *Historia et Rudimenta* occurs in the description of the "removal of the clitoris of young girls,"[5] a custom not known to have been practiced in the Americas. Yet in the seventeenth century, the word *clitoris* not only meant the organ for which the word is used today but also referred generally to any of the outer tissue of the female genitals; the phrase in JAO I, "the barbaric slash of the clitoris on little girls" (see chap. 9), most likely concerns the ritual defloration of young girls, a practice well established in parts of the

5. ". . . la ablación del clitoris de las niñas" (Adorno 1998).

New World and recorded in a Spanish ethnography by 1620 (Hernández [1620] 1996, 238).

Reviewing the arguments that the *Historia et Rudimenta* is a poor-quality modern forgery, one finds none capable of withstanding scrutiny. No one has presented credible evidence that these documents are modern frauds. There are, as Estenssoro, Adorno, and others have rightly noted, many questions about the truthfulness of some of the allegations made in the documents, but such questions do not prove that the manuscripts are modern forgeries produced within recent decades. Certainly, there is no need to adopt a "fundamentalist" approach to the texts, in which the document is rejected utterly if anything is found to be untrue. People in the seventeenth century were as capable of half-truths and fabrications as are people today. There is simply no reason to assume that these documents are recent forgeries, especially given that there is positive evidence that these are early modern documents.

One essential element in proving the age of the *Historia et Rudimenta* and *Exsul Immeritus* is demonstrating that the paper, ink, and other materials therein pertain to the relevant period in the seventeenth century. Ugo Zoppi (2001), of the Physics Division ANSTO, Menai, Australia, conducted radiocarbon analysis on materials taken from both documents in front of two witnesses; A. Bertoluzza, C. Fagnano, M. Rossi, and A. Tinti (2001), of the Università di Bologna, conducted a spectroscope analysis of the colors and inks used in the documents; and Giorgio Gasparotto (2001), also of the University of Bologna, performed an scanning electron microscope analysis and an EDS microanalysis of the metals used in *Exsul Immeritus*. The reports from these analyses reveal that the paper, ink, wax, and metal in the Naples documents are dated to the seventeenth century, with the exception of one page containing evidence of restoration in the nineteenth century. Although it is true that forgers can find blank pieces of old paper to use in faking documents, it is extremely difficult to fake the dates on inks, especially when they are used in the quantity and in the colors found in the two manuscripts. Additionally, the handwriting of the two documents was analyzed by the respected paleographer Luigi Altamura (2001). Altamura found that the styles of handwriting in both sets of texts were appropriate to the respective periods; he also was able to confirm the authenticity of the handwriting samples by Anello Oliva, Pedro de Illanes, and Amadeo di Savoia-Aosta in the documents.

Another source of confirmation of the authenticity of the documents lies in their record of various aspects of Blas Valera's life with the Jesuits—aspects that were completely unknown when the *Historia et Rudimenta* was first published but that have been discovered since. These facts, discussed in the present biography, include (1) the information that Valera's difficulties with the Society of Jesus did not result from illicit relations with a woman but from his "heretical" ideas concerning Andean Christianity (see chap. 8); (2) the assertion that there existed special quipus for recording history, many of which were sent to Garcilaso de la Vega, who lied about them in the *Comentarios reales* (see chap. 6); (3) the severe censorship of Anello Oliva's lifework, resulting in a dramatically changed text that, even so, was denied publication (see chaps. 8, 10); and (4) the conflicted attitudes of Acosta toward Valera and native rights (see chap. 7).

One might suggest that the alleged "forgers" simply looked up all of these facts in the relevant manuscripts to give an air of veracity to their texts, but performing such research would imply a major investment of time as well as a considerably detailed knowledge of Peruvian Jesuit history. My research into his life and career, for instance, has taken over ten years, assisted by grants from the National Science Foundation, the Andrew W. Mellon Foundation, the National Endowment for the Humanities, and Yale University. There are no folders marked "Valera" in any archive; one can locate documents about him only after a time-consuming scrutiny of published and unpublished sources. For example, discovering Montesinos's statements concerning Garcilaso's lies about quipus required studying the four redactions of a text of over eight hundred closely written pages, most of which has never been published; these manuscript redactions exist in four separate archives: the Biblioteca Nacional in Madrid, the Biblioteca de la Universidad de Sevilla, the New York Public Library, and Sterling Memorial Library at Yale University.[6] Finding the rele-

---

6. The manuscripts in Seville (USevilla 1644) and Madrid (BN 1642) were written in the seventeenth century, during Montesinos's lifetime; the Yale manuscript is a crucially important nineteenth-century copy of a lost redaction of the text, the Merced manuscript (ca. 1645). Indications that the manuscript in the New York Public Library (Rich [ca. 1645] 1780) may be the lost Merced manuscript need to be investigated further.

vant sentences in an unpublished portion of the Universitaria manuscript occurred only after a significant investment of time and effort. One might assume that the alleged "forgers" worked more quickly and less thoroughly, but this still would have involved a considerable time commitment, as well as skill in studying archival texts. Who is accused of doing this research? Most importantly, how do the skills and time needed to discover these facts about Valera, Acosta, and Anello Oliva correspond to the accusations that the Naples documents are extremely sloppy forgeries?

There is yet another objection to the idea that the Naples documents were created by forgers who spent considerable time looking up materials on Valera to help substantiate the incredible narrative in these documents. How could the "forgers" know that their lengthy searches through the archives would yield such an extraordinary story as Valera's? Before my research and Gálvez Peña's publication in 1998 of the British Library's unedited manuscript of Anello Oliva, none of the facts mentioned were known about Valera and his circle of Jesuits. Why would the "forgers" have done all of this research as a shot in the dark when there was no reason to believe that it would amount to anything particularly interesting. One might suggest that the alleged forgers came across some of this information about Valera by accident while working on a research project and so decided to investigate further. Yet one is still plagued with questions about who would do this, when they would do it, and what research project would be involved? Certainly, none of the individuals most closely involved with the manuscripts, such as Clara Miccinelli, Carlo Animato, or Laura Laurencich Minelli, have come forward with the data that I have presented in this book.

Confirmation that the Naples documents existed in the seventeenth century has been found recently by two respected Italian scholars, Maurizio Gnerre (Universitá di Napoles L'Orientale) and Francesca Cantú (Universitá di Roma III). In the Roman archive of the Society of Jesus, Gnerre (2001) discovered a short letter that appears to have been part of the group of texts comprising *Exsul Immeritus*. This letter is dated June 25, 1618, and was supposedly written in Alcalá de Henares by someone who signed his name "Exsul Immeritus BV." Apparently addressed to General Mutuo Vitelleschi, the letter refers to BV's simulated death, which he undertook out of obedience. The author, BV, writes that he has completed his mission in his own land and has finished his written work "with its memories and ancient things." BV is waiting to send this work, *Exsul Immeritus,* to General Vitelleschi, the letter continues. Throughout the letter are references to statements and images corresponding to *Exsul Immeritus,* demonstrating that this text did exist in the seventeenth century. The handwriting of the letter also matches that found in the *Exsul Immeritus* documents allegedly signed by Valera. Gnerre is careful to note that this letter is a numbered entry in a volume bound in the nineteenth century, making it virtually impossible for it to be a twentieth-century fake.

A letter located by Francesca Cantú (2001) in a public archive in Rome confirms the existence of allegations in 1610 that Pizarro poisoned Atahuallpa's men. According to this missive from Licenciado Juan Fernández de Boan to the count of Lermos, Don Pedro Fernando Ruiz de Castro, a mestizo in Peru had been proclaiming that Francisco de Chavez denounced Francisco Pizarro for having killed Atahuallpa's best men in Cajamarca with poisoned wine. The letter is dated March 28, 1610, and was written in Lima. Cantú's discovery provides strong evidence for the existence in the seventeenth century of both of the letter purportedly by Chaves in *Exsul Immeritus* and of *Exsul Immeritus* itself, which discusses Chaves's accusations against Pizarro.

These letters located by Gnerre and Cantú were first presented to an academic audience during the 1999 Rome conference on Guaman Poma and Blas Valera sponsored by the Instituto Italo-Latino Americano. Disturbingly, much of the reaction to these documents from the North American and Peruvian scholars attending the conference centered on the suggestion that archives had been planted with fake documents (Mumford 2000, 43). Given that there is not one solid piece of evidence that the *Historia et Rudimenta* and *Exsul Immeritus* are modern fakes, and given that no analysis has revealed any anachronisms or inauthenticities in these two letters, it seems highly problematic to assume that these letters are forgeries.

True Lies and the Mystery of the Texts

While there is no proof that the Naples documents are modern frauds, and significant evidence indicating that they were written in the seventeenth century, their contents have raised numerous questions. Some of the allegations in the documents, such as the story of how the Jesuits claimed falsely that Valera's problems with the Society were due to fornication rather than heresy, imply that the documents were written by someone with an intimate knowledge of the mestizo chronicler and his peers. Other aspects of the two texts, however, can be shown to be false. Much of the criticism of the documents has focused on disproving that Valera could have written the *Nueva corónica y buen gobierno,* attributed to Guaman Poma de Ayala. Leading experts on the *Nueva corónica,* such as Rolena Adorno (1998, 2001) and Xavier Albó (1998), have written convincingly that Valera could not have authored a document exhibiting such a detailed knowledge of the families, local politics, and geography of the Lucanas region of Peru—Guaman Poma's home—and containing such frequent antimestizo diatribes.

However, there are even more fundamental problems with the veracity of the two documents than the question of who wrote the *Nueva corónica.* Most importantly, Blas Valera's signature in the *Historia et Rudimenta* and his handwriting and signature in *Exsul Immeritus* do not match the sample of his handwriting from the Jesuit *Libro de noviciado,* published in facsimile by José Toribio Polo (1907, 552). According to Francisco de Mateos (1944c, 57 n. 92), who possessed a photograph of Valera's signature from the *Libro de noviciado,* Toribio Polo's facsimile matches the signature in the photograph. A comparison of Valera's signature with the writing signed by Valera in the two Naples documents reveals that Valera did not write the sections attributed to him in the Italian manuscripts. Valera's signatures and handwriting in the Naples documents were forged; the question is, by whom?

A second difficulty with the contents of the Naples documents concerns the letter purportedly written by Valera's kinsman Francisco de Chaves denouncing Pizarro for treacherously using poison to capture Atahuallpa. The letter discovered by Francesca Cantú demonstrates that a mestizo in 1610 in Peru expressed the same accusations against Pizarro, attributing them to Chaves as well. This 1610 letter strongly suggests that *Exsul Immeritus*'s purported Chaves letter may well have existed by the early seventeenth century. Certainly, there was no shortage of individuals in sixteenth- or early seventeenth-century Peru who would have been interested in blackening Pizarro's name and perhaps even instigating an investigation into Pizarro's finances. But the brief Chaves letter in *Exsul Immeritus* could not have been the "copious" Chaves account seen by Valera in his father's house, described in the *Relación de las costumbres antiguas*. The author of the *Relación* is emphatic that the Chaves letter "particularly . . . [states] that there were no sacrifices of men or of children among the Peruvians."[7] However, the Chaves letter in *Exsul Immeritus* never once mentions, even remotely, anything about whether the Peruvians practiced human sacrifice; in fact, it makes no statement of any kind about Andean religion or ritual practices. Whereas it is quite possible that someone wrote the Chaves letter in *Exsul Immeritus* in colonial Peru and that this letter found its way into Jesuit hands, this could not have been the letter known by Valera. It is important to remember the vital role played by the purported Chaves letter in Valera's alleged autobiography in *Exsul Immeritus*. If this is not the letter that Valera would have known, the rest of Valera's alleged biography may be suspect also.

Other aspects of the narrative in the *Historia et Rudimenta* and *Exsul Immeritus* also have raised doubts. First, it seems unbelievable that the hundreds of drawings of the *Nueva corónica,* along with the thousand-page text and all of the drawings for Martín de Murúa's chronicle, could have been created by Gonzalo Ruiz, a Jesuit brother who was consistently described in the Jesuit catalogs as "feeble" and good only for "offices of little work."[8] Second, as I mentioned before, the Quechua texts in the *Historia et Rudimenta* date to the mid–seventeenth century, not earlier, and appear to have been written by someone who was not a native speaker. Valera, of course, was not only a native speaker but an accomplished linguist as well, so it is highly unlikely that he wrote them. Third, the Jesuit scholar Xavier Albó (1998, 324) has seriously questioned the likelihood of the story of Valera's faked death and secret voyage to Peru. Finally, the claim that

---

7. ". . . en particular . . . que no hubo sacrificios de hombres ni de niños entre los piruanos" (Blas Valera [1594] 1968, 155).

8. ". . . flacas fuerzas"; " . . . officios de poco trabajo" (entries for Gonzalo Ruiz in the Jesuit catalogs of 1613 [Pius XII Library 1613] and 1601 [Egaña 1981, 270], respectively). By 1613, Ruiz had been assigned to the Jesuit house in Huamanga, where he would spend the rest of his life.

Captain Alonso Valera, not Luis, was Blas's father is also puzzling. So far, no one has found any records confirming the existence of Alonso Valera, not even in the catalog of passengers to the Indies. This is highly surprising given that Alonso was supposedly a military captain closely related to a leading *encomendero*.

These documents, therefore, present a very real mystery. On the one hand, there is strong evidence—such as the letter discovered by Gnerre and the authentication of the signatures of Anello Oliva, Illanes, and Savioa-Aosta—that the documents are genuine seventeenth-century artifacts. On the other hand, the story that they tell is bizarre and contains obvious falsehoods. In response to this conundrum, R. T. Zuidema (2001) has proposed that the *Historia et Rudimenta* is a genuine document dating to before 1750 and possibly containing some portions written by Anello Oliva in 1638. However, he believes that the allegations that Valera wrote the *Nueva corónica* are untrue and that the authors of the *Historia et Rudimenta* had the opportunity to view a portion of Guaman Poma's work, which they incorporated into the document. He views the purpose of the *Historia et Rudimenta* as "very much in line with the Jesuits' reinterpretation of Inca culture for propagandistic purposes," a reinterpretation popular among a certain subgroup of Jesuits in Peru (see Mumford 2000, 45). Borja de Medina likewise has suggested that these documents are authentically old but represent "a fictitious composition originating in the climate of conflict between creoles and peninsulars"[9] in which one side took Valera as their symbolic leader. Juan Ossio, an expert on the *Nueva corónica,* also acknowledges that while there is no doubt that Guaman Poma wrote the monumental work attributed to him, the Naples documents seem to express the authentic sentiments of certain Jesuits in the seventeenth century (see Mumford 2000, 44–45).[10] Ossio has speculated that a faction of Jesuits may have been dedicated to vindicating Valera's reputation and may have attributed the *Nueva corónica* to him as part of that effort.

---

9. "... una composición ficticia originada en el clima de conflicto criollo-peninsular" (cited as a personal communication in Albó 1998, 344). See also Medina 1999.

10. For a description of the anti-Spanish opinions of another Peruvian Jesuit, Martín de Funes, see Piras 1998. Like Valera, Funes, who was involved in setting up the famous Jesuit reductions in Paraguay, suffered at the hands of his superiors for his political opinions.

The opinions of Zuidema, Borja de Medina, and Ossio that the manuscripts are "true lies"—authentic documents containing false-hoods that express the frustrations and desires of certain Jesuits in Peru—seem to fit the evidence most closely. It also seems highly prob-able that Anello Oliva played a major role in creating the Naples doc-uments, perhaps even forging the texts signed by Valera. Adorno (1998, 388–89) has argued that it would have been very unlikely for Anello Oliva to have written the passages attributed to him in the *Historia et Rudimenta,* because of the document's criticisms of Gar-cilaso de la Vega. In Anello Oliva's *Las vidas de los varones insignes,* she remarks, Anello Oliva praises Garcilaso highly, in contrast to the critical comments about Garcilaso's veracity found in the Naples doc-uments. However, if one reads further in Anello Oliva's work, one finds the chronicler quite willing to state categorically that Garcilaso was wrong about a variety of issues. In chapter 2 of *Las vidas,* in a section carrying the notation "Refutation of the Commentator Gar-cilaso,"[11] Anello Oliva argues at length that Garcilaso's account of the foundation of the Inca Empire by Manco Capac is completely wrong. Later in his work, Anello Oliva again maintains that Gar-cilaso's *Comentarios reales* is untrue, this time in its description of the savageness of the native Peruvians before the rise of the Incas. In this instance, interestingly, Anello Oliva ([1631] 1998, 95–96) explicitly cites Valera's *Vocabulario,* with its discussions of the pre-Inca kings, as proof that Garcilaso is incorrect. Finally, Anello Oliva sharply dis-agrees with Garcilaso's defense of the actions of the Dominican Father Vicente de Valverde on the fateful day when Atahuallpa was captured by Pizarro. In a long marginal note, Anello Oliva strongly condemns Valverde's actions of inciting the Spanish to attack the Inca emperor and states that Garcilaso's defense of Valverde is unbeliev-able: "For all of these reasons, what Garcilaso says is not credible to me; I praise his piety, but not his ease in writing about such serious matters, which call out for firmer foundations than he gives . . ."[12] Hostility to the Dominicans present at the Spanish conquest of the Incas is, of course, an important feature of the Naples documents. *Las*

---

11. "Refútase al Comentador Garçilasso" (Anello Oliva [1631] 1998, 37).

12. "Por todas estas raçones no se me haçe creyble lo que diçe Garçilasso; aunque alabo su piedad, pero no la façilidad en escribir cosas tan graves que piden más firmes fun-damentos de los que da . . ." (ibid., 132).

vidas, rather than ruling out Anello Oliva's participation in writing the Naples document, reveals that the Jesuit questioned Garcilaso's truthfulness on several occasions, including one in which he cited Valera against Garcilaso.

Albó has also suggested that Anello Oliva could not have assisted in the creation of the *Historia et Rudimenta* and *Exsul Immeritus.* Because of the chronicler's "peaceful, devout, and prudent character," Albó writes,[13] it is doubtful that he would have participated in the type of "conspiracy" described in the Naples documents. However, René Millar Carvacho's recent investigations into the Peruvian Jesuits between 1630 and 1650 has revealed a very different picture of the Italian chronicler. The image of Anello Oliva that emerges from Millar Carvacho's research (1999) is of a troubled, unbalanced, and angry man, criticized for his imprudent conduct and lack of caring toward his subordinates. On one occasion, he publicly attacked a married woman on the street in front of her husband. While he was in charge of the Jesuit college in Callao, he discharged his duties in such a "deplorable" fashion that he had to be removed from his post.[14] In 1635, General Vitelleschi wrote that had he received reports earlier about Anello Oliva's troublesome conduct, he would never have allowed him to be chosen as superior (Millar Carvacho 1999, 163).

Anello Oliva's anger against the Spanish conquistadors, whom he considered guilty of an unjust conquest leading to the horrific destruction of the native peoples, is amply expressed in his original manuscript of *Las vidas de varones insignes.* This manuscript, begun in 1608, was completed twenty-three years later, in 1631. It apparently was an extraordinary work, comprising four volumes, which covered the Inca history of Peru as well as detailed lives of important Jesuits in the Andes. Unfortunately, most of the work has been lost; only volume 1 of Anello Oliva's magnum opus remains today. The original manuscript of this work, preserved in the British Library, includes lengthy quotations from Las Casas condemning Spanish abuses of the native Americans. Chapter 6, for example, is devoted almost entirely to Las Casas's emotional descriptions of the savage treatment meted out to Peruvian Indians by their Spanish conquerors. However,

---

13. ". . . su carácter tranquilo, devoto y prudente" (Albó 1998, 323).
14. ". . . desempeño deplorable" (Millar Carvacho 1999, 163).

almost all of the portions describing Spanish atrocities (along with numerous other passages) are crossed out with a thick line. Until Gálvez Peña's publication of this manuscript in 1998, it was unknown that long passages in Anello Oliva's work had been censored by his superiors. The other edition of *Las vidas* was published in 1895 by Juan Francisco Pazos Varela and Luis Varela y Orbegoso. This edition was based on Anello Oliva's final manuscript, housed in the Biblioteca Nacional in Lima (the library has since been destroyed by fire). In that manuscript, all of the offensive passages were omitted. In studying Anello Oliva's manuscripts, then, we see that his angry denunciations of Spanish atrocities were censored from his work, much as the *Historia et Rudimenta* claims they were.

In fact, the only portion of Anello Oliva's anti-Spanish diatribe that was allowed to remain in his text were citations from the medieval mystic St. Bridget of Sweden, which he applied to the New World. Well versed in medieval apocalyptic literature, the chronicler apparently cited numerous prophetic revelations about the Indies in the lost portions of his text, according to the surviving index.[15] In the remaining passages about St. Bridget, Anello Oliva states that she had received direct revelations of the "horrendous cruelties" that would occur in Peru after the Spanish invasion. Not only does the chronicler describe the evils that the saint foresaw for the Indies, but he also mentions the punishment awaiting those Spaniards who abuse the Indians. According to Christ's revelations to Bridget, "their teeth will break, their right hand [will be] cut off, and their right foot [will be] withered."[16] Anello Oliva's use of St. Bridget's apocalyptic imagery in *Las vidas de varones insignes* is not dissimilar to that found in *Exsul Immeritus*.[17]

Despite the removal from his work of most of Anello Oliva's harsh

---

15. For example, he quoted the "prophetiça Bernardino," the "revelaçiones especialíssimas a Mari Díaz, santa muger," and "algunas propheçias [de Cristo] singulares," according to the index (Anello Oliva [1631] 1998, 339, 355, 340). It is not known whether Anello Oliva was related to a Padre Anello from Naples who was investigated by the Inquisition for his involvement in a mystical *alumbrada* cult in the 1580s (see BN ca. 1585).

16. ". . . sus dientes serán quebrados, su mano derecha cortada, y su pie derecho dejarretado" (Anello Oliva [1631] 1998, 180). See Hyland and Hyland 1999.

17. Interestingly, the references to mystics are not the only evidence of mysticism in *Las vidas*. In another passage that was crossed out by censors, Anello Oliva ([1631] 1998, 245) advocates a quietistic approach to the Jesuit *Spiritual Exercises,* one that would lead laypeople, including Indian confraternity members, to a mystical union with God, beyond

condemnations of the Spanish, he still was forbidden to publish it. According to Millar Carvacho, there were several reasons for the general's decision not to publish this work. Alonso Messía, Anello Oliva's superior in Peru, had stamped Anello Oliva's final manuscript—the objectionable portions removed—with permission to publish. General Vitelleschi, however, was quite upset that Messía had done so before receiving final approval from Rome; he indicated his displeasure in a letter dated December 20, 1634. Millar Carvacho (1999, 166–67) has suggested that procedural questions in the licensing of the work, its anti-Spanish content, and the general's unhappiness with Anello Oliva's conduct all contributed to the Society's failure to publish *Las vidas de varones insignes*.

In 1638, in the general's letter to the Peruvian province, Vitelleschi forbade publication of Anello Oliva's work (Pius XII Library 1638). This must have come as a deep disappointment to the chronicler, who had dedicated some twenty-three years of his life to researching and writing the four volumes. Did he identify at this point with Blas Valera, whose tragic story he probably had heard in Naples from Lucio Garcete or perhaps had learned in later years in Peru? It is after this date that JAO's portions in the *Historia et Rudimenta* include the story of Valera's faked death and his secret literary production in Peru. Anello Oliva certainly possessed both the means and a motive for helping to create the Naples documents. His extensive knowledge about the Jesuits in Peru would have served as a basis for the information in the texts, from the description of the conflicted attitude of Acosta toward native rights to the claim that special historical quipus had been sent to Garcilaso de la Vega, who did not acknowledge them in the *Comentarios reales*. Anello Oliva also possessed a reason for the anger against the Jesuits expressed in the *Historia et Rudimenta* and *Exsul Immeritus*. Once the general had forbidden the publication of his work, there was nothing he could do to reverse this decision and no other press to which he could go. In the refusal to publish his book, he had legitimate cause for frustration against his order. It seems highly possible that he may have written at least por-

---

words. Not only was his idea that Indians and other laypeople could experience the Ignatian exercises a radical departure from the norm, but the quietistic, mystical approach to the exercises was rejected by the Society.

tions of the Naples documents to set down his forbidden anti-Spanish sentiments under the name of Valera, a Jesuit who also suffered for his criticisms of the conquest and his vision of Andean Christian society. Along with a vindication of Valera, however, *Exsul Immeritus* also demonstrates an appreciation for Juan de Mariana, a Jesuit silenced and imprisoned by the Jesuits in the early seventeenth century for his radical anti-Spanish, antimonarchical political theories. Mariana's ideas were not widely distributed until the seventeenth century, making it unlikely for the real Valera to have had any acquaintance with them. Of course, a Valera who had not really died in 1597 but who lived until 1619 would have been able to have known Mariana, as *Exsul Immeritus* claims, thereby bringing together two of the most radical Spanish Jesuits of Anello Oliva's lifetime.

Whoever wrote the two Naples documents also harbored a deep grudge against Guaman Poma de Ayala. While there is no evidence that Anello Oliva was involved in any controversy with the native writer, it long has been believed that Anello Oliva had access to at least portions of the *Nueva corónica*. Years ago, Raúl Porras Barrenechea (1986, 305, 500) speculated that Anello Oliva in all likelihood viewed a section of Guaman Poma's work, given certain similarities shared by Anello Oliva's and Guaman Poma's texts and no others. Guaman Poma is known to have been involved in at least one very lengthy legal dispute over possession of land in the central highlands (Guaman Poma de Ayala [1590–1616] 1987b), and it is not impossible that he may have clashed with Anello Oliva, who was apparently a difficult person, disliked by his subordinates.

It seems quite probable that Anello Oliva wrote the portions of the *Historia et Rudimenta* attributed to him and highly likely that he wrote at least part of *Exsul Immeritus* as well. One major question remaining is whether these documents were one man's anguished vision or part of a larger Jesuit movement; we know, for example, that one of the Jesuits mentioned in the documents as a sympathizer with the movement, the Latin professor Jerónimo de Montesinos, was at times at odds with his superiors and may have collaborated with Anello Oliva.[18] The *Historia et Rudimenta* seems to have been passed

---

18. In 1599, Aquaviva wrote that Montesinos could not be promoted because of his activities in Quito, but the general does not specify what these activities were (Egaña 1981, 562–63). In an unpublished letter by Aquaviva from 1607, the general writes "escriven del

on after 1618 among at least some native people, but it is simply impossible to answer this question at this stage. To address this and many other issues, however, it is essential to have a published version of *Exsul Immeritus* available. At the time of this writing, although Laurencich Minelli has had a transcription of the main text prepared for several years, it is still awaiting publication.

Incidentally, one last objection commonly made to the authenticity of both the *Historia et Rudimenta* and *Exsul Immeritus* is that the second document seems to answer all of the questions raised by the first (e.g., Mumford 2000, 43–44). For example, after the discovery of *Exsul Immeritus* was announced, several scholars went to great length to demonstrate that Valera could not have written the *Nueva corónica* because of the detailed information about Lucanas in it. To this point, Laurencich Minelli has responded that *Exsul Immeritus* claims that Guaman Poma was allowed to add personal information to the chronicle to give it greater veracity (see Albó 1998, 325–42). But the perception that the second document answers the questions posed by the first is more apparent than real. It is, after all, *Exsul Immeritus* that raises the most fundamental problems of the text: (1) the discrepancy between Valera's real handwriting and that in Valera's alleged autobiography in the document and (2) the dissimilarity between the Chaves letter known to Valera and that in *Exsul Immeritus*. These issues would have been obvious to any self-respecting forger. Valera's handwriting, for example, is reproduced in an article from 1907; it would have been a simple matter for a forger to invent a reason why Valera's purported autobiography was merely dictated by the exiled Jesuit instead of written in his hand. Rather than providing easy answers for issues raised by the *Historia et Rudimenta, Exsul Immeritus* reveals two of the fundamental reasons why these texts cannot be taken at face value.

---

colegio del Cuzco que el P. Jerónimo de Montesinos se a enmendado notablemente en su modo de predicar" (Pius XII Library 1607b); apparently, Montesinos's preaching had been displeasing to his superiors. The Jesuit catalog of 1607 states that Montesinos was a native of Lima, thirty-eight years old, healthy, and a professor of Latin. In 1607, Anello Oliva was in Santa Cruz de la Sierra (Pius XII Library 1607a). Montesinos is listed also in the 1613 catalog (Pius XII Library 1613).

The Implications of the "Naples Documents"

What is the meaning of these documents for the study of Valera? The evidence indicates that they were written after his death. While the authors intended to honor Valera, they blended truth and fiction into a convoluted mix that still cannot be entirely separated. Among the confirmable facts about Valera in the Naples documents are (1) the reasons for his difficulties with the Society, (2) the description of his following among the Indian nobility in the Nombre de Jesús confraternity, (3) his idealism regarding Christian evangelization in Peru, and (4) his creation of a unique native quipu writing system expressive of his religious ideology, samples of which were sent to Garcilaso de la Vega.

Foremost among the lies told about Valera in these documents is the fabrication that he wrote the *Nueva corónica* and then falsely attributed it to Guaman Poma. The *Nueva corónica* diverges in a great many ways from Valera's theology and historiography of the Andes, while it accords with Guaman Poma's other known testimony. The claims about Valera as the author of Guaman Poma's extraordinary text may represent, as Borja de Medina has suggested, a Jesuit attempt to vindicate Valera, along with an effort to discredit the Indian chronicler. The autobiography allegedly written by Valera is clearly faked, perhaps by Anello Oliva, so the information in it cannot be taken as necessarily true. The narrative of Valera's false death, return to Peru, and later return to Spain seems incredible, although there is no actual evidence to either support or deny the possibility of these events.

Most troubling for the biographer of Valera is the documents' tale of the Jesuit's personal history. The story of the rape and murder of Valera's Indian mother by the brutal Alonso Valera, brother of Luis, is particularly disturbing. However, the absence of any mention of Alonso in any colonial records that have come to light suggests that he, too, may be a fabrication. Although he was supposedly a military captain, he cannot be found in the catalog of passengers to the Indies, in any of the notarial records or *cabildo* books relating to Chachapoyas, or in any of the very detailed contemporary accounts of the Peruvian civil wars by Pedro Gutierrez de Santa Clara or Diego Fernández. Garcilaso's *Comentarios reales* is the only source to mention

Alonso Valera, stating that *Alonso* was the name of Blas's father. It is not clear, however, either whether Garcilaso's claim was the inspiration for the idea that Blas's true father was Alonso or whether the chronicler possessed a secret knowledge about his fellow mestizo. Concerning the documents' history of Blas's mother, Francesca, we have no way of knowing whether she was actually the daughter of the native healer Illavanqa. It is possible that this story represents a genuine oral memory of Valera that was passed on to the author of *Exsul Immeritus*. Yet it might also be another fabrication.

There is no doubt in my mind that the documents were written after Valera's death and therefore cannot necessarily tell us any new information about his tumultuous life. These documents make no credible argument that Valera was the author of the *Nueva corónica*. The evidence indicates to me that the documents were written by one or more Jesuits who identified with Valera's legacy and wished to express ideas forbidden by the Society. Nonetheless, the debate over whether the *Historia et Rudimenta* and *Exsul Immeritus* are seventeenth-century forgeries, modern fakes, or entirely authentic manuscripts will undoubtedly last for a long time to come. It seems likely that discussions of Valera's life and thought will occupy center stage in Peruvian studies for many years.

"... an owl among the ruins ..."

The emotionalism of the controversy over the Naples documents reveals the degree to which the issues that Valera cared about are still vital to us today. It is important that we do not allow the debates over these Italian manuscripts to obscure his very real contributions to the struggle for native rights in Peru. During his lifetime, he assiduously collected indigenous legends and histories from local peoples throughout Peru. In Cuzco, he organized a circle of native elites to discuss Andean traditions and religion in light of the Spanish conquest and helped to develop a phonetic form of quipu "writing." Through his many writings, he argued for the natural justice and virtue of Inca society and Inca religion. His four works include his magnum opus, the *Historia Occidentalis,* which, although it is lost, has profoundly influenced generations of readers through the remnants of it preserved by Garcilaso de la Vega.

In his concern for the welfare of the indigenous peoples of Peru and in his courageous efforts to defend their civilization and forge a new vision of Andean Christianity, Valera was truly a "Las Casas of the Andes." However, unlike Las Casas, who was rewarded with a bishopric for his stance on behalf of the native Americans, Valera was imprisoned, flogged, and suspended from saying mass because of his beliefs. His health broken and his reputation damaged, he was then exiled to Spain, carrying with him the knowledge that his vision of native Andean society was not shared by his Jesuit superiors in Peru. His case was even taken as the Jesuit justification to deny mestizos admission into the Society, a policy that would remain in place until the Jesuit expulsion from South America in 1768. We have no writings directly from Valera expressing his sentiments about the trials he underwent. Yet we do know that from the time of his house arrest onward, he daily recited the seven penitential psalms in Latin; surely, one suspects, he must have identified with the words of the psalmists.

> Have pity on me, O Lord, for
> I am languishing; . . .
>
> (Psalm 6)

> For my days vanish like smoke,
> and my bones burn like fire.
> Withered and dried up like grass
> is my heart;
> I forget to eat my bread, . . .
> I am reduced to skin and bone.
> I am like a desert owl;
> I have become like an owl among the ruins,
> I am sleepless and cry out . . .
>
> (Psalm 101)

Murdered at the hands of English pirates, Valera never got to plead his case before Rome, as he had requested in 1586 from his underground prison cell. It is hoped that now, over four hundred years after his death, his ideas will finally have a hearing.

APPENDIXES

APPENDIX A

Father Jerónimo Valera, O.F.M.,
on Native Rights,
January 12, 1599 (AGI 1599)

Dudas que se ofrescen sobre si el virrey deste Reyno podrá licitamente repartir yndios para labrar las minas que de nuevo se han descubierto ó descubriesen siendo útiles y prouechosas en conformidad de lo que cerca desto manda su Magestad en tres capítulos de cartas y de lo que le paresce a esta audiencia conforme al acuerdo que sobre ello hizo de que van las copias en esta relación.

Suponese para esto por notoria la nescesidad que hay de que las minas se labren y en la que esta su magestad de que nos consta ser muy grande y que de todos sus reynos en solo los de las yndias tiene socorro de hazienda para defensa de la cristiandad y que este sale de las minas las quales sin el trauajo de los yndios no se podrán labrar ni veneficiar los metales de que se saca la plata, y que si esto çesase o viniese en notable diminucion, como se puede entender que vendra no descubriendose minas de nuevo y labrandolas pues las antiguas se van acabando y bajando la ley, yrreparable sería el daño que los enemigos de nuestra santa fee podrán hazer en los rreynos de su Magestad y ultramarinos y en estos como más largamente esta aduertido en la

239

junta de letrados que el señor Virrey don francisco de Toledo hizo para rrepartir yndios a el cerro de Potossí y en el rrepartimiento último del señor Marques de cañete virrey destos reynos para el mismo cerro en trece de nouiembre de nouenta y tres años.

Deuese también aduertir quan neçessario sea para la conseruaçion deste rreyno que las minas se labren pues la sustancia principal dél consiste en la plata que della sale sin la qual es euidente la diminucion y pobreza en que todas las cossas vendrían çessando el comercio como cesaria necesariamente faltando la plata que lo sustenta.

I. Supuesto todo lo susodicho se pregunta si será licito dar yndios a los descubridores y dueños de minas que estan descubiertas y de nuevo se descubrieren para veneficio dellas siendo de ymportancia y prouecho con las condiciones y calidades de paga y buen tratamiento conthenidas en las hordenanças del señor visorrey Francisco de Toledo.

II. y en caso que sea licito rrepartir yndios para el veneficio de las dichas minas de que distancia y por que tiempo se podrán dar y en que cantidad se podrán dar y en que cantidad supuesta la que tubieran de tributarios los rrepartimientos de donde se dieren.

III. yten si estando tan apocados como estan con otros seruicios y rrepartimientos los yndios como son sementeras, tragines, tanbos, edificios y obrages y guardas de ganados de donde se prende sacar las minas, se podran comutar en parte o en todo estos seruicios reduciendolos al del veneficio de las minas advirtiendo el maior trauaxo y riesgo que en este ay asi se les cargaran mas yndios de rrepartimientos para no causar este rrepartimiento en las demas.

IIII. y si las minas que se descubrieren de nuevo fueren en comarcas de donde van yndios a otras más distantes se quedaran en las que assi descubrieren por rraçon de su mayor comodidad ecepto el cerro de potossi por estar aquellas tan asentadas y fundadas que seria de yncombeniente quitarles los yndios.

Hase de ver con los demás papeles de susorreferidos el que va con los de lo que se propuso por parte de los dueños de minas en la nueva españa sobre esta misma materia que aunque en lo particular deste rreyno no haze el caso en lo general es de ymportancia.

I. Para rresponder a este casso se supone por cossa certíssima ser cossa licita rrepartir yndios para labor de las minas descuviertas en este rreyno por las rraçones y causas que muchas vezes por hombres doctos se an dado en aquesta dubda y el numero de el rrepartimiento paresce ser justo el que por los señores virreyes destos rreynos se ha hecho en señalar la septima o sexta parte de los yndios de rrepartimiento para labrar las dichas minas.

II. Lo segundo se presupone que agrauar mas este rrepartimiento en suvirlo a la quarta o quinta parte de los yndios para labrar las dichas minas seria cossa rigurossa y en alguna manera ynjusta pues resultaria no solo en detrimento de los mismos naturales por hirse acauando con tan exesiuo trauajo pero tambien sub-cederia notable daño a este rreyno y de los demas de su rreal magestad pues por tener en el tiempo presente mas plata con que defenderlos y sustentarlos podria subceder en el futuro tanta falta de yndios para el seruicio de las minas que fuese notable la falta de plata para su conseruación como la esperiencia nos enseña con este seruicio de las minas yrse cada dia disminuyendo el numero de los naturales deste reyno.

III. Lo tercero se presupone que pues el fin principal de las minas y su administracion es el prouecho que de ellas se saca para la def-fensa de la fee y defensa de los rreynos de su Magestad catholica hauiendo minas y no pudiendose acudir a la labor de todas ellas solas aquellas se deben labrar para las que les huuiere suficiente seruicio y de quien se saque mayor prouecho.

Supuesto lo dicho rresponde que para las minas de nueuo descu-biertas no es cossa conuiniente agrauar mas el rrepartimiento de los yndios para su administracion lo qual se prueua con la evidencia moral que con este rreyno se tiene de la notable diminucion que con el rrepar-timiento ya otras uezes hecho de la sesta o septima parte se halla en los naturales desta tierra y por rremediar con más eficacia la necesidad presente no es justo se deje de preuenir la futura con humana provi-dencia que siempre tan necesaria es en casos semejantes.

A lo que se pregunta si sera licito comutar en parte o en todo los yndios rrepartidos a los tambos, sementeras, obrages & para labrar las dichas minas nos parece que en ninguna manera se haga lo primero porque segun la practica comun hordinaria rrelacion y aun generales quejas de los señores de ganado obrage y sementeras, y de los españoles que exercitan los caminos deste reyno no solo no hay yndios sobrados en estos ministerios pero antes ay gran falta dellos y vese ser anssi verdad porque como cada día se van multiplicando más los españoles en este rreyno ay necesidad de más seruicio personal de los naturales para las cosas tocantes a la vida comun.

Lo segundo y más principal porque cuando dos cosas ocurren y entranbas necessarias a las quales juntamente no se puede satisfazer la que es de menor necesidad se a de dejar para acudir a las más urgentes pues con esto de dos vienes se escoge el mejor y de dos males se evita el mayor a lo qual obligacion como consta ex capitulo non medioc-riter de consecrat dist 5 et cau. duo mala 13 dist. et cau. iurauit et cau. non solum 22. q. 4 et facit cau. sic viue 16. q. 1 y ansi lo enseña arist. lib. 5 ethico duorum bonorum appositorum melius est semper eligen-dum et lib. 3 thopicorum eligendum est duobus omino, similibus id. ex quo maius bonum sequitur pues sin duda es cierto que aquestas cosas sobredichas son más nescesarias en este reyno que la multipli-cacion de las minas que el prouecho que de ellas se saca para el sus-tento de la vida comun de tal suerte son las sobredichas cosas nesce-sarias que no hauiendo suficiente cantidad de sementeras, tragines y ni suficiente seruicio para los pasageros en los pueblos y tambos lo uno sesaria el comercio y trato que ay de unas partes a otras en este reyno y ya que no fuese en todo a lo menos en parte y tan grande que fuese en notable daño de la tierra y lo otro abria tanta necesidad de sustento corporal que los pobres y aun los que no son padeciessen gran detrimento asi de hambre como de otras cossas tocantes a la vida comun y assi nos parece que de ninguna manera se haga nuevo rrepartimiento de yndios ni se quiten de las sementeras obrages y para labrar las minas de nuevo descuviertas pero si estas pareciesen ser mejores que las que se labran o van labrando apliquense los yndios de las otras a estas por causas de su mayor vtilidad que es el fin que en ellas se pretende y esto nos parece salio meliore iudicio en san fran-cisco de lima en 12 de henero de 1599 años.

[signed] fray hyeronimo valera, fray cristoval chauero, fray francisco de otaloras, fray bernardo gamarra, fray cristoual clauero, fray ben-ito de huertas

APPENDIX B

Testimony of Father Lucio Garcete, S.J., to the Inquisitors of Panama City, August 11, 1591 (AHN 1591)

Lucio Garsete Religiosso de la compañía de Jesus. digo que por descargo de mi consciencia y no por odio ni rancor de nuestro Cong.te. Quel padre Juan de Atienca provincial ques actualmente de la dicha compañía en el piru con parecer de sus consultores a lo que sospecho, especialmente del padre Esteuan Cabello, mandó al Padre Valentin de Carauntes que entonces era Maestro de Novicios, que en ciertos libros de nuestro instituto, que se yntitulan compendio de Privilegios, y ay uno que se llama compendio comun, y otro compendio indico engrudase papelicos blancos, ciertos privilegios tocantes en perjuizio de los casos reservados que tiene el Sancto Officio, y en otras partes del dicho compendio cortase con la tigera cierta hoja en que se les consede a los superiores facultad de absolver de casos de Heregía, y de otros casos tocantes al sancto officio y licencias de leer libros pro-hiuidos, y asi se hizo y lo mismo se me mandó a mí quando vine a Panama, y entiendo que se mandó a todos los superiores del Piru, lo qual se hizo segun entiendo, sin primero pedir licencia al Sancto Officio, y a fin de que se encubriesen. E los privilegios que tienen al

Sancto Tribunal de la ynquissicion, y por otra parte el dicho Provincial, y los que el quisiere, se quedaron con las dichas facultades, y el de aduertir que hizo el dicho Padre Provincial la sobre dicha diligencia, quando supieron de la prission de los nuestros en Valladolid por orden del Illustríssimo senor Cardenal de Toledo Inquissidor mayor que fue por causa de los dichos preuilegios. y dubdo mucho si en la prission en que el dicho Padre provincial tubo por espacio de tres años en Lima al Padre Valera si fue por algun caso del Sancto Officio porque fue estrechissima y larga prission Valiendose con el o con otros de semejantes previlegios. Tambien el dicho Padre Provincial publico, que los nuestros auian salido libres gracias a dios. siendo que se supo de cierto que todos salieron con su penitencia a un que se rieta.

Lucio Garcete

En la ciudad de Panama a onze dias del mes de Agosto de mil y quinientos y noventa y un años. Ante el muy Reverendo padre Fray Pedro Ortiz, Guardian del Monasterio de señor San Francisco desta ciudad por la Commission que tiene del Sancto Officio. Pareció el padre lucio garsete de la companía de Jesus, rector que ha sido de la companía de Jesus, y presento este memorial scripto e firmado de su nombre y ante todas cosas juró en forma de derecho de dezir verdad y dixo que lo contenido en el dicho memorial es verdad. y lo dize y declara por descargo de su consciencia. y que la letra y firma del dicho memorial es suya y de su mano y letra y por tal la reconoce y prometió de guardar secreto desta su declaracion So pena de excomunion. y perjurio y auiendose le leydo esta su declaracion se rratifico en ella y dixo ser asi verdad por el juramento que hizo y que no ha hecho por odio ni enemistad. y el de treynta y seis años. lucio garsete. fray pedro ortiz. ante mi Joan lorenzo perez.

References

Manuscripts Consulted

Archivo General de Indias, Seville (AGI)

1583a   Testimony of Diego de Agüero. Lima, August 30. Audiencia de Lima, legajo 126.

1583b   Testimony of Diego de Porras Sagredo. Lima, August 30. Audiencia de Lima, legajo 126.

1583c   Testimony of Licenciado Francisco Falcón. Lima, August 30. Audiencia de Lima, legajo 126.

1599   Padre Jerónimo Valera, O.F.M. on native rights. Lima, January 12. Audiencia de Lima, est. 70, caja 1, legajo 33.

Archivo Histórico Nacional, Madrid (AHN)

1571–73   Procesos penitenciados y deliberados. Lima, March 1571 to February 1573. Inquisición, libro 1027, fol. 18a.

1580a   Charges against Oxnam and crew. Lima, March. Inquisición, libro 1027, fols. 107a–b, 143a.

1580b   Testimony of Catalina Paxna, Ana Paxna, and Juana de Manarion against Melchior Hernández, O. de M. Inquisición, libro 1027, fols. 77a–78a.

1580–81a   Procesos pendientes. Lima, April 1580–April 1581. Inquisición, libro 1027, fols. 69b, 118a–125b, 172b–173a.

1580–81b   Procesos penitenciados. Lima, April 1580–April 1581. Inquisición, libro 1027, fols. 126b, 161b–162a.

1581–82a Relación de negocios sentenciados e determinados. Lima, April 1581–February 1582. Inquisición, libro 1027, fol. 195a–197a.

1581–82b Sentence against Luis López, S.J. Lima, October 1581–March 1582. Inquisición, legajo 1654, exp. 14.

1582 Proceso contra Luis López, S.J. Lima, March 19. Inquisición, libro 1027, fol. 195b.

1590 Letter by Don Antonio de Arpide y Ulloa. Lima, April 30. Inquisición, libro 1035, fols. 14b–19b.

1591 Testimony of Lucio Garcete, S.J. Panama City, August 11. Inquisición, libro 1035, fol. 227a–b.

1595 Proceso contra Ricardo Haquines. Lima, November 4. Inquisición, libro 1036, fol. 122a.

N.d.a Proceso contra Miguel de Fuentes, S.J. Lima. Inquisición, libro 1027, fol. 195a–b.

N.d.b Sentence against Miguel de Fuentes, S.J. Lima. Inquisición, legajo 1647, exp. 2.

Biblioteca de la Universidad de Sevilla (USevilla)

1644 Fernando de Montesinos. *Memorias historiales i políticas del Perú.* MS 332/35.

Biblioteca Nacional, Madrid (BN)

[1594] *De las costumbres antiguas de los naturales del Piru.* MS 3177.

[ca. 1585] Copia de las proposiciones de Sor Julia, Padre Anello y Joseph alubrados. Naples. MS 2440, fols. 110a–113b.

1642 Fernando de Montesinos. *Memorias antiguas i nuevas del Pirú.* MS 3124.

British Library (BL)

1620 Melchior Hernández, O. de M. *Memorial de Chiriquí.* C62, i, 18.9.

1631 Juan Anello Oliva, S.J. *Varones insignes en sanctidad de la Compañía de Jesús de la provincia del Perú.* Additional MS 25.327.

Harkness Collection, Library of Congress (Harkness)

1538–45 *Libro del cabildo de San Juan de la frontera de Chachapoyas.* Peru, no. 1031.

1568a Carta de venta de Antonio López a Diego de Porras. Lima, May 25. Peru, fol. 866a.

1568b Letter by Antonio López concerning Santiago del Cercado. Peru, fol. 852a.

1569 Carta de venta de Baltasar de los Reyes a Diego de Porras. Lima, May 16. Peru, fol. 868a.

Latin American Manuscript Collection, Yale University (Yale)

1508–1634 *Indice de bullas, brebes, y montorios . . . en el Archivo del Collegio de San Pablo.* Series II, box 2, folder 2.

1645 Fernando de Montesinos. *Memorial sobre las minas de Indias.* Formerly lost manuscript about Montesinos's invention of a new method for processing silver. Series I, box 2, folder 23.

References

[ca. 1645] ca. 1860   Fernando de Montesinos. *Memorias antiguas historiales del Perú.* Handwritten copy by Brasseur de Bourborg of the "lost" 1780 copy of the Merced MS. Series II, box 2, folder 15.

Lilly Library, Indiana University at Bloomington (Lilly)

    1600   Testimony of Bishop Luis López de Solís about the Jesuits of Quito. July 24. Latin American MSS, vol. 21, folder 3, fols. 86a–94b.

Pius XII Manuscript Library, St. Louis University (Pius XII Library)

    1583   José de Acosta. *Información y respuesta sobre los capitulos del concilio Prounicial del Perú del año de 83 de que apellaron los procuradores del clero.* Pastells Collection, roll 1, vol. 9, 749–73.

    1607a   Catálogo año/607. Archivum Romanum Societatis Iesu, roll 122, Peru 4.

    1607b   Letter from General Aquaviva to the Peruvian province. Archivum Romanum Societatis Iesu, roll 120, Peru 1.

    1612   Antonio Pardo, S.J. Mission a Chachapoyas. Archivum Romanum Societatis Iesu, roll 125, Peru 13.

    1613   Catálogo año/613. Archivum Romanum Societatis Iesu, roll 122, Peru 4.

    1638   Letter from General Vitelleschi to the Peruvian province. Archivum Romanum Societatis Iesu, roll 122, Peru 2a.

Rich Collection, New York Public Library (Rich)

    [ca. 1645] 1780   Fernando de Montesinos. *Memorias antiguas historiales del Perú.* Formerly lost 1780 copy of the lost Merced MS. Rich 75.

Works Consulted

Acosta, José de

    1953   Testimony on Mestizo Ordination, 1583. In *Los Mercedarios en el Perú en el siglo XVI,* ed. Victor Barriga, Vol. 4:279–81. Arequipa.

    1954   *De Procuranda Indorum Salute.* In *Obras del P. José de Acosta,* ed. Francisco de Mateos. Madrid: Biblioteca de Autores Españoles. Originally written in 1577.

    1987   *Historia natural y moral de las Indias.* Ed. José Alcina Franch. Madrid: Historia 16. Originally written in 1590.

Adorno, Rolena

    1986   *Guaman Poma: Writing and Resistance in Colonial Peru.* Austin: University of Texas Press.

    1998   Criterios de comprobación: El manuscrito Miccinelli de Nápoles y las cronicas de la conquista del Perú. *Anthropológica* 16:374.

    2001   Contenidos y contradicciones: La obra de Felipe Guaman Poma y las aseveraciones acerca de Blas Valera. <http://ensayo.rom.uga.edu /filosofos/peru/guaman/adorno.htm>. (February 2002).

Albó, Xavier

    1998   La *Nueva corónica y buen gobierno:* Obra de Guaman Poma o de Jesuitas? *Anthropológica* 16:307–48.

REFERENCES

Alcina Franch, José
    1971   El Atlántico y América antes de Colón. *Cuadernos Hispanoamericanos* 256:22–43.
    1987   Introduction to *Historia natural y moral de las Indias,* by José de Acosta. Ed. José Alcina Franch. Madrid: Historia 16.

Altamura, Luigi
    2001   Relazione di consulenza concernente la verifica di scritture. In *Guaman Poma y Blas Valera: Tradición andina e historia colonial,* ed. Francesca Cantú, 143–70. Rome: Antonio Pellicani Editore.

Alvarado, Juan de
    1965   Memoria de cosas primeras que acontecieron en los Chachapoyas. In *Relaciones geográficas,* vol. 4, ed. Marcos Jimenez de la Espada. Madrid. Originally written in 1550.

Anello Oliva, Giovanni (Juan)
    1895   *Historia del Perú y varones insignes en santidad de la Compañía de Jesús.* Ed. J. F. Pazos Varela and L. Varela y Orbegoso. Lima. Originally written in 1631.
    1998   *Historia del reino y provincias del Perú y vidas de los varones insignes de la Compañía de Jesús.* Ed. Carlos Gálvez Peña. Lima: Pontificia Universidad Católica del Perú. Originally written in 1631.

Animato, Carlo, Paolo Rossi, and Clara Miccinelli
    1989   *Quipu: Il nodo parlante dei misteriosi Incas.* Genoa: Edizioni Culturali Internazionali.

Arriaga, Pablo Joseph de
    1921   *La extirpación de la idolatría en el Perú.* Lima: Colección de Libros y Documentos Referentes a la Historia del Perú. Originally published in 1621.
    1968   *The Extirpation of Idolatry in Peru.* Trans. Clark Keating. Lexington: University Press of Kentucky. Originally published in Spanish in 1621.

Ascher, Marcia, and Robert Ascher
    1981   *Code of the Quipu.* Ann Arbor: University of Michigan Press.

Atienza, Blas de
    1953   Testimony of Fr. Blas de Atienza, August 30, 1583. In *Los Mercedarios en el Perú en el siglo XVI,* ed. Victor Barriga, vol. 4:266–72. Arequipa.

Augustine of Hippo, St.
    1984   *Concerning the City of God against the Pagans.* Trans. Henry Bettenson. London: Penguin Books.

Avalos y Figueroa, Diego de
    1602   *Miscelánea austral.* Lima.

Barnes, Monica
    1992   Catechisms and Confessions: Distorting Mirrors of Andean Societies. In *Andean Cosmologies through Time,* ed. Robert Dover, Katherine Seibold, and John McDowell, 67–94. Bloomington: Indiana University Press.

1996　A Lost Inca History. *Latin American Indian Literatures Journal* 12, no. 2:117–31.

Barnes, Monica, and David Fleming

1991　Filtration-Gallery Irrigation in the Spanish New World. *Latin American Antiquity* 2:48–68.

Barriga, Victor

1933　*Los Mercedarios en el Perú en el siglo XVI.* Vol. 1. Rome.

1939　*Los Mercedarios en el Perú en el siglo XVI.* Vol. 2. Arequipa.

1942　*Los Mercedarios en el Perú en el siglo XVI.* Vol. 3. Arequipa.

1949　*Mercedarios ilustres en el Perú: El Padre Diego de Porres.* Arequipa: Talleres Graficos la Colmena.

1953　*Los Mercedarios en el Perú en el siglo XVI.* Vol. 4. Arequipa.

1954　*Los Mercedarios en el Perú en el siglo XVI.* Vol. 5. Arequipa.

Bartra, Enrique

1967　Los autores de catecismo del Tercer Concilio Limense. *Mercurio Peruano* 470:359–70.

Bauer, Brian S.

1992　*The Development of the Inca State.* With a foreword by Gary Urton. Austin: University of Texas Press.

1998　*The Sacred Landscape of the Inca: The Cusco Ceque System.* Austin: University of Texas Press.

Bauer, Brian S., and David Dearborn

1995　*Astronomy and Empire in the Ancient Andes.* Austin: University of Texas Press.

Behar, Ruth

1989　Sexual Witchcraft, Colonialism, and Women's Powers: Views from the Mexican Inquisition. In *Sexuality and Marriage in Colonial Latin America,* ed. Asunción Lavrin, 178–206. Lincoln: University of Nebraska Press.

Bermudez Plata, Cristóbal, ed.

1940　*Catálogo de pasajeros a Indias I (1509–1534).* Seville: CSIC.

1942　*Catálogo de pasajeros a Indias II (1535–1538).* Seville: CSIC.

1944　*Catálogo de pasajeros a Indias III.* Seville: CSIC.

Bertoluzza A., C. Fagnano, M. Rossi, and A. Tinti

2001　Primi risultati dell'indagine spettroscopica micro-Raman sui documenti Miccinelli *(Historia et Rudimenta* e *Exsul Immeritus).* In *Guaman Poma y Blas Valera: Tradición andina e historia colonial,* ed. Francesca Cantú, 181–90. Rome: Antonio Pellicani Editore.

Betanzos, Juan de

1987　*Suma y narración de los Incas.* Ed. Carmen Martin Rubio. Madrid. Originally written in 1551.

1996　*Narrative of the Incas.* Trans. Roland Hamilton and Dana Buchanan. Austin: University of Texas Press. Originally written in Spanish in 1551.

REFERENCES

Burgaletta, Claudio

    1999   *José de Acosta SJ (1540–1600): His Life and Thought*. With a foreword by John W. O'Malley. Chicago: Loyola Press.

Burkhart, Louise

    1989   *The Slippery Earth: Nahua-Christian Moral Dialogue in Sixteenth-Century Mexico*. Tucson: University of Arizona Press.

Cantú, Francesca

    2001   Guaman Poma y Blas Valera en contraluz: Los documentos inéditos de un oidor de la Audiencia de Lima. In *Guaman Poma y Blas Valera: Tradición andina e historia colonial,* ed. Francesca Cantú, 475–519. Rome: Antonio Pellicani Editore.

Carmona Moreno, Felix

    1993   *Fray Luís López de Sólis, OSA: Figura estelar de la evangelizacion de América*. Madrid: Editorial Revista Agustiniana.

Caurson, Barbara

    1879   *The Jesuits: Their Foundations and History*. Vol. 1. New York.

Christian, William A., Jr.

    1989   *Local Religion in Sixteenth-Century Spain*. Princeton: Princeton University Press.

Church, Warren

    1996   Prehistoric Cultural Development and Interregional Interaction in the Tropical Montane Forests of Peru. Ph.D. diss., Yale University.

Cieza de León, Pedro

    1923   *The War of Las Salinas*. Trans. Sir Clements Markham. London. Originally written in Spanish in 1553.

    1986   *Descubrimiento y conquista del Perú*. Ed. Carmelo Saénz de Sant Maria. Madrid: Historia 16. Originally written in 1553.

Clancy, Thomas H.

    1976   *An Introduction to the Jesuit Life*. St. Louis.

Cobo, Bernabe

    1952   *Historia del nuevo mundo*. Ed. F. Mateos. Biblioteca de Autores Españoles, vols. 91–92. Madrid. Originally published in 1653.

    1953   *Inca Religion and Customs*. Ed. and trans. Roland Hamilton. Austin: University of Texas Press. Originally published in 1653.

Confesionario para curas de Indios con la instrucción contra ritos y exhortaciones para ayuda a bien morir

    1585   Lima: Antonio Ricardo.

Conklin, Harold

    1991   Doctrina christiana, en lengua española y tagala. In *Vision of a Collector: The Lessing J. Rosenwald Collection in the Library of Congress,* ed. Kathleen Mang and Peter VanWingen, 36–40. Washington: Library of Congress.

Cook, Alejandra Parma, and Noble David Cook

    1991   *Good Faith and Truthful Ignorance*. Durham: Duke University Press.

References

Cook, Noble David

   1981   *Demographic Collapse: Indian Peru, 1520–1620.* Cambridge: Cambridge University Press.

Córdoba y Salinas, Diego de

   1651   *Cronica de la religiosissima provincia de las doze aposteles.* Vol. 3. Lima.

Cummins, Tom

   1994   Representation in the Sixteenth Century and the Colonial Image of the Inca. In *Writing without Words,* ed. Elizabeth Hill Boone and Walter D. Mignolo, 188–219. Durham: Duke University Press.

Declaración de los quipucamayocs a Vaca de Castro

   1922   In *Informaciones sobre el antiguo Peru,* 3. Lima: Colección de Libros y Documentos Referentes a la Historia del Perú. Believed to be originally written in 1542.

Decoster, Jean-Jacques, and Brian S. Bauer

   1997   *Justicia y poder, Cuzco, siglos XVI–XVIII: Catálogo del Fondo Corregimiento Archivo Departamental del Cuzco.* Cuzco: Centro Bartolomé de las Casas.

Domenici, Davide, and Viviano Domenici

   1996   Talking Knots of the Inka. *Archaeology* 49, no. 6:54–55.

Durand, José

   1961   Blas Valera y el Jesuita Anónima. *Estudios Americanos* (Seville) 109–10:73–94.

   1987   Los últimos días de Blas Valera. In *Libro de homenaje a Aurelio Quesada Sosa,* 409–20. Lima.

Duviols, Pierre

   1974–76   Une petite chronique retrouveé: Errores, ritos supersticiones, y ceremonias de los Indios de la provincia de Chinchaycocha. *Journal de la Société des Americanistes* 63:275–97.

   1977   Los nombre quechua de Viracocha, supuesto Dios Creador de las evangelizadores. *Allpanchis* (Cuzco) 10:53–63.

   1989   Las cinco edades primitivas del Perú según Guaman Poma de Ayala: Un método de computo original? In *Time and Calendars in the Inca Empire,* ed. Mariusz S. Ziolowski and Robert M. Sadoski, 7–16. BAR International Series, vol. 479. n.d.

Egaña, Antonio de

   1954   *Monumenta peruana.* Vol. 1. Rome: Monumenta Historica Societatis Iesu.

   1958   *Monumenta peruana.* Vol. 2. Rome: Monumenta Historica Societatis Iesu.

   1961   *Monumenta peruana.* Vol. 3. Rome: Monumenta Historica Societatis Iesu.

   1966a   *Monumenta peruana.* Vol. 4. Rome: Monumenta Historica Societatis Iesu.

REFERENCES

1966b   *Historia de la Iglesia en la América Española*. Madrid: Biblioteca de Autores Cristianos.

1970   *Monumenta peruana*. Vol. 5. Rome: Monumenta Historica Societatis Iesu.

1974   *Monumenta peruana*. Vol. 6. Rome: Monumenta Historica Societatis Iesu.

1981   *Monumenta peruana*. Vol. 7. Rome: Monumenta Historica Societatis Iesu.

Espinosa Soriano, Waldeman

1967   Los señoríos étnicos de Chachapoyas y la alianza hispano-chacha. *Revista Histórica* 30:233–70.

Estenssoro, Juan Carlos

1997   Historia de un fraude o fraude histórico? *Revista de Indias* 57, no. 210:566–78.

Esteve Barba, Francisco

1968   Estudio preliminar. In *Crónicas peruanas de interés indígena*. Madrid: Biblioteca de Autores Españoles.

Falcón, Francisco

1918   *Representación . . . sobre los daños y molestias que se hacen a los Indios*. In *Informaciones acerca de la religión y gobierno de los Incas*, ed. Horacio Urteaga, 135–76. Lima: San Martín. Originally written in 1567.

Fernández de la Mora, Gonzalo

1993   El proceso contra el Padre Mariana. *Revista de Estudios Políticos* (Madrid) 79:47–99.

Fernández García, E.

1990   Blas Valera es el "Jesuita Anonimo," autor de la *Relación de las costumbres antiguas de los naturales del Perú*. In *La evangelización del Perú, siglos XVI y XVII: Actas del Primer Congreso Peruano de Historia Eclesiástica*. Arequipa.

Fry, Timothy, ed.

1980   *The Rule of Saint Benedict*. Collegeville, Minn.: Liturgical Press.

Gálvez Peña, Carlos

1998   Prologue to *Historia del reino y provincias del Perú*, by Giovanni Anello Oliva. Ed. Carlos Gálvez Peña. Lima: Pontificia Universidad Católica del Perú.

Garcilaso de la Vega, El Inca

1944a   *Comentarios reales de los Incas*. Ed. Ángel Rosenblatt. Vol. 1. Buenos Aires: Emecé Editores. Originally published in 1609.

1944b   *Comentarios reales de los Incas*. Ed. Ángel Rosenblatt. Vol. 2. Buenos Aires: Emecé Editories. Originally published in 1609.

1987   *Royal Commentaries of the Incas and General History of Peru*. Part 1. Trans. Harold V. Livermore. Austin: University of Texas Press. Originally published in Spanish in 1609.

References

Gasparotto, Giorgio
2001 Studio al microscopio elettronico a scansione (SEM) e microanalisi EDS delle parole chiave metalliche allegate a *Exsul Immeritus*— indagine preliminare. In *Guaman Poma y Blas Valera: Tradición andina e historia colonial*, ed. Francesca Cantú, 191–94. Rome: Antonio Pellicani Editore.

Gnerre, Maurizio
2001 La telaraña de las verdades: El f. 139 del tomo *Cast. 33* del Archivum Romanum Societatis Iesu (ARSI). In *Guaman Poma y Blas Valera: Tradición andina e historia colonial*, ed. Francesca Cantú, 195–245. Rome: Antonio Pellicani Editore.

Godoy Aguirre, Mario
1997 La música en la catedral de Quito: Diego Lobato de Sosa. *Revista Musical de Venezuela* 34:83–94.

González de la Rosa, Manuel
1907 El Padre Valera, primer historiador Peruano. *Revista Histórica* 2:180–99.

1908 Los "Comentarios reales" son la réplica de Valera a Pedro Sarmiento de Gamboa. *Revista Histórica* 3:296–306.

1909 Polémica histórica: Las obras del Padre Valera y de Garcilaso. *Revista Histórica* 4:301–11.

Gose, Peter
1996 Oracles, Divine Kingship, and Political Representation in the Inka State. *Ethnohistory* 43, no. 1:1–32.

Goti Ordeñana, Juan
1999 *Del Tratado de Tordesillas a la Doctrina de Derechos Fundamentales en Francisco de Victoria*. Valladolid: Universidad de Valladolid.

Griffiths, Nicholas
1996 *The Cross and the Serpent: Religious Repression and Resurgence in Colonial Peru*. Norman: University of Oklahoma Press.

Guaman Poma de Ayala, Felipe
1987a *Nueva crónica y buen gobierno*. Ed. John V. Murra, Rolena Adorno, and Jorge L. Urioste. Vols. 1–3. Madrid: Historia 16. Originally written in 1615.

1987b *Y no ay remedio*. Ed. Elías Prado Tello and Alfredo Prado Prado, with an introduction by Pablo Macera. Lima: Centro de Investigación y Promoción Amazónica. Originally written in 1590–1616.

Hampe Martínez, Teodoro
1996 *Cultura barroca y extirpación de idolatrías: La biblioteca de Francisco de Avila (1648)*. Cuzco: Centro Bartolomé de las Casas.

1998 *Santo Oficio e historia colonial*. Lima: Ediciones del Congreso del Perú.

2001 Una polémica versión sobre la conquista del Perú: Es auténtica la *Relación* de Francisco de Chaves (1533)? In *Guaman Poma y Blas*

REFERENCES

Valera: Tradición andina e historia colonial, ed. Francesca Cantú, 343–64. Rome: Antonio Pellicani Editore.

Haro Alvear, Silvio Luis

1965 *Atahualpa Duchicela.* Ibarra: Imprenta Municipal de Ibarra.

Hartmann, Roswith

1986 Un predicador quichua del siglo XVI. In *Primer Simposio Europeo sobre Antropología del Ecuador,* 291–301. Quito: Ediciones Abya-Yala.

Hernández, Melchior

1996 *Memorial de Chiriquí.* In *Religiosos Mercedarios en Panamá (1519–1992),* ed. Juan Zaporta Pallares, O. de M., 233–47. Madrid: Revista Estudios. Originally written in 1606.

Hiltunen, Juha

1999 *Ancient Kings of Peru: The Reliability of the Chronicle of Fernando de Montesinos.* Helsinki: Suomen Historiallinen Seura.

Hocart, A. M.

1970 *Kings and Councillors: An Essay in the Comparative Anatomy of Human Society.* Chicago: Chicago University Press.

Huarochirí Manuscript, The.

1991 Ed. and trans. Frank Salomon and George Urioste. Austin: University of Texas Press. Originally written ca. 1607.

Hyland, Sabine

1994 Conversion, Custom, and "Culture": Jesuit Racial Policy in Sixteenth-Century Peru. Ph.D. diss., Yale University.

1996 A Concubine Redeemed: The 1603 Case of Luisa, "Indian of Chile." *Manuscripta* 40, no. 3:173–79.

1998a Illegitimacy and Racial Hierarchy in the Peruvian Priesthood: A Seventeenth-Century Dispute. *Catholic Historical Review* 84, no. 3:431–54.

1998b The Imprisonment of Blas Valera: Heresy and Inca History in Colonial Peru. *Colonial Latin America Historical Review* 7, no. 1:43–58.

2000 Introduction to Yale University's Latin American Manuscript Collection. *Yale University's Latin American Manuscript Collection, series II. Primary Source Microfilms.*

2001 Montesinos y los reyes de Wari. In *Huari and Tiwanaku: Modelos vs. evidencias, primera parte,* ed. Peter Kaulicke and William H. Isbell, 641–48. Lima: Boletín de Arqueología Pontificia Universidad Católica del Perú.

2002 Woven Words: The Royal Khipus of Blas Valera. In *Narrative Threads: Explorations of Narrativity in Andean Khipus,* ed. Gary Urton and Jeffrey Quilter, 151–70. Austin: University of Texas Press.

in press. Biblical Prophecy and the Conquest of Peru: Fernando de Montesinos'. *Memorias historiales. Colonial Latin American Historical Review.*

References

Hyland, Sabine, and William Hyland
    1999   Juan Anello Oliva and St. Bridget of Sweden: Medieval Visions in a Seventeenth-Century Chronicle of Peru. Paper presented at the First International Congress of Peruvianists, Harvard University.

Jensen, DeLamar
    1992   *Renaissance Europe: Age of Recovery and Reconciliation.* Lexington: D. C. Heath.

Julien, Catherine
    2000   *Reading Inca History.* Iowa City: University of Iowa Press.

Klaiber, Jeffrey
    1976   The Posthumous Christianization of the Inca Empire in Colonial Peru. *Journal of the History of Ideas* 37, no. 3:515.

Las Casas, Bartolomé de
    1986   *Tratados I.* Mexico City: Fondo de Cultura. Originally published in 1552.
    1992   *The Devastation of the Indies: A Brief Account.* Trans. Herma Briffault, with an introduction by Bill Donovan. Baltimore: Johns Hopkins University Press. Originally published in Spanish in 1552.

Laurencich Minelli, Laura
    1994   *La misteriosa scrittura dell' antico Perú.* Bologna: CUSL.
    1996   *La scrittura dell' antico Perú.* Bologna: CUSL.
    1997   Note sull'autenticitá del documento seicentesco *Historia et Rudimenta Linguae Piruanorum. Thule* 2–3:239–44.
    1998   *Historia et Rudimenta Linguae Piruanorum:* Un estorbo o un acontecimiento? *Anthropológica* 16:349–68.
    1999   Carta a Rolena Adorno: Un complemento a la polémica sobre Guaman Poma. *Anthropológica* 17:422–27.
    2000   Blas Valera leader di un movimento neo-inca cristiano? Una prova ulteriore dell' autenticitá del ms. *Historia et Rudimenta Linguae Piruanorum.* In *Studi americanistici in Italia: Risultati e prospettive,* ed. L. Gallinari, 261–85. Cagliari: CNR.
    2001a   Presentación del documento *Exsul Immeritus Blas Valera Populo Suo.* In *Guaman Poma y Blas Valera: Tradición andina e historia colonial,* ed. Francesca Cantú, 111–42. Rome: Antonio Pellicani Editore.
    2001b   Un aporte de *Exsul Immeritus Blas Valera Populo Suo* y de *Historia et Rudimenta Linguae Piruanorum* a la historia peruana: La figura del cronista Blas Valera. In *Guaman Poma y Blas Valera: Tradición andina e historia colonial,* ed. Francesca Cantú, 247–72. Rome: Antonio Pellicani Editore.

Laurencich Minelli, Laura, Clara Miccinelli, and Carlo Animato
    1995   Il documento seicentesco *Historia et Rudimenta Linguae Piruanorum. Studi e Materiali de Storia delle Religioni* 61:363–413.
    1998   Lettera di Francisco de Chaves alla Sacra Cattolica Cesarea Maestá:

Un inedito del sec. XVI. *Studi e Materiali de Storia delle Religioni* 64:57–92.

Lerche, Peter

1995   *Los Chachapoya y los simbolos de su historia.* Lima.

Lisi, Francesco Leonardo

1990   *El Tercer Concilio Limense y la aculturación de los indígenas sudamericanos: Estudio crítico con edición, traducción, y comentario de las actas del concilio provincial celebrados en Lima entre 1582 y 1583.* Salamanca: Universidad de Salamanca.

Loaysa, Francisco

1945   Introduction to *Las costumbres antiguas del Perú,* by Blas Valera. Ed. Francisco Loaysa. Lima.

Lohmann Villena, Guillermo

1970   El Licenciado Francisco Falcón (1521–1587): Vida, escritos y actuación de un procurador de los Indios. *Anuario de Estudios Americanos* 27:131–94.

1999   *Las minas de Huancavelica en los siglos XVI–XVII.* Lima: Pontificia Universidad Católica del Perú.

Lopétegui, León

1942   *El Padre José de Acosta y las misiones.* Madrid.

López, Luís

1889   El Visorey Francisco de Toledo. In *Colección de documentos inéditos para la historia de España,* ed. José Sancho Rayon and Francisco de Zadalburu, 94:472–525. Madrid. Originally written in 1581.

López de Gomara, Francisco

1965   *Hispania victrix: Primera y segunda parte de la historia general de las Indias.* Ed. P. Guibelalde. Madrid. Originally published in 1553.

MacCormack, Sabine

1985a   The Fall of the Incas: A Historiographical Dilemma. *History of European Ideas* 6, no. 4:421–45.

1985b   The Heart Has Its Reasons: Predicaments of Missionary Christianity in Early Colonial Peru. *Hispanic American Historical Review* 65:443–66.

1991   *Religion in the Andes: Vision and Imagination in Early Colonial Peru.* Princeton: Princeton University Press.

1994   *Ubi Ecclesia?* Perceptions of Medieval Europe in Spanish America. *Speculum* 61, no. 1:74–100.

2000   Processions for the Inca: Andean and Christian Ideas of Human Sacrifice, Communion, and Embodiment in Early Colonial Peru. *Archiv für Religionsgeschichte* 2, no. 1:110–40.

Markham, Clements

1920   Introduction to *Memorias antiguas historiales del Perú,* by Fernando de Montesinos, ed. and trans. Philip Ainsworth Means. London: Haklyut Society.

References

Martines, Lauro
  1979   *Power and Imagination: City-States in Renaissance Italy.* New York: Vintage Books.
Marzal, Manuel M.
  2001   Blas Valera y la verdadera historia incaica. In *Guaman Poma y Blas Valera: Tradición andina e historia colonial,* ed. Francesca Cantú, 387–400. Rome: Antonio Pellicani Editore.
Mateos, Francisco de
  1944a   *Historia general de la Compañía de Jesús en la provincia del Perú.* Vol. 1. Madrid.
  1944b   *Historia general de la Compañía de Jesús en la provincia del Perú.* Vol. 2. Madrid.
  1944c   Introduction to *Historia general de la Compañía de Jesús en la provincia del Perú.* Vol. 1. Madrid.
  1954   Introduction to *Obras del P. José de Acosta,* ed. Francisco Mateos. Vol. 73. Madrid: Biblioteca de Autores Españoles.
Means, Philip
  1928   *Biblioteca Andina.* New Haven.
Medina, Borja de
  1999   Blas Valera y la dialéctica "exclusión-integración" del otro. *Archivum Historicum Societatis Iesu* 68, no. 136:229–68.
Meicklejohn, Norman
  1988   *La Iglesia y los Lupaqa de Chucuito durante la colonia.* Cuzco.
Metraux, Alfred
  1962   *Les Incas.* Paris.
Miccinelli, Clara, and Carlo Animato
  1999   Missionari gesuiti nella terra degli Incas. *Societatis Rivista dei Gesuiti Dell' Italia Meridionale* 47, nos. 5–6:191–201.
Millar Carvacho, René
  1999   El govierno de los Jesuitas en la provincia peruana, 1630–1650." *Historia* (Santiago) 32:141–76.
Mills, Kenneth
  1997   *Idolatry and Its Enemies: Colonial Andean Religion and Extirpation, 1640–1750.* Princeton: Princeton University Press.
Mogrovejo, Toribio Alfonso de
  1921   Diario de la segunda visita pastoral del arzobispo de los Reyes Don Toribio Alfonso de Mogrovejo. *Revista del Archivo Nacional del Perú* 2, no. 1. Originally written in 1593.
Molina, Cristobal de
  1989   *Fábulas y mitos de los incas.* Ed. Henrique Urbano and Pierre Duviols. Madrid: Historia 16. Originally written in 1575.
Molina, Tirso de
  1974   *Historia general de la orden de Nuestra Señora de las Mercedes.* Ed. Manuel Penedo, O. de M. Vol. 2. Madrid. Originally written in 1639.

Montesinos, Fernando de
  1882   *Memorias antiguas historiales y políticas del Perú.* Ed. Jiménez de la Espada. Madrid: Miguel Ginesta. Originally written in 1644.
  1920   *Memorias antiguas historiales y políticas del Perú.* Ed. and trans. Philip Ainsworth Means. London: Haklyut Society. Originally written in 1644.
  1930   *Memorias antiguas historiales y políticas del Perú.* Ed. Horacio H. Urteaga. Lima: Libreria e Imprenta Gil. Originally written in 1644.
Mumford, Jeremy
  2000   Clara Miccinelli's Cabinet of Wonders. *Lingua Franca* 10, no. 1:36–45.
Murra, John V.
  1975   *Formaciones económicas y políticas del mundo andino.* Lima: Instituto de Estudios Peruanos.
Murúa, Martín de
  1987   *Historia general del Perú.* Ed. Manuel Ballesteros. Madrid: Historia 16. Originally written in 1613.
Muscutt, Keith
  1998   *Warriors of the Clouds: A Lost Civilization in the Upper Amazon of Peru.* Albuquerque: University of New Mexico Press.
Niles, Susan A.
  1999   *The Shape of Inca History: Narrative and Architecture in an Andean Empire.* Iowa City: University of Iowa Press.
Olechea, Juan B.
  1972   Los Indios en las ordenes religiosas. *Missionalia Hispanica* 86:241–56.
O'Malley, John
  1995   *The First Jesuits.* Cambridge: Harvard University Press.
O'Reilly, Terence, S.J.
  1991   The *Spiritual Exercises* and the Crisis of Medieval Piety. *The Way Supplement* 70.
Oviedo y Valdés, Gonzalo Fernández de
  1547   *Coronica de las Indias.* Salamanca.
Pagden, Anthony
  1982   *The Fall of Natural Man: The American Indian and the Origins of Comparative Ethnology.* Cambridge.
Pease, Franklin
  1973   *El Dios creador andino.* Lima: Mosca Azul Editores.
Pérez Fernández, Isacio, O.P.
  1986   *Bartolomé de las Casas en el Perú, 1571–1573.* Cuzco: Centro Bartolomé de las Casas.
Pina, Fermín del
  1990   Edición de crónicas de Indias e historia intelectual, o la distancia entre José de Acosta y José Alcina." *Revista de Indias* 50, no. 190:861–78.
Piras, Guiseppe
  1998   *Martín de Funes SI (1560–1611).* Rome: Edizioni di Storia e Letteratura.

References

Polo de Ondegardo
  1985a Instrucción contra las ceremonias y ritos que usan los Indios. In *Doctrina christiana y catecismo*, fols. 1–5. Madrid. Originally published in 1584.
  1985b Los errores y supersticiones de los Indios sacadas del tratado y averiguación que hizo el Lic. Polo. In *Doctrina christiana y catecismo*, fols. 7–16. Madrid. Originally published in 1584.

Porras Barrenechea, Raúl
  1950 Cronicas perdidas, presuntas y olvidadas sobre la conquista del Perú. *Documenta* 2, no. 1:179–243.
  1986 *Los cronistas del Perú y otros ensayos (1528–1650)*. Lima: Banco de Crédito del Perú.

Porres, Diego de
  1953 Instrucciones que escribió el P. Fr. Diego de Porres para los sacerdotes que se ocuparon en la doctrina y conversión de los Indios. In *Los Mercedarios en el Perú en el siglo XVI*, ed. Victor M. Barriga, 4: 174–77. Arequipa. Originally written ca. 1585.

Pricot, Luis
  1962 *América indígena: El hombre américano*. Barcelona.

Puente Brunke, José de la
  1992 *Encomienda y encomenderos en el Perú*. Seville.

Rafael, Vicente L.
  1993 *Contracting Colonialism: Translation and Christian Conversion in Tagalog Society under Early Spanish Rule*. Durham: Duke University Press.

Ramírez, Susan E.
  1996 *The World Upside Down: Cross-Cultural Contact and Conflict in Sixteenth-Century Peru*. Stanford: Stanford University Press.

Relación de idolatrías en Huamachuco por los primeros agustinos
  1918 In *Informaciones acerca de la religión y gobierno de los Incas*, ed. Horacio H. Urteaga, 3–56. Lima: San Martín. Originally written in 1560.

Relación de la religión y ritos del Perú hecha por los padres agustinos
  1992 Ed. Lucila Castro de Trelles. Lima: Pontificia Universidad Católica del Perú. Originally written in 1560.

Riva Agüero, José de la
  1908 Garcilaso y el Padre Valera, respuesta a una crítica. *Revista Histórica* 3:46–49.
  1909 Polémica histórica: El Señor González de la Rosa y las obras de Valera y Garcilaso. *Revista Histórica* 4:312–47.
  1954 *La historia en el Perú*. Madrid: Maestre.

Román y Zamora, Jerónimo
  1575 *Repúblicas del mundo*. Medina del Campo.

Rosán, Laurence J.
  1967 Proclus. In *The Encyclopedia of Philosophy*, vol. 5, 479–82. New York: Macmillan Publishing.

REFERENCES

Rosny, León de

1870   *Les escritures figuratives et hieroglyphiques des differents peuples anciens et modernes.*

Rowe, John H.

1982   Inca Policies and Institutions Relating to the Cultural Unification of the Empire. In *The Inca and Aztec States, 1400–1800,* ed. George A. Collier, Renato Rosaldo, and John D. Wirth, 93–118. New York: Academic Press.

Salles-Reese, Verónica

1997   *From Viracocha to the Virgin of Copacabana: Representations of the Sacred at Lake Titicaca.* Austin: University of Texas Press.

Salomon, Frank

1986   *Native Lords of Quito in the Age of the Incas: The Political Economy of North Andean Chiefdoms.* Cambridge: Cambridge University Press.

1991   Introduction to *The Huarochirí Manuscript,* ed. and trans. Frank Salomon and George Urioste, 1–40. Austin: University of Texas Press.

2001   How an Andean "Writing without Words" Works. *Current Anthropology* 42, no. 1:1–27.

Sandoval, Alonso de

1647   *Tomo primero de Instauranda Aethiopum Salute.* Madrid: A. de Paredes.

Sansevero, Prince of [Raimondo di Sangro]

1750   *Lettera apologética.* Naples.

Santisteban Ochoa, Julian

1946   *Los cronistas del Peru.* Cuzco.

Santo Tomás, Domingo de

1891   *Arte de la lengua quichua.* Ed. Julio Platzmann. Leipzig: B. G. Teubner. Originally written in 1560.

Sarmiento de Gamboa, Pedro

1960   *Historia de los Incas.* Biblioteca de Autores Españoles, vol. 135. Madrid. Originally written in 1572.

1972   *History of the Incas.* Trans. Sir Clements Markham. London: Dover Publications. Originally written in Spanish in 1572.

Schjellerup, Inge

1997   *Incas and Spaniards in the Conquest of the Chachapoyas: Archaeological and Ethnohistorical Research in the North-eastern Andes of Peru.* Göteborg University, Department of Archaeology, Series B, Archaeological Theses, no. 7. Göteborg.

Schneider, B.

1967   Aquaviva, Claudius. In *The New Catholic Encyclopedia,* Vol. 1:89–90. New York: McGraw Hill.

Sharon, Douglas

1978   *Wizard of the Four Winds: A Shaman's Story.* New York: Free Press.

References

Spalding, Karen
    1984   *Huarochirí: An Andean Society under Inca and Spanish Rule.* Stanford: Stanford University Press.

Tentler, Thomas
    1977   *Sin and Confession on the Eve of the Reformation.* Princeton: Princeton University Press.

Tierney, Brian
    1997   *The Idea of Natural Rights: Studies on National Rights, Natural Law, and Church Law, 1150–1625.* Atlanta: William E. Eerdmans Publishing.

Toribio Polo, José
    1907   Blas Valera. *Revista Histórica* 2:544–52.

Urbano, Henrique
    1992   Introduction to *Varias: Antigüedades del Perú.* Madrid: Historia 16.

Urteaga, Horacio, ed.
    1918   *Informaciones acerca de la religion y gobierno de los Incas.* Lima: San Martín.

Urton, Gary
    1990   *The History of a Myth: Pacariqtambo and the Origin of the Inkas.* Austin: University of Texas Press.
    1994   A New Twist in an Old Yarn: Variation in Knot Directionality in the Inca Khipus. *Baessler-Archiv Neue Folge* 42:271–305.
    1997   *The Social Life of Numbers.* Austin: University of Texas Press.
    1998   From Knots to Narratives: Reconstructing the Art of Historical Record Keeping in the Andes from Spanish Transcriptions of Inka Khipus. *Ethnohistory* 45, no. 3: 409–38.
    1999   *Inca Myths.* London: British Museum Press.
    2001   A Calendrical and Demographic Tomb Text from Northern Peru. *Latin American Antiquity* 12:127–47.

Valera, Blas
    1945   *Las costumbres antiguas del Peru.* With an introduction by Francisco Loayza. Lima. Originally written in 1594.
    1968   *Relación de las costumbres antiguas.* Ed. Francisco Esteve Barba. Biblioteca de Autores Españoles, vol. 209. Madrid. Originally written in 1594.

Valera, Jerónimo
    1610   *Commentarii ac Quaestiones in Universam Aristotelis ac Subtilissimi Doctoris Ihoannis Duns Scoti Logicam.* Lima.

Valtierra, Ángel, S.J.
    1956   El Padre Alonso de Sandoval S.J. In *De Instauranda Aethiopum Salute,* v–xxxvii. Bogotá: Empresa Nacional de Publicaciones.

Vargas Ugarte, Rubén, S.J.
    1963–65   *Historia de la Compañía de Jesús en el Perú.* 4 vols. Burgos: Aldecoa.

REFERENCES

Velasco, Juan de
    1977   *Historia del reino de Quito en la América Meridonial.* Quito. Originally written in 1789.

Wiener, Charles
    1880   *Pérou et Bolivie, récit de voyage.* Paris: Librarie Hachette.

Zamora, Margarita
    1988   *Language, Authority, and Indigenous History in the "Comentarios reales de los Incas."* Cambridge: Cambridge University Press.

Zaporta Pallarés, Juan, O. de M.
    1996   *Religiosos mercenarios en Panamá (1519–1992).* Madrid: Revista Estudios.

Zoppi, Ugo
    2001   I documenti Miccinelli: Il contributo offerto dalle analisi radiometriche. In *Guaman Poma y Blas Valera: Tradición andina e historia colonial,* ed. Francesca Cantú, 171–80. Rome: Antonio Pellicani Editore.

Zuidema, R. Tom
    1990   *Inca Civilization in Cuzco.* Trans. Jean-Jacques Decoster. Austin: University of Texas Press.
    2001   Guaman Poma, Blas Valera y los escritos jesuitas sobre el Perú. In *Guaman Poma y Blas Valera: Tradición andina e historia colonial,* ed. Francesca Cantú, 365–86. Rome: Antonio Pellicani Editore.

Index